Families in a Working World
The Impact of Organizations
on Domestic Life

Families in a Working World
The Impact of Organizations on Domestic Life

by Margaret R. Davis

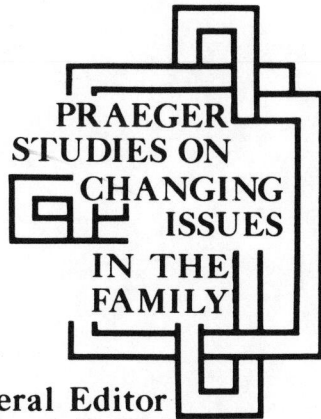

PRAEGER
STUDIES ON
CHANGING
ISSUES
IN THE
FAMILY

General Editor
Suzanne K. Steinmetz

PRAEGER

PRAEGER SPECIAL STUDIES • PRAEGER SCIENTIFIC

Library of Congress Cataloging in Publication Data

Davis, Margaret R., 1931–
  The impact of organizations on family life.

  (Praeger studies on changing issues in the family)
  Bibliography: p.
  Includes index.
  1. Family—California—San Francisco Bay region—
Case studies. 2. Social institutions—California—San
Francisco Bay region—Case studies. 3. Family—Case
studies. 4. Social institutions—Case studies.
I. Title. II. Series.
HQ555.C2D38   306.8'5   82–446
ISBN 0-03-059774-9   AACR2

306.85
D 263f

Published in 1982 by Praeger Publishers
CBS Educational and Professional Publishing
A Division of CBS, Inc.
521 Fifth Avenue, New York, New York 10175 U.S.A.

© 1982 by Praeger Publishers

23456789   145   987654321

Printed in the United States of America

84-3884

This book is most fondly dedicated to my own Ray, Janet, and Robert; to my mother; and to all the families who made it possible.

Acknowledgments

The studies on which this book is based were conducted at Stanford University with financial support provided by the National Institute for Mental Health. I am deeply grateful to the assistance and support provided by my advisors, professors W. Richard Scott, John W. Meyer, and Joan E. Talbert. My thanks are due also to professor William G. Ouchi for his help in recruiting subjects and to Barbara Rosenblum for her comments on an earlier draft on the manuscript.

Foreword

In modern societies, work (i.e., paid employment) normally occurs in an organizational setting. Davis questions whether there is a difference between the operation of rational social structures, such as organizations, and the emotional oriented, expressive group known as the family. Davis's thesis, a powerful one, which she amply supports, is that as more and more women enter the work force, they and their husbands must deal with the mechanism for dividing the work labeled "housework" and child care. No longer does the woman have eight hours a day in which to perform these tasks; now she must do them in 4.8 hours.

While, historically, we have dealt with two kinds of social structures—rational, bureaucratic organizations and face–to–face emotionally-bonded primary groups—we now find that these two distinctions have merged. No longer can they be considered separate worlds. We must address the impact of the organizational setting on the family, in terms of dual careers, single employed parents, and organizational demands that impinge upon family times—as well as how families goals are impacting on the organizational setting when families demand Flextime, shared jobs, and maternity and paternity leave and resist arbitrary company transfers.

Weber's rational bureaucratic organizational versus Cooley's primary group, Durkhiem's mechanic solidarity of folk society versus organic solidarity of the large impersonal organization, and Parson's instrumental (male provider) versus expressive (female nurturant) roles will all need to be reevaluated in a society in which family roles comingle with work roles and merge these traditional distinctions.

Davis suggests that a job is a cluster of tasks or activities so arranged as to be reasonably doable within the allotted work day or week. Thus we find that one might follow a job description and be able to measure the person's efficiency by seeing how adequately those tasks are performed. In contrast, Davis notes that family norms ignore the issue of available time and tend to divide tasks exclusively by sex and age. She also suggests that the low status attached to "women's work" may have resulted from the lower status of women in general. Whether sex-typing has its origin in biology or in unequally distributed resources, it is obviously maintained through cultural transmission of norms and values.

Families in a Working World might well have been titled "Who's doing the Housework." Davis reports findings from time-budget studies showing that employed women spend an average of 4.8 hours per day on housework, while their full-time homemaking sisters spend 8.1 hours per day. Although teenagers provide some help with housework, and husbands of employed women with young children provide about 2.6 hours of help a day, in homes where there are no young children both employed and nonemployed women receive only 1.6 hours of help per day from their spouses.

In an earlier study by Davis, she found that in 1972, for every hour a woman was employed outside the home, her husband contributed two and one-half minutes of housework. In 1976 this contribution increased to five minutes for every hour a woman was employed outside the home. Although the ratio is improving, five minutes of help around the house for every hour of employment outside the home is not an equitable trade-off. If the time the employed wife spends on housework is reduced by 23 minutes per hour, who then is performing the work that she can no longer do?

Contemporary women must reconcile the dual set of expectations placed on them: fulfill the rational, bureaucratic, organizational goals via gainful employment and, at the same time, fulfill the residual expectations of mother, housekeeper, lover, and social partner. If a woman chooses to stay home and take care of her home and children, then she suffers the loss of self-esteem and self-concept that society gives to those who are gainfully employed. The problem intensifies because the man who works long hours outside the home is looked at as aggressive, upwardly mobile, and a hard worker who is trying to provide for his family—positive attributes.

A woman, however, who is supposed to assign the highest priority to family duties, will be viewed as not caring for her children, not placing a high value on her family's needs, and negligent in fulfilling her major role if she exhibits the same qualities. If she does succeed, the question is always raised: "at what cost to her family?" Thus the woman faces a unique dilemma: how does she juggle these two very important aspects of her life? To which does she place the higher priority? To which drummer does she march?

The alternative is to become "super mom": the marvelous house-keeper who rarely has any outside help, the cook who fulfills the do-it-yourself, back-to-natural-food fad by baking bread and canning and preserving her own homegrown vegetables, the interior designer who paints and decorates her own house, all while holding down a full-time job with upwardly mobile aspirations. Of course, this myth-ical woman also has model children and is probably on the school board, an officer in PTA, and Cub Scout leader.

Unfortunately, we wonder how long women can juggle these multiple demands with equally high priorities before stress reduces their resources and without support from society.

Davis raises several questions that we must consider. What factors other than the wife's employment seem to affect a husband's willing-ness to do housework? Do the emerging equalitarian attitudes en-courage role sharing? If, as the data suggest, employed women spend less time on housework than full-time housewives (and husbands and children only relieve part of this burden), then what happens to all of the undone housework? Are families becoming so efficient, so ration-alized and organized that they are able to complete the same amount of work no matter how much the available time diminishes?

Davis observes that by efficiently organizing one's work, assign-ing priorities to the different tasks, and streamlining these tasks so that they can be performed in the allotted time, respondents believe that they can accomplish both jobs.

An underlying theme of *Families in a Working World* is Kohn's generalization theory, which states that successful modes of accom-plishing tasks in one area of life, such as the workplace, tend to be applied to other areas of activity, such as the family. Thus as women are exposed more and more to the rational, organized system of the bureaucratic work world, these ways of handling tasks will then be applied to their home life—making family work, housework, and child care more efficient, more rationally organized, and more like the model of the bureaucratic system.

The 30 in-depth interviews with couples support the expectations that those in managerial, supervisional positions will be more likely to report successful domestic organization, thus projecting the myth of "super woman"; that is, the woman who has the higher prestige or supervisory managerial job (i.e., the successful career woman) will also tend to be viewed as the successful homemaker and parent.

This relationship is the most clearly illustrated in the interview with Bob, a graduate assistant, and Nancy, who is employed full-time. They have an unbelievably busy life with numerous hobbies, social activities, and extra educational activities. Nancy plans ahead, stocks up for months, and makes desserts and all of the baby's food ahead by grinding up meat and freezing it in ice cube trays. Nancy describes a schedule in which being three minutes early threw their timing off and caused a problem:

> I was three minutes off in my timing, waking my husband three minutes early, so he had the baby ready three minutes before I was due to talk out the door.... I get ready to leave for work, prepare the baby's bottles and food for the day. He gets up and dresses baby, then walks down the stairs and hands me the baby just as I am ready to go out the door.

With schedules accounting for each minute, one wonders how this couple might react on that "typical" day when the car won't start, the washer overflows, the dog has gone into labor, and the baby suddenly gets diarrhea!

Families in a Working World provides needed insight on the organizing of household task in a society with diminished time for these activities.

In the 1950s and 1960s a large number of families could manage on the one-earner income. The second earner, the wife, often saw her contribution in terms of increasing the standard of living: the second car, the vacation home, camp and college for the children.

In the 1970s the wife's income became necessary to maintain the standard as rising energy costs, double digit inflation, and soaring interest rates produced a widening gap between the family's expectations and the achievement of their goals. The wife's income was as likely to be used to pay the electric bill as it was to be providing funds for the children's summer camp.

In the 1980s families are increasingly turning to moonlighting to pay for the extras, in the form of overtime as well as with second jobs. Extending Davis' thesis, one wonders how long families can continue to perform household duties that maintain the same standards with continually diminishing time.

Suzanne K. Steinmetz
Series Editor

Table of Contents

List of Tables
and Figures

Introduction

With increasing numbers of married women entering the labor force, the issue of how organizations affect family life has become increasingly salient. My interest is how these changing relationships between the family and the organizations in its environment affect family roles and activities.

Most sociological theory tends to treat the family group as a type of social structure quite distinct from the formal organizations that dominate modern life. The conceptual barriers between the two kinds of social group are so strong that a sort of "myth of separate worlds" has arisen. Rosabeth Kanter describes the myth like this:

> In a modern industrial society work life and family life constitute two separate and nonoverlapping worlds, with their own functions, territories, and behavioral rules. Each operates by its own laws and can be studied independently (1977, p. 8).

One apparent result of this "myth" has been a reluctance of social scientists to delve into the ways that organizations affect the functioning of the modern family. This is in spite of the fact that we all know that work and school organizations have a major influence on such important facets of family life as the time parents can spend with children, their social activities, scheduling of meals, and so on.

The bulk of this monograph is devoted to findings from an exploratory study in which 30 families were asked to describe in detail how their family life was affected by their ties to work organizations.

This project was broad in scope, in that I was interested in uncovering any factors that people felt were important. However, I had a rather narrow aim also, and this was to gain support for a theoretical argument that, in effect, challenges the myth discussed above. The gist of this argument is that as family ties to organizations increase, the family will become more "rationally" organized and less "traditional" in its orientation toward domestic work. Or, to put it another way, the more people in families are members of organizations too, the more we will find household work becoming organized.

A definitional note as to what I mean by "household work" is in order here. Throughout this book, such terms as household work, housework, and domestic chores are used more or less interchangeably. There is a popular tendency to think of "housework" as primarily comprising those tasks that are traditionally performed by women—such as, cooking, laundry, and cleaning. However, in general, my interest is in *all* the work of a household, including tasks traditionally performed by males—such as, yardwork and maintenance and repair of appliances.

The rest of this book is organized as follows. Chapter 1 summarizes the sociological theories that, in my opinion, have done much to produce and maintain a "myth of separate worlds." In Chapter 2, I outline my theoretical argument that increased commitments to organizations will result in family life increasingly reflecting organizational norms and values.

The effects of a wife's employment on the family's division of labor have been investigated by a number of researchers. As this topic is a key concern of the present study, some of the relevant literature is summarized in Chapter 2.

The remaining chapters in the book deal with findings from interviews with husbands and wives in 30 families. These families were all husband-wife intact, and all had at least one child under the age of 18 living at home. Eleven of the wives were employed full-time. A core set of questions, covering my interests, was raised in each interview; however, the subjects were encouraged to respond freely in any way they chose and to introduce any issues they felt were important in meshing work and home lives. The interview findings have been organized into six chapters. The first of these covers dimensions of work life reported to have most effect on domestic life. Other chapters deal with the rational organization of housework, family functions, the family's division of labor, sex-role ideology, and children's activities.

The concluding section summarizes the implications of the findings here for sociological theories of the family. In particular, I hope to convey my own overall conclusion, which is that the conceptual boundaries that have so long divided families from organizations tend to hinder rather than further our understanding of family life. Families and organizations are part of the *same* world, and both kinds of social unit are affected by prevalent expressive and instrumental norms and values. A family is united by affective bonds among members and is influenced by traditional modes of behavior. But it is also a task-oriented unit, guided by many of the same norms of rationality that permeate other task-oriented units in society.

Note: The quotes from interviews with husbands and wives that appear in this book are exactly as transcribed from interview notes. Only names of persons and places have been changed to preserve anonymity.

PART ONE:
THEORETICAL BACKGROUND

CHAPTER *I*

The Myth of Separate Worlds

Historically, sociologists have distinguished between two kinds of social structure. The first is the rational bureaucratic organization, as described by Max Weber (Henderson and Parsons, 1947); the second is the primary group, as conceptualized by Cooley (1923). The typical work organization, of course, belongs in the first category; the family unit is invariably classified in the second. When one considers that these two forms of social group are treated by social scientists as though they were nonoverlapping, even antithetical, it is easy to see how a "separate worlds" belief might arise. We will first review some seminal ideas concerning social bonding to find the origins of conceptual family-organization distinctions.

FORMS OF SOCIAL COHESION

The term, primary group, was used by Charles Horton Cooley to refer to those social groups based on primary relationships. A primary relationship between two individuals is characterized by a unique and holistic orientation to each other and involves emotion or affect. Secondary groups, by contrast, are those where people join together in explicit pursuit of their common, usually narrowly defined, interests or goals—like producing a product, pursuing a hobby, supporting a common cause, and so on. A secondary relationship among individuals is thus limited in scope and is emotionally neutral.

Societies have similarly been characterized according to the extent to which they are dominated by primary or secondary forms of social cohesion. For instance, the German sociologist, Ferdinand Tönnies, suggested that folk or rural societies (which he termed Gemeinschaft) are those based on primary relationships, whereas urban societies (Gesellschaft) are characterized by formal or secondary relationships (Tönnies, 1887). People do not join a Gemeinschaft—they are born into it; by contrast, membership in a Gesellschaft is voluntary and is based upon the rational pursuit of self-interest.

The French sociologist, Emile Durkheim, introduced the terms, "mechanical" and "organic" solidarity, to describe the different ways that integration is achieved in the two kinds of society (Durkheim, 1933). In the folk society, there is mechanical solidarity; cohesion occurs because members share a common set of norms and values. As societies become larger and more complex, they tend to move away from the mechanical toward an organic form of solidarity, where people are linked on the basis of social and economic exchanges with one another.

More recently, Adams has argued that as societies move in one direction their family units tend to move in the reverse direction (Adams, 1971, pp. 88–89). He says that in all mechanically solidary societies composed of self-sufficient family-kin units, these units are organically integrated by a clear division of labor. As society in general becomes more differentiated, families increasingly are united by bonds of affection rather than a set of practical interdependencies as implied by the organic concept.

FAMILY FUNCTIONS

The changed orientation with respect to the predominant form of social bonding is also said to be accompanied by changes in the kinds of functions performed by the family. Some say that the family shrinks in importance as bureaucratic organizations increasingly take over what were once family functions.[1] Others (e.g., Vincent,

---

[1] For example, see Ogburn and Tibbits, 1933; Ogburn and Nimkoff, 1955, pp. 15, 45–48, 129–30, 244–47; Sorokin, 1941, p. 187; Zimmerman, 1947, pp. IX, 782–83, 802 ff.; Sorokin, 1937, vol. V., p. 776; Anshen, 1949, p. 4.

1966) suggest that what is occurring is a change in the kinds of functions performed by families. For example, although a bureaucracy may now be educating children, the family is still responsible for seeing that children attend school and meet school-imposed requirements.

One group of sociologists, Eugene Litwak and his associates, have developed some critieria for specifying which kinds of tasks are best performed by primary groups, such as families, and which by bureaucratic organizations. They suggest that families are much better suited than organizations to handle three kinds of tasks: (1) those where so little knowledge is required that the ordinary person can perform them as well as the expert—for example, dressing and feeding children, shopping, and other domestic chores; (2) those where knowledge is so lacking that there is no existing body of expertise on which to draw—for example, childrearing in general; (3) those where knowledge is so complex "it cannot be put together in time to make a decision" (Litwak, 1968, pp. 468–81).

FAMILY ROLES

Talcott Parsons popularized the concepts of "instrumental" and "expressive" to describe different role orientations (1951, pp. 45–67). Instrumental activities are related to the deliberate planning and execution of tasks and are evaluated as the means to preconceived ends. A secondary group thus has an instrumental orientation. Expressive activities, on the other hand, are related to the fulfillment of personal gratifications and are valued as ends in themselves. The primary group is said to have an expressive orientation. Zelditch expanded this idea by characterizing the husband-father as the family's "instrumental leader," because the husband-father generally deals with the instrumental world outside the family, and the wife-mother as "expressive leader," as she is generally responsible for managing purely domestic affairs (1955). This kind of conceptualization has been attacked by feminists in recent years as representing masculine stereotypes of male and female roles. However, in defense of Parsons and his associates, the predominant family type at the time of their writing was the husband-breadwinner and wife-homemaker family; thus, their image of family structure was at least consistent with current reality.

As organizations have become increasingly dominant in society, family analysts have increasingly emphasized the expressive nature of family life. Adams, I believe, captures this popular sentiment when he says the family "has come to be the seat of primary relationships... a refuge from a segmented and impersonal urban life" (1971, p. 88).

SEPARATE WORLDS—FACT OR FANTASY?

One consequence of the tendency to dichotomize social groupings in the ways discussed above is that those people who study formal organizations tend *not* to study families, and vice versa. However, organizational theorists long ago were obliged to face the fact that people do not simply shed their expressive selves upon entering an organizational setting. Primary groups, in the form of friendship groups and informal networks, may be found anywhere that people congregate on a regular basis. These affect-based groups have been shown to influence such important organizational concerns as the way that work is scheduled and performed, how much or little of it gets done, who gets appointed to what position, and so on.[2]

Looking at the other side of this coin, no one can deny that a most important part of family life is instrumental, or task-oriented, in nature. Most of the responsibilities with which modern families are legally and socially charged, particularly with regard to minor children, are associated with instrumental activities: seeing that family members are fed, clothed, housed, and so on. In short, all the *work* of a household—cooking, cleaning, shopping—is instrumental.

Furthermore, I do not believe we can or should distinguish between family work and organization work along the dimensions suggested by Litwak. It may be recalled he proposed that primary groups are better suited than bureaucratic structures to perform tasks that are simple and easily learned, or for which there is no existing body of expertise, or that require quick and complex decisions.

In fact, organizations are extremely well suited to perform simple tasks—the move toward differentiation and specialization in complex organizations has the underlying aim of ensuring that "anyone can do it." We should not be misled by the fact that organizations often

---

[2] The way that researchers are constantly rediscovering the primary group as an essential key to understanding organizational processes is discussed in Katz and Lazarsfeld (1955).

require incumbents to have formal qualifications for a job, even when that job is a counterpart of a domestic work role—jobs like chef, maid, bookkeeper. This is not so much due to inherent differences in the nature of the work performed in each setting as to the fact that organizations are consciously governed by rational norms, which call for incumbents to have rational qualifications, while families are not. (Perhaps a lot of family grief would be alleviated if society were to require potential spouses and parents to have appropriate qualifications for these "jobs.")

It might be true, as Litwak suggests, that the average parent can perform as well as the expert when it comes to childrearing. I am not sure, however, that this issue has ever been systematically investigated. Certainly it is likely that many other domestic tasks, such as cooking, money management, home decorating, and many others, can benefit from expertise—at least to as great an extent as tasks in nondomestic settings.

Finally, it is not clear that organizations are any less suited, or families any better suited, to make decisions that call for complex knowledge and quick action. Decisions like this are regularly faced in both kinds of setting. Some organizations—in particular, those in an uncertain or constantly changing environment—are structured so as to build in the capacity for just this kind of decision making. Typically, they do so by becoming less "bureaucratic"—for instance, by relying more on individual discretion and less on formal rules (Burns and Stalker, 1961; Thompson, 1967).

Probably the most important dimension along with the kinds of work setting differ is that of the scale of operation of tasks performed. Obviously, the problems and decisions involved in producing daily meals for the average family will differ substantially from the problems and decisions involved in producing daily meals for a thriving restaurant. The average family does not have the resources available for large-scale operations; the average organization would not find production on as small a scale as the family to be profitable. Aside from this difference in the typical scale of operations, however, family tasks are qualitatively similar to many of the tasks regularly performed in organizational settings.

We will now compare "traditional" family norms and "rational" organization norms as they relate to two facets of task activity: (1) the division of labor, or how work is allocated, and (2) the way that work is planned or arranged.

DIVISION OF LABOR

Organization norms stress the allocation of tasks according to such rational specifications as the incumbent's skill, training, or experience. In addition, the issue of time is at least implicitly taken into account in assigning work in an organization. In general, jobs (with a "job" consisting of a cluster of tasks or activities) are designed so that the tasks assigned can reasonably be performed within the allotted work day or week. By contrast, family norms ignore the issue of time available and other rational critieria by focusing exclusively on sex and age as the bases for the division of labor.

We know that the division of labor by sex within families is remarkably consistent across all modern industrial nations and even across social classes (Szalai, 1972). However, sex-typing of work also regularly occurs in the organizational domain, notwithstanding its supposedly rational norms and values. Theories abound concerning the origin of the tendency to sex-type activities in society. They fall into two broad categories: the biological or "functional" group, and the conflict or power group.

Biological Theories

Theorists in the first tradition see sex-role division as more or less inevitable, or as the "best way" to handle matters. In a family context, these people would argue that for biological reasons it is functional for women to handle domestic and child-care tasks and for men to handle tasks that require physical strength or mobility. According to this argument, women who bear and nurse children are both best fitted and most desirous of taking care of them. This means they must stay close to the home, and it is thus reasonable for them to have charge of such domestic tasks as cooking, cleaning house, doing the laundry, and so on. On the other hand, men, who do not have this special relationship with their children, are better fitted for tasks that require leaving the home, such as hunting, or commuting to the city.

Tiger and Shepher are amongst those who argue for the inevitability of the traditional division of family labor (1975). They point to the fact that even women in the kibbutzim of Israel—communities designed to eliminate sexual inequality—have, over time, pressed for more involvement with their children, a development not parallelled by the men of the kibbutzim. This, these writers conclude, is evidence of the strong biological pull between mothers and children that survives regardless of social arrangements designed to overcome it.[3]

It is not clear how arguments of this kind explain the sex-typing of occupations, except insofar as certain occupational roles are considered analogous to domestic roles. For example, secretaries and teachers might be viewed as surrogate wives and mothers. However, this explanation breaks down when we look at the evidence from an historical or international point of view. At one time, for instance, secretaries were mostly male; in different societies at different times, teachers have mostly been male; male physicians predominate in the United States today, but female physicians predominate in the Soviet Union and China.

Conflict Theories

Theorists in the conflict or power tradition deny the inevitability of existing sexual divisions. They explain these as arising from unequal exchange relationships between the sexes. Power accrues to those who control the most important resources in such exchanges. In past times, physical strength was probably the most crucial individual resource and, thus, the chief basis for the distribution of power. Collins (1971) suggests that physical strength has likely dwindled in significance over time as the use of physical force has come to be regulated by the state, and that, in modern times, access to an economic market is probably the most important individual resource. Thus, he, along with many other present-day writers, foresees that redistribution of economic wealth on a more equal basis between the sexes will result in a leveling of the sex-based power differential.

This kind of argument becomes circular when it is used to explain the family division of labor. As any undesirable work is supposedly imposed on the less powerful by the more powerful, and men have always been the more powerful, we must assume that domestic work is undesirable or women would not be doing it.

---

[3] There is another explanation that might account for their findings. This is that some individuals, both men and women, are more personally desirous of increased contact with their children. Women of the kibbutz can find support for any such desires in the conventional norms that apply in Israeli society generally; men of the kibbutz with similar desires have no similar source of cultural endorsement.

Some kind of reconciliation of these competing approaches seems to offer the most convincing overall explanation. For biological reasons, certain tasks undoubtedly have been more appropriate for men or for women. The greater physical strength of men undoubtedly was, and maybe still is, a basis for their having the upper hand in any conflict between the sexes. The low status attached to women's work has come about because women have generally been the lower status of the two sexes. Thus, any occupation or activity that women take over tends to lose status. Regardless of whether sex-typing has its origins in biology or in unequally distributed resources, there is no doubt it is maintained through the cultural transmission of norms and values. Sokoloff describes "cultural determinism" as being based on the overriding assumption of "the plasticity of human beings and responsiveness to normative pressures of their cultures" (1980, p. 15). And, of course, some argue that there is a tendency to justify arrangements that are culturally convenient by proclaiming them to be biological necessities (Oakley, 1980, p. 8).

There is, incidentally, little systematic evidence available concerning the roles of *children* in modern families. Some writers suggest that with modernity children have become freer of parental control, parents are less authoritarian, discipline is more lax, and there seems less insistence on regular contributions by children to either domestic tasks or family income.[4]

PLANNING OF WORK

Organizations typically have quite explicit standards regarding the way work is supposed to be done. There is a large body of literature devoted to such topics as the way activities are planned, coordinated, and scheduled in organizations. By contrast, the issue of how or if people in a family setting arrange their household work has received little attention from either historians or sociologists.

There are, however, indications from studies of professional working women that the pressure of time leads some people to become more "organized" in their approach to housework. Safilios-Rothschild (1976) talks about the elaborate and precise time schedules needed

---

[4] For discussions of the changing relationships between parents and children, see Ariès, 1962 and Shorter, 1975.

by the dual-career families she studied in order to coordinate their activities. Rapoport and Rapoport (1976, p. 169) write of the "great attention to efficiency of organization" of a dual-career family in their study and of the tendency of another such family to "apply similar administrative practices of negotiation and rational management [at home] as at work" (p. 231).

Oakley, in *The Sociology of Housework* (1974), suggests that housewives are likely to be satisfied with housework the more they succeed in organizing it. She says that the specification of standards and routines for housework "serves as proof that housework is work; the spelling out of these rules . . . places housework in the same category as other work" (p. 104). Her findings suggested that the highly organized women in her study were, in fact, more satisfied than the less organized women; however, dissatisfied housewives outnumbered the satisfied in all groups. Her study did not attempt to identify factors associated with greater or lesser tendencies to organize housework.

SUMMARY

One phenomenon of modern industrial-urban life is the growth of the bureaucratic organization as a means of structuring activity. Underlying this social form is the idea of *rationality*—work is carried out in such a way as to maximize efficient performance in the light of preconceived ends. This is in contrast to *traditional* social groupings where people relate to one another according to circumstances of their birth, or personal emotions, and where activity is governed by custom rather than by rational thought. Families have come to be regarded as pockets of traditionalism in a world dominated by rational organizations. However, the family is a task-oriented work unit as well as a collection of loving individuals. We cannot hope to understand family processes, let alone shape sensible social policies, without paying full attention to the instrumental as well as the expressive side of family life. Sociological theory has tended to draw too strong a boundary between rational social groups like organizations and primary groups like families. This boundary is, I would argue, permeable in both directions.

In the next chapter, I shall focus more on the impact of organizations on family life and argue that we can expect to find families becoming more rational in their approach to domestic work as family ties to organizations increase.

CHAPTER **II**

The Impact
of Organizations
on Family Life

Probably most individuals in most modern industrial nations spend the major portion of their waking lives in an organizational setting of some kind. To a great extent, family life itself is patterned around the time constraints imposed by external schedules—for example, of work organizations, schools, and so on.

Some clarification is in order regarding the use of such terms as "organization" and "organized group." An organization is *any social group that is structured according to rational principles*—or that is formed and maintained to carry out explicitly instrumental objectives. Thus any social group that exists to carry on a business—whether it be an industrial complex, a consortium of professionals, or a mom and pop grocery store—is an organization in this sense. Obviously, these "organizations" will vary extensively in their degree of bureaucratization (in the Weberian sense) and in the extent to which informal or affective norms are permitted to affect the organization's activities. To repeat, what they have in common is the fact that they are all formed and maintained to perform certain instrumental functions and that these functions legitimate their existence. Of course, there are many people who earn a livelihood outside the context of an organization, even using a definition this broad.

To some degree, every single affiliation with an organized group outside the family places some constrictions on the individual. The

13

amount of constraint is likely to be a function of (1) the extent to which the affiliation is viewed as mandatory rather than optional, (2) the amount of time involved, and (3) the amount of individual flexibility permitted in scheduling. Membership in philanthropic or recreational organizations may be viewed as completely optional; however, once undertaken, even these commitments may require the individual to set aside specific hours in a schedule established by the institution, not the individual.

There is no doubt, of course, that ties to school and work organizations are likely to be viewed as least optional. Children of certain ages are legally required to attend school. Usually at least one adult in the family has to work to earn money, and in our society this generally involves working for an organization. Furthermore, the demands of these important organizations tend to override purely domestic concerns. Total neglect of the latter is, of course, frowned on; nevertheless, the family is expected to adapt to, to mold its schedule around, an externally-imposed timetable. Assuming that activities within a family group are interdependent, we can say that the greater the number of ties to organizations any one family has, the more difficult it will be to arrange domestic activities.

The whole situation becomes particularly complicated when the wife takes on important external commitments. A husband who works long hours outside the home can justify the neglect of his domestic duties by claiming that he is performing his chief function of breadwinning with extra zeal. This is not true for the wife. She is *supposed* to assign highest priority to family duties. This then is the modern woman's dilemma. If she goes out to work and consequently neglects her family, she is morally reprehensible. If she works but refuses to neglect her family, she probably never will progress very far with her career. If she does not go out to work, she denies herself the primary avenue in modern society for obtaining prestige, self-validation, and other important rewards.[1]

---

[1] This issue is discussed by Michael Young and Peter Willmott, 1973, Chapters IV and X. Incidentally, a study by Christine Bose (1980) shows that the occupation of "housewife" is ranked higher in prestige than many blue collar women's occupations, which suggests that women who can aspire no higher than such occupations may value the housewife status more highly than women with better occupational changes.

An additional problem is that the traditional sex-typing of domestic tasks imposes far heavier time demands on the wife than on the husband; thus, if a working-wife family maintains the traditional division of family labor, this places a double burden on the wife—both in an absolute sense of the time required of her and in terms of her contribution relative to that of her husband.

The "working-wife phenomenon" of recent decades has been the subject of intense interest and concern to scientists and laymen alike because it implies that a real shift is occurring in U.S. family roles. By 1978, the majority of married women with employed husbands were themselves employed (Bureau of Labor Statistics, 1978, Table A-9). Particularly striking has been the increase in the proportion of mothers with young children who work, for although the care of a household is always time-consuming, it is particularly so when there are children in the home. Furthermore, many—if not most—working wives regard their income as crucial and their work affiliation as being as "involuntary" as their husband's.[2]

There are two ways in which we can expect increased family ties to organizations to result in the family's becoming less "traditional" and more "rational," or organized, in its approach to domestic work. One is based on the time constraints that organizational commitments impose on the individual, and thus on the whole family. The second is based on the increased exposure to organizational values and norms that occurs when an individual spends more time in an organizational setting.

The argument with respect to time constraints is as follows: (1) The more time an individual spends on organizational activities, the less time he or she has available for domestic activities. (2) As time available for domestic activities becomes scarce, family members will seek ways to conserve time or use it more effectively. (3) In modern societies, there is a widespread assumption of causality between a rational orientation to organizing activity and the most effective use of time. (4) Therefore, as time available for domestic activities becomes scarce, family members will try to become more rationally organized in performing family work.

---

[2] See Hoffman and Nye, 1974, pp. 26–38, for a review of studies showing that "financial need" is most often cited as the most important reason that wives take jobs.

The second argument relates to the acquisition of organizational norms and values. In modern societies, some degree of exposure to rational norms is inevitable for everyone but a hermit; nevertheless, it is most likely that individuals who have direct affiliations with organizations have the best chance of getting such exposure. Melvin Kohn and his associates have developed what can be described as a "generalization theory" of human behavior. According to this theory, individuals tend to apply strategies that are successful in one setting to other settings that make similar demands on them (Kohn, 1969; Kohn and Schooler, 1973; Schooler, 1972; Mortimer and Simmons, 1978). Incorporating this theory, we can summarize our second argument as follows. (1) Members of organizations receive more exposure to rational norms and values than do nonmembers. (2) Individuals tend to transfer practices and attitudes learned in one setting to other settings. (3) Therefore, members of organizations are more likely than nonmembers to apply rational organizational practices to their domestic activities.

IMPLICATIONS OF FAMILY RATIONALITY

There have not been any studies, to my knowledge, that systematically examine the way that families organize their housework, so the following discussion is purely speculative. I would expect that the rational family, in contrast to a nonrational family, will more carefully plan and schedule activity and make deliberate attempts to find efficient ways to use time and perform tasks. The rational family will more fully utilize traditionally slack resources—for example, by having the children and the husband help with the housework when the wife is employed. Although organizational norms dictate that rational criteria be used to assign tasks—and availability of time is one such criterion—it is hard to predict with confidence that the rational family will completely abandon the traditional sex-typing of chores. As we have already discussed, sex-typing occurs even in organization settings.

A consequence of admitting the possibility of family rationality is that we might fruitfully be able to apply findings from the organizational literature to predict and explain family work patterns. One such finding is that organizations in a relatively undemanding and unchanging environment can coordinate their internal activities by means of a centralized authority system and a set of rules and procedures. This would apply, for example, to a company that manufactures a single product and that has a steady market for this product. By contrast, when environmental demands are unpredictable and constantly changing, to be effective the organization must decentralize—that is, create relatively autonomous rather than interdependent subunits, and it must rely less on standardized procedures and more on individual discretion in making decisions.[3] This might be the case, for example, with a company that tailors its products to customer demands, that is faced with a changing and unpredictable market, or that is subject to community and political pressures. One can imagine the same general finding applying to families also. If everyone's timetable is fixed and unvarying, the family might operate quite well with a basic set of rules and authority structure. The more complex and changing the external demands on the family, the more we might expect to see the family relying on each individual member to make decisions as the need arises and, perhaps, even to become self-sufficient ("decentralized") by handling his or her own meals, shopping, laundry, and other tasks.

The growing predominance of dual-earner families in U.S. society represents an important change in the number and nature of family-organization linkages. Of all family-organization linkages, affiliations with a work organization are the least likely to be viewed as optional and the most likely to be constraining in terms of demands on the individual's time. Throughout the rest of this book, my focus is largely on differences between dual and single earner families in the way they relate to work organizations and the way they structure their household activities.

THE EFFECTS OF EMPLOYMENT ON HOUSEWORK

One aspect of this total picture is the impact of a wife's employment on the family division of labor. As it happens, this issue has been quite extensively researched. Two rather different ways of measuring housework have been used, and the method seems to have some effect on the kinds of results reported.

---

[3] See the discussions by Galbraith (1973), Lawrence and Lorsch (1967), Perrow (1970), and Thompson (1967).

The first method is to ask about the *relative* amounts of time spent on various household tasks by family members. For example, the respondent might be asked, "Who does the cooking in your family?", and given a choice of five responses: wife always, wife usually, both husband and wife equally, husband usually, husband always. Using this way of measuring housework, results quite consistently indicate that husbands of employed wives do more housework than do husbands of nonemployed wives, although the employed women continue to be responsible for most of the housework.[4] In general, these findings hold for people in different social classes.[5] When adolescent children are present, it is they—rather than the husband—who most relieve the wife (Bahr, 1974). Families with employed wives tend to utilize paid help with housework more than do families with nonemployed wives; however, this applies mostly in families in higher income groups (Powell, 1963; Olsen, 1960).

The second method of measuring housework focuses on *absolute,* rather than relative, amounts of time spent. Time budget studies, for example, ask respondents to complete a detailed daily log of activities, with weekly estimates being inferred from the time recorded on the sampled day's log. Studies using this method tend to report either no effect of a wife's employment on the husband's housework time, or, at most, a very tiny positive effect. One study by Walker (1970), for example, reported that husbands of both employed and nonemployed women spent the same average amount of time, 1.6 hours per day, in housework. However, employed mothers with children under two years of age received over one hour per day more help from their husbands than their nonemployed counterparts. Also, for mothers working more than 15 hours per week, almost 30 percent of the total housework was done by teenagers; for women working less than this or not at all, only 20 percent was contributed by the teenagers. The strongest impact of the wife's employment in Walker's study was on

---

[4] Among the most widely cited of such studies are those by Blood and Wolfe (1960), Nye and Hoffman (1963), Young and Willmott (1973), and Hoffman and Nye (1974). The article by Bahr in the book by Hoffman and Nye, gives a good summary of this literature.

[5] It may be that race affects these findings. Joan Aldous (1969) found that in lower-class black families, husbands are *less* likely to help with housework and child care when wives work. The opposite was true with the lower-class white males in her sample.

the amount of housework the wife herself did: employed women spent an average of 4.8 hours per day as compared with 8.1 hours per day for nonemployed women.[6]

Another study investigating the impact of working hours on housework hours is one performed by the author using data from the Panel Study of Income Dynamics (PSID). The results confirm those reported above. For example, I found that on the average every hour a woman works outside the home reduces the time she spends on housework by 23 minutes. For husbands in that study, every hour the wife was employed increased housework time by about five minutes. There is a detailed discussion of the methods and findings of this analysis in the appendix.

We are left now with several questions to explore. For example, what factors other than the wife's employment affect a husband's willingness to do housework? If employed women spend so much less time on housework than full-time housewives do—and, at the same time, their husbands and children take on only a part of the burden—then what happens to all the undone housework? Do these families become so efficient—so rational and organized—that the same amount of work gets done no matter how much the available time shrinks?

We come now to Part Two of this work, which presents findings from interviews with 30 families, during which these and other issues relating to family functioning in an organizational environment are explored in some depth.

---

[6]Walker (1970) and Walker and Gauger (1973). See also Meissner, Humphreys, Meis, and Scheu (1975), pp. 424–39. Many time budget studies are reviewed by Pleck (1977), pp. 417–27.

PART TWO:
EXPLORATORY
INTERVIEW STUDY

CHAPTER **III**

The Interviews

When the issues under investigation are complex and not well understood, conventional survey research is of limited utility. In the present case, for instance, it would be difficult to design a standardized questionnaire and be confident that it was a valid instrument for capturing the kinds of family dynamics I am interested in here. These interviews were conducted in order to gain some firsthand knowledge about family links to organizations—in particular, to work organizations—and the processes through which those links affect family life.

The 30 families involved were questioned about such issues as the way that employment demands affect home life, the processes leading to different kinds of housework allocation, the number and kinds of household tasks done, the extent to which and ways in which norms of "organizational rationality" influence the performance of family work, and so on.

SELECTION OF SAMPLE

Random sampling methods are not appropriate for a project like this. What is needed is the deliberate selection of families who vary along certain specific dimensions of interest, but who are as homogeneous as possible with respect to other characteristics that are not being examined here but that might influence results.

Employment of the wife is an important family link to organizations that is expected to affect domestic life, and thus approximately equal numbers of employed and nonemployed wives were selected. Specifically, there were 11 full-time and four part-time employed women, two full-time students, and 13 full-time housewives. Of the men, four were students and the remaining 26 were employed full-time.

All families lived in the San Francisco Bay Area, were white, and consisted of both husband and wife and at least one child under the age of 18.

Subjects were recruited from two sources. Ten families were obtained by the "network" approach, starting with student families at Stanford University who were then asked to recommend friends whose families had the appropriate characteristics. Everyone approached at this stage agreed to participate. The remaining 20 families were obtained through a study conducted by Professor William G. Ouchi of the Stanford Graduate School of Business. The Ouchi sample contained 80 individuals from two large electronics firms and represented staff and line management, clerical and assembly workers. The first 20 of these individuals who met my criteria and who agreed to participate were included.

All the employed individuals, men and women, worked for an organization as I have defined it—that is, a social group that is structured according to rational principles. Nearly all worked for a large bureaucratic organization. Characteristics of the interviewees will be discussed in more detail below.

INTERVIEWING PROCEDURES

Questions were asked in open-ended fashion, and the respondents were encouraged to talk freely. I explained to all respondents that I was attempting to determine the ways that family life was affected by the organizational ties of family members, and toward the end of each interview I asked them to volunteer information about factors they felt were important but that I had neglected to cover.

All interviews were conducted at the respondents' homes. Most took place in the evening—before, during, or after dinner.

In 18 of the 30 cases, both husband and wife were present; in the remaining cases, only the wife took part. As the interviews progressed, I made more deliberate efforts to have both spouses present as it became evident that this increased the amount of and the nature of information obtained. Jessie Bernard (1972) writes that every married couple represents not one marriage but two. This was brought home to me in a few cases where I started by interviewing the wife alone, and the husband joined us later. In these instances, I was surprised at the different picture of family life that emerged when reports from the husband were added to the wife's earlier report. In particular, there were sometimes large discrepancies between the reports of each on the amount of time each spent on housework. This point is discussed further in Chapter 7.

Interviews lasted from about one to three hours each, the length of the interview being controlled largely by the subjects. Some answered questions briefly; others elaborated at length. A large family, especially one with older children, tended to produce more lengthy interviews because there was more information to report. Interviews with both spouses present averaged two hours each, as compared to just over one and one-half hours each for single-spouse interviews. Short interviews are not necessarily less useful than long ones, however, because some respondents are able to convey much pertinent information in a brief period of time.

CHARACTERISTICS OF FAMILIES INTERVIEWED

Table 3.1 gives the distribution of families by family size, age of youngest child, age of husband and wife, education and occupation of husband and wife, and time spent on paid employment and other organizational affiliations by husband and wife.

Most families consisted of four persons (53 percent). There were roughly equal numbers of three- and five-person families (20 and 17 percent, respectively), and only a few (10 percent) had six or more persons. The youngest child was aged five or under in 40 percent of the families, at least six but not over 12 in 37 percent, and at least 12 but under 18 in the remaining 23 percent.

The average educational level of husbands and wives was quite high. Forty percent of the husbands and 33 percent of the wives reported having a bachelor's degree, with an additional 40 percent of husbands and 13 percent of wives having an advanced degree. Most of the men (73 percent) and over half the employed women were in professional or managerial occupations. As mentioned earlier, half the women were full-time housewives or students.

Table 3.1.
Aggregate Characteristics of Families Interviewed[a] (N = 30)

Characteristics	No.	Percent
Family Size		
3	6	20
4	16	53
5	5	17
6	3	10
Age of Youngest Child		
5 or younger	12	40
6–11	11	37
12–17	7	23
Age of Husband		
Under 25	0	0
25–34	12	40
35–44	12	40
45–54	6	20
Age of Wife		
Under 25	0	0
25–34	14	47
35–44	11	37
45–54	5	17
Education of Husband		
High school	4	13
Some college	1	3
College degree	12	40
Advanced degree	12	40
Not ascertained	1	3
Education of Wife		
High school	6	20
Some college	7	23
College degree	10	33
Advanced degree	4	13
Not ascertained	3	10
Occupation of Husband		
Professional	3	10
Managerial	19	63
Clerical and sales	1	3
Blue collar	3	10
Student	4	13
Occupation of Wife		
Professional	6	20
Managerial	2	7

Table 3.1. (continued)

Characteristics	No.	Percent
Clerical and sales	3	10
Blue collar	4	13
Student	2	7
Housewife	13	43
Weekly Work Hours of Husband[b]		
31–40	4	13
41–50	6	20
51–60	16	53
61 and more	4	13
Mean for all husbands = 51.9 hours		
Weekly Work Hours of Wife[b]		
None	13	43
1–10	1	3
11–20	2	7
21–30	1	3
31–40	2	7
41–50	8	27
51–60	3	10
Mean for all wives = 22.7 hours		
Mean for working wives = 40.0 hours		
Weekly Hours Spent on Other Organizational Affiliations by Husband		
Less than 1	16	53
1–10	12	40
11–20	2	7
Mean for all husbands = 2.9 hours		
Weekly Hours Spent on Other Organizational Affiliations by Wife		
Less than 1	8	27
1–10	14	47
11–20	5	17
21–30	1	3
31–40	2	7
Mean for all wives = 7.6 hours		
Mean for housewives = 17.5 hours		

[a]All the families interviewed were white, resided in the San Francisco Bay Area, had at least one child under the age of 18 living at home, and consisted of the married couple and their children only. Children who have left home are not included when family size is calculated.

[b]This includes hours of full-time college attendance and commuting time.

The husbands, on the average, spent far more time on their jobs or full-time college than did the wives. For men, the mean number of hours per week spent on work and commuting time was 51.9; for employed wives, the equivalent mean was 40 hours per week (and 22.7 hours per week for all wives).

"Other organizational affiliations" are organized activities outside the home besides paid employment and full-time schooling—such as voluntary work of various kinds, including work with children's organized groups, and part-time educational activities such as night school classes. Wives, on the whole, spend more time in such activities than do husbands, with an average of 7.6 hours per week as compared to 2.9 hours for the husbands. For full-time housewives, the average rises to 17.5 hours per week. As will be discussed in Chapter 9, much of this consists of time spent on children's extracurricular activities.

Table 3.2 lists each family interviewed in chronological order and gives age and sex of children; occupation and weekly hours spent at work or full-time college by husband and wife; weekly housework hours reported for husband, wife, and children; and hours spent by each family member on other organizational activities. The chief purpose of this table is to provide a ready descriptive reference for the reader when specific family case histories are being discussed.

One cautionary note to the reader is in order at this point. In the chapters that follow, findings are often presented in tabular form. These tables should be interpreted as simply *descriptive* of the findings from this group of families. Given the size and nature of the sample, results should not be taken as generalizable to any other population. What is most important in a qualitative enterprise such as this is to try to uncover the processes that underlie any dominant patterns that emerge and the processes that account for any exceptions to the predominant pattern.

Findings from the interviews have been assembled by topic. Each of the six chapters that follow cover one topic. Chapter 4, Work and the Family, describes the facets of work organizations that most seem to affect family life. Chapter 5, Rationalization of Family Work, addresses a central concern in this study—the extent to which families try to organize household work in a rational way and the factors that account for a greater or lesser degree of domestic organization. Chapter 6, Family Functions, deals with the kinds of instrumental tasks families perform and factors that affect the time individuals devote

Table 3.2.
Characteristics and Weekly Time Allocation of Families Interviewed

Interview Number[a]	Age and Sex of Children	Occupation	Hours Employment or Full-time College (including commute)	Hours Housework	Hours Other Organizational Affiliations[b]
1	F 12, 10	(H) Architect	40	5	3.5
		(W) College student	32	10–14	4–14
		(C) Students	0	5	4–14
2	F 1.5	(H) College student	45+	NA	0
	M 5	(W) Housewife	0	26–37	17
		(C) 1 student	0	0	0
3	F 13 mos.	(H) Computer management	46–50+	2.5	3
		(W) Housewife	0	17–25	6
		(C) None	0	0	1
4	F 11, 9	(H) Architect & part-time instructor	50–60	NA	0
	M 14, 12	(W) Part-time tennis instructor	20	20–28	5
		(C) Students	0	7+	High
5	F 2	(H) College student & computer programmer	42.5	5–6	9+
	M 6	(W) Housewife	0	34–46	6
		(C) 1 student	0	0	0
6	F 8	(H) Student & research asst.	40–60	16.25	0
	M 4.5, 1.5	(W) Housewife	0	27–39	6.5

Table 3.2. (continued)

Interview Number[a]	Age and Sex of Children	Occupation	Hours Employment or Full-time College (including commute)	Hours Housework	Hours Other Organizational Affiliations[b]
		(C) 1 student	0	NA	2
7	F 4 mos.	(H) Copywriter	54	2-6	0
		(W) Housewife	0	40-56	9+
		(C) None	0	0	0
8	M 10 mos.	(H) College student & research asst.	51.5	7.5-10.5	.5
		(W) Schoolteacher	57-61	7.5-10.5	1.5
		(C) None	0	0	0
9	M 15, 9	(H) Lawyer	52-56	3.5	2
		(W) College student	48	12+	11.5
		(C) Students	0	3	11+
10	F 13, 10	(H) Corporation management	50-56+	8-10	0
		(W) Sales manager	50-56+	8-10	0
		(C) Students	0	8-10	1
12	F 14	(H) Personnel manager	55+	2-4	0
		(W) Housewife	0	NA	0
		(C) Student	0	0	0
13	F 14; M 19, 12	(H) Real estate salesman	40	10+	0
		(W) Personnel clerk	50	10+	0
		(C) Students & part-time workers	3-20	10+	0

#	Children					
14	M 7, 2.5	(H)	Financial manager	47	8	2
		(W)	Compensation manager	52.5+	30	0
		(C)	1 student	0	Low	2
15	F 16, 10 M 18	(H)	Personnel manager	57.5–62.5	Low	1–4
		(W)	Housewife	0	25–30	4.5
		(C)	Students & summer work	NA	Low	High
17	F 14 M 17	(H)	Roofer	40	0	0
		(W)	Assembly worker	46+	25+	0
		(C)	Students	0	5+	0
18	M 9, 7	(H)	Labor relations manager	50–57.5	1	8–10
		(W)	Housewife	0	12+	36+
		(C)	Students	0	0	20+
19	M 10, 7	(H)	Product line manager	50–52.5	8–12	16
		(W)	Housewife	0	16	10–17
		(C)	Students	0	4–5	3–6
20	F 16 M 13	(H)	Group personnel manager	45–55	6	2+
		(W)	Schoolteacher	40	10–15	.5
		(C)	Students	0	10–14	9–20
21	M 3.5	(H)	Program manager	50–52.5	9+	7–
		(W)	Production engineering asst.	45	14+	7–
		(C)	None	0	Low	0
22	M 9, 8, 4, 14 mos.	(H)	Division manufacturing manager	52.5–57.5	2–6+	15
		(W)	Housewife	0	70	9
		(C)	3 students	0	15	3–5
					(except for baby)	(except for baby)

Table 3.2. (continued)

Interview Number[a]	Age and Sex of Children	Occupation	Hours Employment or Full-time College (including commute)	Hours Housework	Hours Other Organizational Affiliations[b]
23	M 17, 16	(H) Mechanic & part-time handyman	62	2+	.5
		(W) Assembly worker	50	16–18	1–10
		(C) Students & part-time workers	0–23	2–5	0
24	F 10	(H) Marketing manager	49	15	0
		(W) Secretary	49	15	0
		(C) Student	0	3.5	1–2
25	F 10	(H) Division controller	50–55	18	1.5+
	M 8	(W) Part-time nurse	Avg. 2 but ranges from 0–28	27.5	15–27
		(C) Students	0	6–8	3.5–13.5
26	F 16	(H) Electronics manager	47.5	20	0
	M 14, 12	(W) Nurse	45	20	1
		(C) Students & part-time work for daughter	NA	4	0
27	M 3.5, 1	(H) Navy electrician	36	12–20	6
		(W) Assembly worker	44+	24	6
		(C) None	0	0	1.5
28	F 17, 14	(H) Technical director	50–60	3	0
	M 15	(W) Part-time medical asst.	22+	18	0

#	Children	Member	Occupation[b]			
		(C)	Students	0	2	High
29	M 11, 9	(H)	Engineering manager	55	4–5	7
		(W)	Housewife	0	24–26	6.5
		(C)	Students	0	2	9+
30	F 4 / M 8 mos.	(H)	Personnel manager	62.5+	10	0
		(W)	Housewife	0	56	2
		(C)	None	0	Low	0
31	M 8.5, 6	(H)	Owner, auto dealership	72.5+	0	0
		(W)	Housewife	0	32	29–33
		(C)	Students	0	2	8–10
32	F 14 / M 16, 13, 9, 4	(H)	Operations manager	55–62.5	4–6	0
		(W)	Housewife & substitute schoolteacher	0–45	28	12 (but 0 if she is working)
		(C)	Students	0	4–6	3+

[a]Data from Interviews #11 and #16 were omitted from analyses because the families did not meet selection criteria.

[b]Other organizational affiliations include college courses, such as night school courses, taken without a degree in mind; children's after-school activities; civil, political, or religious volunteer work.

NOTE: If there is more than one child in the family, time estimates refer to average time spent *per child* unless otherwise indicated.

to domestic work. Chapter 7 focuses on Who Does the Housework, an issue around which much of the current struggle between the sexes revolves. Chapter 8, Sex Role Ideology, delves into the normative beliefs underlying male and female roles in the family. Finally, Chapter 9 describes two child-related issues: the organized extracurricular activities of children, and parent-initiated leisure activities to foster "family togetherness."

CASE STUDIES

Near the beginning of each topic-oriented chapter, there is a case study describing in some detail an interview with a single family. One of the chief reasons for including these case studies is to make at least a few of the families "come alive" for the reader. Thus, in addition to illustrating the topic of the chapter in which it appears, each case study also describes the family's experiences and attitudes concerning many of the topics of the other chapters. Chapter 4, for example, describes how one couple—Jean and Larry—views the impact of work on the family. It also relates Jean and Larry's reports on the division of family labor, the rational organization of housework, children's activities, sex-role ideology, and so on. In short, the case study presents a holistic view of a particular family, while the rest of the chapter organizes findings from all 30 families around one topic.

Individuals are referred to by name (not, incidentally, their real names) whenever their story is presented in some detail, as in the case studies. Sometimes, families are referred to by interview number so that the interested reader may check their characteristics in Table 3.2.

We move now to the first issue that the interviews set out to explore: the employment-related factors that most affect family life.

CHAPTER IV

Work and the Family

This chapter examines some facets of work organizations that affect family life. Before presenting findings from all 30 families, I describe an interview with just one couple, Jean and Larry. Their lifestyle and patterns of activity are quite acceptable in today's United States, but only a few years ago might have aroused widespread disapproval.

Jean and Larry both have full-time jobs. They have two young sons, aged seven and two and one-half years. For nearly all their lives, the two boys have been left with sitters while their parents were at work. Both Jean and Larry enjoy and are quite highly committed to their jobs. After leaving high school, Jean worked as a secretary for many years. She was promoted two years ago to the position of personnel representative and very recently received yet another promotion to the position of compensation administrator. Larry, who has a bachelor's degree, is a financial manager.

Jean and Larry (Interview #14)

Our interview took place on a hot summer evening. It was a fairly old, moderate-income housing tract. I steered between the campers, trucks, cars and bikes lining the curbs to park my own car. There were men in the front yards gathered around the vehicles at the curb talking and shouting to one another.

Inside the house, there was an immediate change of atmosphere from the hot noisy bustle outside. The house was cool and quiet and, in the tiny living room where I sat anyway, immaculately tidy. It was a very small house. The room where we sat was large enough to accommodate no more than four easy chairs and a couple of small coffee tables. Jean seated me and asked if I would like some cold white wine. She said:

> I can really use a glass of wine right now. It's nice to unwind for a while after work.

Jean's husband was out "riding his bike" when I arrived. The older son was watching television in another room. The younger was in bed; however, as soon as we started talking, he called out for his mother. She gave me a wry smile and said something like, "I knew I hadn't gotten my first call yet." She fetched the little boy from his bedroom, and he sat on her lap for a while, watching me curiously. Later, he wandered off to watch television with his older brother, who also occasionally came in to look at me. Jean made no attempt to direct their behavior, but whenever they had questions or requests, she immediately stopped talking to me to respond to them.

Jean was in her early 30s. She had married at the age of 18 straight out of high school. She and Larry lived in Chicago during the first few years of their marriage. She worked at various clerical and secretarial jobs. Then they moved to California and decided to start a family. It was their joint decision that Jean stay home with the children, at least while they were little.

> Jean: I didn't really enjoy that. I thought that I would, but I didn't. So when Paul [older boy] was 17 months, I went back to work.

I asked her:

> Why didn't you enjoy being at home? Were you bored?
>
> Jean: Very bored. I never had any adult companionship. All the women around here [their neighborhood], all they talked about all the time was their children. That's all we talked about. I needed to do things, to feel that I've accomplished things by myself. I really enjoy working.

A noisy clattering in the kitchen a few moments before indicated that her husband had returned from his bike ride. He walked into the room in time to hear me ask:

How did your husband feel about your returning to work?

Jean: He was very reluctant at first.

Larry gave me a cheerful "Hi" and then made a face at his wife's response as if to confirm that he had indeed been reluctant to have her return to work.

The contrasting personal styles of Jean and Larry became evident very quickly. Jean was well-dressed, calm, spoke clearly and usually quietly, as if she was accustomed to putting on a good face to strangers (perhaps in the context of her job). Larry was more spontaneous. Casually dressed, good-looking, with a cheerful engaging smile, he would frequently disagree with his wife's responses. Often the dialog would become a sort of debate in which each was trying to convince me that he or she was right and the other was wrong. This dialog was always lighthearted, even humorous, but I wouldn't be surprised if the discussion between them in the absence of outside observers sometimes became quite heated and bitter.

Jean described their typical work day. She leaves home about 7:00 a.m. and returns about 5:30 p.m., five days a week. She always leaves the house at the same time in the morning but sometimes is home later depending on her workload that day. As for Larry, Jean laughed as she said, "He leaves at five minutes of 8:00. He starts work at 8:00 and gets home 5:15 to 5:30." About once a month, Larry has to put in overtime to get month-end reports done.

Jean takes the children to the sitter's on the way to work. They eat breakfast at the sitter's. She picks them up again after work. If she finds she's going to be home late, she either asks the sitter to keep them for a while longer or calls Larry to pick them up instead. Jean is very satisfied with her sitter, a woman in her late 50s. Jean says she never seems to object to having the children stay late and is willing to take care of them even if they are sick.

We discussed the desirability of leaving children with sitters. Jean and Larry were in agreement that it was "really good for the kids." They feel their children have a grand time at the sitter's, playing with the other children there. And Jean feels she appreciates them more:

> I enjoy them much more when I don't have so much of them. When I was at home all the time, I used to get so bitchy with Paul. Didn't I, Larry? I would be screaming at him all the time. It was almost as if I was their maid—always picking up after them. Now I really appreciate my kids more, not seeing so much of them.

She added, repeating her earlier comments, "A great deal is due to my sitter." Jean feels that without having such a perfect sitter at her disposal, she would probably rethink her decision to work.

> **Q:** So there's no doubt in your mind, Jean, that you'd rather be trying to juggle your work and home schedules than simply staying home?
>
> **Jean:** It's really due to the jobs I've had. If I'd had a dull job that I didn't enjoy, I'd probably feel different. I've really enjoyed all the jobs I've ever had, except for the bank. I had a job with a bank once for six months. I didn't like that. But I've always enjoyed working and I don't like housework.

I had heard that Jean's present employer has a reputation for being good to work for and asked what had caused her to apply there. She said it was "just because they had a job open." But she went on to say that she was delighted with her choice:

> It is a super company, really super. The trust and the honesty. It's very personal, but not to the point where people are interfering in your personal life.

Her last comment was of interest to me, because I had heard some people describe this particular company as the sort of "familial" organization said to be characteristic of Japan. In that sort of organization, the line between the employee's personal and company life is reportedly not very strongly drawn. Jean elaborated:

> At [her last company, also a large corporation] they were controlling your personal life. Both my husband and I used to work there. You know, if people wanted to get a divorce, the company didn't want them to talk about it at work. They didn't want people to know that their managers were divorced. That there was something wrong with their personal lives. They weren't handling things properly. I was a secretary then, and if, say, my boss and I wanted to go out after work just for a drink, we couldn't do it. It would get him into a lot of trouble.

Jean said this was a situation she more or less took for granted until she moved to her present employer:

> I really didn't realize how bad it was until I came to work here and saw how different things were. Of course, that was in Chicago; maybe things are different in California or something.

She likes the "personal touch" in her present company also—the fact that people are always addressed by their first names, rather than "Mr. This and Mr. That," and the fact that the two senior partners in the company "walk around like normal everyday people."

Jean's company has a flexible scheduling policy; Mike's employer doesn't. When I queried Jean on flexible scheduling and how it affected her life, her comments were very positive:

> I can do just about anything I want. It's not like a sales office where we have to be there at certain times for the customers. We just deal with other employees. All of us come in at different hours. [She backtracked a bit.] Well, it's kind of the usual hours, you know. But sometimes someone says "I'll be late tomorrow. I won't be in till 9:00." It's really very flexible.

I asked how flexible Larry's working hours were and Jean replied for him:

> It's not as flexible as mine, but he doesn't have trouble getting time off. He needs flexible hours; he always prefers to go in later in the morning. I can go into work very early. If I went in at 8:00, it would cause a lot of problems because of the traffic. It can take 45 minutes in heavy traffic. I can get home in only 20 minutes sometimes [i.e., by carefully planning her hours].

Larry's expression made it plain that he felt she was overstating the benefits of flexible scheduling. He argued, "But you're really operating under set hours."

> Jean: But I don't have to. I can leave at 4:00 if I want to.
>
> Larry: I just can't see that it benefits you that much.
>
> Jean: Flex hours aren't set up so that each day is different. You establish the schedule that best suits you, and stick to it.

This echoed other comments I'd heard about flexible scheduling. The flexibility lies mainly in establishing a schedule in the first place.

> Q: Do you prefer to have a predictable schedule?
>
> Jean: It's much better to stick to one schedule. The kids just wouldn't take to having each day different. We have enough problems with them

now. Like at the weekends, we let them sleep really late. Then on Monday mornings, it's a real problem getting them up.

Jean went on to explain that she could take time off in the middle of the day if she wanted to, but she doesn't like to do this. Everyone in the office has an established schedule. You get to know what the schedules of other people are, and, similarly, they rely on your being available at certain times. She feels it is important for her career to have a predictable work schedule.

Predictability is, of course, an important component in the concept of rationality because predictability enables one to gain a larger degree of control over one's environment. Jean believes very strongly in the idea of rational organization of one's time and activities as a way to successfully combine the worlds of work and home and to gain the most mileage, as it were, out of every day. She was one of several women I interviewed who claimed that being employed made her use her time more efficiently, so that she often got as much, if not more, done around the house when she worked as when she stayed home.

> As far as the housework goes, I don't enjoy housework. [It makes no difference] if I have 12 hours to do something or two hours. I didn't do any more when I was at home than I do when I work. If I'm on a schedule, I can do things better, quicker, more efficiently.

Her husband had been listening intently, as though this were a topic that had never arisen between them and he found it interesting. He questioned her about her last statement, "What do you mean?"

> **Jean:** I just don't do anymore when I'm home all the time. When I'm working, I just get more organized and more efficient.
>
> **Q:** Can you think of any particular jobs that don't get done as much or get eliminated entirely when you're working?
>
> **Jean:** No, not really, There's just no appreciable difference.

We discussed some of the ways that Jean organizes her life as a working wife and mother.

> **Jean:** From the moment I get up in the morning until at least 7:00 in the evening, every moment is carefully planned. At lunchtime, I plan the shopping that needs to be done. Like today, I took a package to the

post office—it was someone's birthday. Then I stop at the vegetable stand on the way home because it's more convenient that way than on the way to work. When I go shopping for clothing, I often go at lunchtime, or sometimes after work. I often order from the catalog too to save time. People at work are just amazed when they see how much I order that way. Then sometimes I'll get four or five outfits in one lunchtime. You get really efficient when you have to.

Larry interrupted, "You buy four or five outfits at a time?" in a tone of incredulity. Jean explained:

Yes. Maybe two for Paul, two for Jimmy, one for me. Oh, not all for me! [But she added] Although sometimes when I get depressed, that's just what I'll do.

At a later point in our talk, I asked Jean what kinds of things most upset her daily life, and she returned to her concern with having things organized and predictable:

Right now, things are very structured for me, very organized. So if anything at all in my day goes helter skelter—like, say, Mike calls and says someone is coming over in the evening for dinner—that really upsets me. I like to have at least 24 hours notice. I like to have my general schedule for the day all set at work and at home, and if anything gets out of whack, that bothers me for the whole day.

Q: Why is this? Is it because time is so short for you? Or is it a personality thing?

Jean: Oh, it's a personality thing. That's just me. I like things tidy and arranged.

When I explained that I was going to ask about household chores and who usually performed them, there was a brief silence and Larry swung around in his chair to face his wife.

Q: Who usually does the cooking?

Larry: [in a mutter] : Now this is going to be interesting!

Jean: Yes, it is. [Firmly] I do the majority of the cooking.

This is clearly the reponse he thought she was going to give, and he interrupted quickly:

> Yes, but I cook too. At least a couple of times a week.

Jean's pleasantly modulated tone of voice rose for the first time in our talk:

> What! Listen [speaking directly to me], you put down that I do most of the cooking. He cooks sometimes—like maybe twice a month.

A bantering argument ensued. A breakdown, meal by meal, didn't resolve the issue. No one cooks breakfast: the children eat at the sitter's and neither Jean nor Larry eats breakfast. Both adults eat lunch out every day. During the week, Jean says she "always or nearly always" gets dinner, with Larry sometimes cooking at the weekends. Larry would not accept her account, and we ended up with my promising to report both sides of the story: her version that he cooks about twice a month, and his version that he cooks about twice a week.

> Q: How about the dishes?
>
> Jean: I do, always.

A sly grin from Larry confirmed that there was no disagreement here.

> Q: Household cleaning?
>
> Jean: I do just about all of it.
>
> Larry: [with indignation] I disagree! I thought I did just about as much as you do.

Another minor argument broke out with Jean asking over his protesting voice questions like, "When was the last time you vacuumed, for instance?" Again, they did not reach agreement. She held firm to her claim that she did nearly all the cleaning, and he to his claim that he did far more than she gave him credit for.

They agreed on the issue of household help. They have tried in the past to have someone come in to clean.

> Jean: It didn't work out too well though. I was constantly telling them to do something, and then they didn't do it. It's really hard to find someone you can trust. And then the good ones are really expensive.

They both agreed that Jean handles the grocery shopping and all the laundry. Another disagreement arose over who pays the bills.

Larry: We pretty well share.

Jean: [with mock disgust] Oh, don't listen to him. I write out all the checks. I make sure we have enough money in the checking account to cover the checks. He does do the income tax.

As she talked, Larry was making comments like, "That sounds very one-sided," and Jean would give little snorts of laughter, waving her hand at him and looking at me as if to say, "Ignore him."

Q: Larry, what kinds of things do you do around the house?

Larry: The yardwork. I maintain the pool.

Q: Do you fix things? [He looked blank.] Like the car?

Larry: Sometimes. I'm not very mechanically inclined. We usually have the car serviced at the garage.

There was more disagreement when I asked each of them to estimate the number of hours per week each spent on domestic chores. Larry said he spent "about eight hours," and Jean nodded heartily, "Yes, that's what I would have said." However, after considering for a few moments, she said she estimated that *she* spent "about 30" hours a week, and this drew a derisive explosion from Larry. He argued that 15 hours was closer to the time she actually spent. They didn't resolve this disagreement.

Later in the interview, we returned to a discussion of dealing with finances. I asked Jean if she would miss having a source of independent income if she were ever to quit working.

Jean: No, I really don't think of it as my money. We put aside part of it for savings, part for expenses. One chunk goes into payments for my car, a lot of the rest into the checking account. The same is true of Larry's money.

I asked if they planned together what money they would allocate to what use. Her reply was that *she* more or less decided how much they needed to have in the checking account as she was the one who wrote the checks and basically handled their financial affairs. This, of course, confirmed what she had already told me. Only this time Larry didn't contradict her. He listened thoughtfully, as if he really hadn't been aware of her role in this before now, and murmured, half to himself, "That's really something I should be doing."

Jean did give Larry high marks in one area, and this was in taking care of the children. As I talked to them, I noticed that the children were as likely to approach Larry with requests as Jean. In fact, when they called out from another room, he was more likely to attend to them than Jean was. This may have been because they both thought of our interview as primarily Jean's concern; she had been my initial contact. But their discussion on the subject confirmed that Larry was deeply involved in his children's activities and enjoyed them very much. He told me with some pride that he is active in the Indian Guides, a "father-son thing" that is run by the YMCA. He attends meetings three times a month, each lasting two or three hours; they have occasional paper drives, go on outings, and so on. Jean is not involved in any like activities with her sons.

> **Jean:** I find time very scarce on work days. Larry does help me because he keeps the children occupied when I'm busy in the kitchen. He is really a great assist in that way.

The decision as to who will take the children to the doctor and dentist is made according to the work schedule of each parent and who can get time off most readily on the day in question. In cases of emergency, Larry is usually called because his job is closer to home than Jean's. Just recently, for instance, the younger son fell and cut his head badly; Larry was called to take him to the hospital, and Jean met them there later.

> **Q:** How about the kids? Are they encouraged to help around the house?
>
> **Larry:** We've just started with Paul. He cleans his own room now—reluctantly! And he helps me outside too.
>
> **Q:** Does he get an allowance for this?
>
> **Larry:** Yes. That's why he does it. We haven't yet established what he is supposed to do for an allowance. He keeps running around trying to think up things to do.

Larry left the room at this point to tend to the boys, and while he was gone I asked Jean, "Do you think as the boys grow older, they will help you out more at home?'' She laughed and said, "It depends on whether their father is around." Larry walked back into the room, and Jean said, "I told her I didn't want them to grow up like you—chauvinistic!" An appreciative grin from Larry!

Q: Larry, do you do more around the house when Jean is working?

A resounding *"No!"* from Jean, and Larry made good-humored murmurs of agreement.

Q: [to Jean] Have you ever discussed this with him? Or asked him to help more?

General laughter followed from them both, with cries of "Oh, yes" from Jean.

Larry: She keeps mentioning it all the time, but each time she does, I just give her more to do. So it's like negative reinforcement.

This was said with great humor.

Q: [to Jean] So you've more or less given up on trying to convert him?

Jean: You said it. That's exactly it.

Larry grinned across at her and said, "It's a good job you have a sense of humor." (Later, when I was leaving, Jean made a comment to the effect that "He gets away with it because of his charm.")

When they were first married, Jean used to work the swing shift from 3:00 until midnight, so Larry had to cook his own dinner. Jean said, "He's a good cook anyway, so that's no problem for him." He cooks now when she's home late from work, or sometimes he starts the meal and she finishes preparing it. She added firmly that this didn't happen often, and this time he didn't argue with her.

Q: Why do you want to convert him? Because you need the help? A matter of equity?

Jean: [quickly] Yes, it's equity. Also, I would like more time to spare.

Q: What would you do with it?

Jean: I would read.

I asked Larry, "Why don't you help Jean more with the housework?" because by this time there seemed to be an implicit acknowledgment that there *was* inequity here.

> **Larry**: Well, I like it the way it is. I think it's great.

He added, after a slight pause:

> And I think it's equitable. I don't think there's that much difference. She says it's eight to 30—I say it's 10 to 15 [i.e., hours per week that each spends on housework].

Jean was trying to interrupt, but without success, as he increasingly raised his voice to talk over hers.

> **Larry**: I don't think she spends that much time on a daily basis. Jean spends a lot more time at the weekends, it's true, with the grocery shopping and the laundry. But not during the week.

Jean was throwing in scornful little asides, indicating her disagreement. She said that the fact that things seemed to run so smoothly was due to her giving a great deal of time and thought to planning things carefully. Things ran so smoothly, in other words, that Larry simply thought there wasn't much to do. But apparently Larry thinks she takes it all *too* seriously. He looked at her thoughtfully and said rather accusingly, "You look on all of it as a burden. You don't enjoy it at all." Jean was a little taken aback at this and said to me, almost apologetically, "Only when I entertain. I really enjoy it then."

> **Q**: Why is that?

> **Jean**: Well, I try out new dishes then. And I have more time. It's not like after work when I have to rush. We nearly always entertain on Saturdays and Sundays. It's all better planned and scheduled. And they're appreciative. That makes such a difference. You know, when Paul says "Daddy is a better cooker than Mommy," that's such a blow to the ego.

So it seems that Jean's compulsion to be organized results in her being relatively inflexible, and it may be that Larry feels that she is unable to get spontaneous pleasure out of informal or unexpected events. His unexpected accusation put their earlier disagreement about the housework in a new perspective. It may be that he sees her as rather boringly preoccupied with getting things done properly and on time, and a part of his delight in needling her and refusing to cooperate may arise from the same sort of motivation that prompts the naughty schoolboy to bait a tedious teacher!

> **Q:** Would you ever consider working part-time, Jean?
>
> **Jean:** No. I just don't think I could advance in my career with that kind of a schedule. Also, I don't think I would utilize the extra time off that well.

This, of course, ties in with her earlier remarks that she uses her time more efficiently when she *has* to.

> **Q:** Jean, do you feel—deep down—that it is really Larry's responsibility to earn the living?
>
> **Jean:** No. Definitely not.
>
> **Q:** How would you react if he were to quit his job and say he was going to stay home and take care of the house from now on?
>
> **Jean:** [with some indignation] That wouldn't be right. It's a shared re-sponsibility, bringing in the income so that we can enjoy life.

Larry was looking interested at this idea.

> **Larry:** I think I'd go for that. I think I'd be a good houseperson.
>
> **Q:** Would you really do all the housework and take full responsibility for it?

Jean was muttering over our conversation, "Oh, yeah, he'd like it fine as long as I came home and cooked dinner every night."

> **Larry:** Well, probably what would happen is I would enjoy it for a while. [To Jean] Remember that time you were gone for two weeks. I really enjoyed doing everything then.

Another rather lively discussion followed. Jean pointed out that dur-ing the period he was referring to the children had been at the sitter's every day, and he was rebutting with, "Yes, but the sitter has the kids now too." Jean went on, "But you don't have the responsibility all the time, 24 hours." He started to disagree, but changed his mind and said, "Yes, that's right."

> Larry: [to me] I really don't think I'd enjoy it all the time. It would be okay for a while. If I had it to do on a regular basis, I wouldn't want to do it all.

He added, with a mischievous grin at his wife, "Now that I have my bike, I need more free time than ever."

The issue of family roles arose again in a slightly different context when I asked Jean what would happen if she didn't have such a perfect sitter for her children. She had earlier said that she would have to rethink the situation as far as having a full-time job was concerned.

> Jean: The kids are too important to me. I just wouldn't work if I couldn't get a good sitter.
>
> Q: Do you think it would be your duty to stay home and give up your job...

Jean quickly answered "Yes" before I could finish my question.

> Q: ... or do you think Larry has equal responsibility?

Jean thought about this for a few moments.

> Jean: That would depend on who was making the most money. I really think it would.

But this time Larry knew where he stood on the issue of giving up his job.

> Larry: [firmly] I don't think so. We'd have to have a real long discussion about that first. No, I wouldn't like staying home. I wouldn't want to give up my job.

At one point, I asked which one of them most enjoyed being with the children. They both pondered the question for a while and then agreed that probably each one of them enjoys their sons as much as the other does. They have different ways of dealing with the children. Jean tends to be consistently firm with them, while Larry tends to let them run wild and then suddenly get angry if they get too far out of hand. However, both Jean and Larry seem to approve of the other's childrearing practices and feel they balance one another in this respect.

We discussed their family background a little. Larry was the middle one of three sons. His mother "did everything" around the house and was employed full-time from the time Larry was ten years old. He doesn't ever remember her complaining about having to do all the housework. However, he recalls that she did not enjoy having to go out to work and is sure she would have given up her job if their financial situation had permitted. His father worked full-time, and handled the bill paying. He also cooked occasionally. Jean snickered and said, "He made fudge." Larry ignored Jean's comment, and said his father was especially likely to fix the breakfast. He also took care of the yard and the "fixing."

Larry's older brother was ten years older than he and had already left home when the mother went to work. The parents worked the same shift most of the time, and Larry and his younger brother had to fix their own meals most of the time. The mother would frequently leave a list of groceries to be bought, and Larry or the younger brother would go to the store for them. (Incidentally, I could not help but wonder silently during this recital if Larry's remembrance of his past helpfulness would have been challenged by his mother as his accounts of present helpfulness are challenged by his wife!) Larry said he was "supposed" to clean his own room and help his father in the yard and received an allowance for this. He was rather vague as to whether he did, in fact, do much of this work.

Jean was the middle of five children. She had two older brothers and a younger brother and sister. She grew up on a farm. The father and boys worked outdoors primarily. The daughters helped the mother with the house, the garden, the chickens, and the family cow.

In spite of their disagreements over the way they divide household work, Jean and Larry expressed similar attitudes toward sex roles. Both claim to have what can be described as egalitarian views. They told me, for instance, with amusement that some of their neighbors wouldn't let their little boys play with dolls. Jean said this was ridiculous seeing the boys "would grow up to be fathers one day, hopefully." Larry heartily agreed with her.

Q: If you were to become multimillionaires, what changes would you make in your lives?

Jean's instant response was in terms of hiring household help to leave her freer to pursue her career.

> **Jean:** I would bring in a live-in maid. I'd still leave the kids at the sitter's because she's such an excellent sitter. But I'd have a housekeeper to do everything—the cooking, cleaning, everything. I'd have someone to do all the yardwork too.

At first, Larry agreed, "That sounds just great to me too." But almost immediately he retracted.

> **Larry:** I spoke too fast. That's not fine with me. I really would prefer to do some things myself. I get a lot of satisfaction out of it [i.e., the yardwork and other things he does now]. Mostly the satisfaction comes when it's done [laughing], but, yes, I do enjoy it too.

Both pooh-poohed the claims made by some people that a mother's employment is harmful to her children. They feel their own children really enjoy being at the sitter's. However, when we were discussing family togetherness, Larry said:

> After leaving them at the sitter all day, it makes us feel a bit guilty leaving them again in the evening.

Because of this, they seldom go out together without the children. I commented that I'd heard other working couples make similar remarks. Larry just nodded at my comment, but Jean reacted somewhat defensively.

> **Jean:** But you haven't heard couples say it where the wife *doesn't* work? That's really odd to me. After all, any working father leaves the kids all day, doesn't he? And then *he* doesn't feel guilty going out in the evening without them?

I admitted this was true. Jean said she thinks this is probably an instance of the way that traditional stereotypes operate to reinforce the idea that the mother is responsible for the children and that by going out to work she is abandoning them and should feel guilty.

They recounted the camping and skiing trips they took with their children, sometimes with just the four of them and sometimes with other couples and their children along.

> Larry: But it's better when it's just us. Because then we get to talking with the grownups and not paying attention to the kids.
>
> Jean: Yes, but the kids also enjoy themselves [i.e., when other families are there], playing with the other kids.
>
> Larry: Yes, that's right.

Jean is apparently the only working mother she personally knows, either among their own close friends or among the women she works with. It may be she is accustomed to defending her situation to others.

At the end of my visit, we chatted for some time about my study. Jean and Larry's younger son is participating in a research study at a local university, and they are quite fascinated with the idea of social science research on families. The disagreements that arose during the interview over such issues as housework came as no surprise to either of them. As I had surmised, they had covered this territory many times before. They told me with amusement that they had had to respond to questionnaires about their family life in connection with the son's research project and that there also their responses had differed from each other's. They take a somewhat philosophical view toward their differences of opinion, seeing this as a more or less inevitable clash between the sexes. Larry was willing to admit that he frequently attempted to serve his own selfish interests rather than doing what he honestly felt was fair. However, he reiterated his earlier statement that he feels Jean greatly exaggerates the supposed injustices being heaped on her.

When I suggested that the issue of housework is an emotionally laden one in these days of women's liberation, they laughingly agreed.

> Larry: [playfully] Now the minute you leave, you realize violence is going to erupt!

And just before I did leave, he asked, grinning, "Do you find you leave a trail of divorces in your wake?" His wife added, "You should check up a year or so later to find out."

In discussing families in a world of organizations, Young and Willmott say, "the family is not the governing institution but the governed" (1973, pp. 283–84). They mean by this that to an incredible extent a modern family's timetable and activities are determined by the demands placed on it by the organizations in its environment.

Their claim is certainly borne out by the reports of the families I interviewed, at least as far as workday schedules are concerned. The timing of any domestic activity, like mealtime, is typically explained in terms of an organizational commitment. For example, one housewife says:

> We eat at 6:30 because that's when Bill gets home from work—except on Thursdays when we eat at 7:00 because I have to take Brownies from 4:00 to 6:00.

Moreover, it seems to be taken for granted that when a conflict arises between organizational demands and domestic demands, it is the latter that have to adapt to the former. This is true even of such nonessential organizational commitments as children's extracurricular activities.[1]

The discussion that follows is organized around four employment-related issues: hours of work, flexible scheduling, job satisfaction, and the desire to maintain a boundary between work and family.

HOURS OF WORK

Most full-time jobs formally consist of an eight-hour day, five days per week. For most of my respondents, commuting time adds considerably to this. Also, many of them—especially those in managerial positions—put in long hours of overtime (see Table 3.2). A working week of from 50 to 60 hours is not uncommon, especially for the men, although some women work this long a week also. Some of the women have part-time jobs, or jobs that leave their summers free (as with schoolteachers), or jobs that occupy their time sporadi-

---

[1] The only other factor, mentioned by three families with babies, to explain the timing of meals and other domestic activities is the unpredictable behavior of a very young child. If the baby is "fussing" or fails to take an expected nap, meals are delayed and the housework left undone.

cally (as with substitute teachers or nurses). There are, however, seven wives whose working hours equal or exceed those of their husbands.

How then does the length of an individual's work day affect his or her family life? It seems, first, that the discrepancy between the husband's and the wife's working hours is a factor that affects responses. In the seven families where wives work as long or longer a day than their husbands (Jean and Larry are among them), there is considerable bitterness expressed by the two wives whose husbands, they claim, do less than their fair share of household work. In the other five families, the division of household labor is reported to be quite egalitarian.

For the majority of the families interviewed, where the men work longer hours than the wives, wives tend to be philosophical about husbands who help little in the home, excusing this unhelpfulness in terms of the men's relative lack of time for domestic work. (I return to this issue in Chapter 7.)

The prevailing attitude toward long working hours is far from philosophical, however. In 11 families, both husbands and wives expressed discontent at the long hours of—as it happens, in all cases—the husbands. In all these families, wives either do not work or work only part-time. The chief complaints are (1) the husband is excluded from family dinnertime, and (2) the husband cannot spend enough time with the children in after-school activities, such as sports.

Dinnertime

In five families, the men almost never eat dinner with the rest of the family during the week. Susan (Interview #29), a nonemployed wife with two school-aged sons, says:

> He used to get home at 6:30 [but], it got later and later. I like to eat early. I like to eat at 5:00. [Now] we just don't have dinner together.[2]

For many families, a joint evening meal is a vital family institution. It is a time of communication among family members, usually without intrusion from individuals outside the family. It seems to serve several functions, not the least of which is the promotion of a feeling of family solidarity. It also serves to facilitate parental control over children. It seems sometimes that the *wife* of a husband who

---

[2] The case of Max and Susan is presented in Chapter 9.

cannot be included in the family dinnertime is more upset than he at this situation. In one family (Interview #32), the husband's working day has been extended by the demands of a new job. His wife feels strongly about the desirability of a joint evening meal. Even though the youngest child is only four years old, she will keep dinner until the husband returns—and this is sometimes as late as ten o'clock in the evening. This situation is causing considerable tension in their family, and the wife is hoping to persuade her husband to change his job.

Arranging a communal dinnertime is not seen as a problem in those families where both husband and wife work full-time. In these cases, preparations for dinner are started late, after one or other spouse returns from work, and only rarely does the family start a meal without both workers being present.[3]

Children's Activities

Long working hours make it difficult for a father to participate in his children's after-school activities, and in several families this was cited as a source of discontent. One business executive (Interview #25) explained how much he and his wife enjoyed exercising with their children at a nearby "parcourse" in the evenings. They are sad that they can very seldom do this, because his superior frequently calls late afternoon meetings. The wife says:

> The kids are supposed to go to bed at 8:00 during school, so by the time
> Ken gets home, it's usually too late.

The issue of children's organized after-school activities is discussed in Chapter 9. It seems the importance of such activities for children is more likely to be stressed in homes where mothers are *not* employed. In the families where wives work long hours, participation by parents in children's activities was not mentioned as a problem. It seems in these cases parents expect the children to handle their own activities after school.

---

[3] Obviously, this situation might be very different in families where husband and wife work different shifts. I had only one familiy in this situation (Interview #27), and their case is atypical in that the husband works for the U.S. Navy and they live on base. He goes home for a long noontime break, during which time his wife is home and the family eats dinner. In the evening, when she is working, he often packs a sandwich lunch and drives the children to her workplace where they all have a picnic supper during her meal break.

Overtime

Respondents who work long hours were asked why the overtime is necessary. Most of them are not paid for overtime, thus extra income is not the immediate aim. However, most seemed to feel that this extra effort is necessary in order to "get ahead" in a career or to "do a good job." To quote:

> It's the responsibility that goes with the job [i.e., to see the work gets done] (Interview #26).

> There's just that much work to do. It's to satisfy myself (Interview #30).

Another man (Interview #29) described a training session for new managers that he had attended at which the consensus had been that it is essential to put in overtime to advance one's career. He said:

> It's funny. Everyone said you have to put in extra time to get ahead. [But it wasn't the instructor who said this.] It was the consensus of the class that we had to work overtime.

These comments can be contrasted with those of one dual-worker couple where neither husband nor wife work long hours (Interview #20).

> **Husband:** Friends are always saying you can't make it unless you put in a lot of extra hours. But I've proved that you can.

> **Wife:** He spends more time on his family than anyone else in this neighborhood, *and* he's been extremely successful in his work.

> **Husband:** I always say if you can't get it done in eight hours, you're either not doing it properly or you need two people. It's a matter of priorities. I could work 16 hours a day if I wanted to. Some people cut it off at 7:00 or 8:00; I cut it off at 4:30 or 5:00.

When I repeated these comments to men who complained about overtime, the response was that this kind of attitude is fine for those who have "made it" but is simply not appropriate for someone who is struggling to learn a new job and trying to do it well.

There was little evidence that these men were working long hours in a deliberate effort to escape family responsibilities. Only one (Interview #10) said that he had, in the past, sometimes come home late in order to avoid his quarrelsome family.

FLEXIBILITY IN SCHEDULING

People's attitudes toward flexible scheduling were asked about in every interview—both because this has been widely touted as a possible solution to the problems of combining work and family demands and because half these respondents worked for a company with an official Flextime policy.

Three of the husbands had occupations where, in principle, their working hours were completely flexible. In only one of these cases, however, did the flexibility result in the individual having full control over his schedule. In this case, the man is a successful architect with his own business (Interview #1). He feels he can alter his hours and take time off to suit his own whims. His wife is a full-time college student. She, too, builds flexibility into her schedule by selecting programs with few required courses, dropping out for a semester whenever she feels like it, and only undertaking commitments (like volunteer work) that permit her to schedule the meetings. She says, "My commitment is to people, not schedules." This family was unique among those I interviewed as far as the high degree of control over schedule is concerned. Such control in their case is undoubtedly facilitated by the husband's success in his business and his arrival at a career plateau where he is able to "cruise" in comfort.

Two other husbands also have flexible schedules, but have not enjoyed such success in their occupations. One is also an architect with his own business (Interview #4). He, however, feels himself to be at the beck and call of his clients, fearing to turn down any request for an appointment for fear of losing business. Another man (Interview #13), a realtor, is in a similar position. Flexibility for him means that none of his time is free from interruption by potential clients, and he does not dare refuse any request for an appointment.

In 11 of the families interviewed, at least one adult worked for a company with a formal flexible scheduling policy. This permits employees to select their own working hours within a certain range of daytime hours. These families were asked to report how this policy affects them and to compare their present situation with other experiences they may have had with conventional work schedules.

Those in top level managerial positions unanimously reported that the company's flexible scheduling policy makes little difference to their lives. Most claim that executive positions afford a fair degree of flexibility in scheduling, no matter what the formal company policy is. On the other hand, the freedom they describe—to go in late in the morning or take time off for personal errands—is largely offset by the fact that most regularly work far longer than the required eight hours a day.

Lower-level employees (in clerical or blue collar jobs) spoke of flexible scheduling with favor—principally because it permits an employee some discretion in establishing an initial schedule. (The desire to avoid rush hour traffic was mentioned by most as a key factor in deciding on a schedule.) However, these employees—along with the executives—explained that they feel they would be violating informal company norms, if not formal rules, by too frequently varying their working hours. Because other employees expect to find people at their desks at certain hours, work routines for the entire office would be disrupted by an individual's abrupt or frequent changes in routine. Recall Jean's comments:

> Flex hours aren't set up so that each day is different. You establish the schedule that best suits you and stick to it.

Seemingly, a regular routine simplifies not only work life but domestic life also, as changes in the work routine lead to new problems of coordinating husband's, wife's, children's and sitter's schedules.

In summary, flexible scheduling has some advantages in enabling individuals to establish a fairly satisfactory schedule in the first place. From this point on, both from the point of view of fellow workers and from the family's point of view, most people interviewed consider it best to stay with a regular routine.

As it happens, the Flextime policy affecting these workers does not actually permit very much individual flexibility or control over schedule. A rather different version of flexible scheduling has been experimented with in other countries whereby individuals are completely free to choose their working hours—that is, there are no restrictions on time of day or days of the week worked, as long as a total number of hours is worked per week or per month. Obviously, such a scheme permits a far greater degree of personal control over schedule than the kind of flexible scheduling enjoyed by the families interviewed and would permit a more useful investigation of the effects of flexibility of working arrangements on family life.[4]

---

[4] For a comprehensive review of different kinds of flexible scheduling plans, see Wade (1974).

JOB SATISFACTION

The ability to find satisfaction, challenge or fulfillment in one's job undoubtedly has an important impact on an individual's mental health, and thus indirectly on his or her family life also. Many respondents echoed Jean's and Larry's opinions that a life without a job would be empty and boring. Not only does a job expand one's intellectual world, but, for many women, the very fact that employment makes being a housewife a part-time activity leads to an increased enjoyment of housewifery.

Certainly, there is some evidence that for full-time employed wives one consequence of enjoying their work is an increased determination to find solutions to domestic problems caused by their employment. Beth (Interview #23), for example, is an assembly worker who really enjoys not only the money but also the stimulation and company of others that her job provides. She is quite ambitious and attends night school in order to "better herself." When Beth started working full-time a few years ago, their three young sons had no supervision after school and this led to difficulties. The boys would get into fights with other neighborhood children or play wild games that resulted in property damage or personal injury. Beth described to me the many different ways in which she and her husband tried to resolve this problem. Finally, they decided to work different shifts so that the boys would get the needed supervision.

Similarly, other employed women who enjoy their jobs appear to regard problems caused by their employment as challenges, which they tackle with determination. In contrast, the few women who find their jobs boring and unsatisfying (as did the wives in Interviews #17, #24, #27) all say that the only real solution to domestic problems caused by their employment is for them to give up work.

MAINTAINING FAMILY BOUNDARIES

There is clear consensus among respondents concerning the importance of restricting an employer's influence over the employee's private life. Recall Jean's indignation at a former employer who, she claimed, tried to control employees' personal lives and her satisfaction with her present company, which is "a super company ... very personal, but not to the point where people are interfering in your private life."

Rather surprisingly, the desire for noninterference often seems to be reflected in people's attitudes toward company-sponsored social events also:

> The fact I don't work in a very social company—picnics and parties— has an effect on our lifestyle. I really like this. My position is I like leaving work when I leave (Interview #30).

What is particularly interesting is that in 11 of these families one or more members worked for a large company that prides itself on its familial concern for its employees. Although employees of this company reported that the company sponsors a number of social events, the fact that there was no pressure put on them to attend such events was cited by all to be a highly desirable feature of the company. A common comment when asked what they liked most about this "familial" company was that expressed by one couple (Interview #20): "They realize employees have a life of their own outside the company." Another man (Interview #22) compared his former place of employment unfavorably with his present employer:

> They used to have a local tavern that was a company meeting place. All the men used to stop off for a drink after work. At [present "familial" company] no one does that—everyone goes home after work. They're much more family-oriented.

It is paradoxical that many of these same respondents are relative newcomers to California and complain, sometimes bitterly, about the difficulties of making friends. One man (Interview #32) pointed out that his next-door neighbor was killed in an air crash over a year ago, but he has only just heard about it. His wife described her unsuccessful attempts to make friends with the neighbors:

> I knocked on every door in the neighborhood to invite people over to a coffee klatsch. People were friendly. They invited me in. I talked to some of them for over half an hour or so. *But* only two people came.

She added, with a rueful laugh, that no one had reciprocated. Similar stories were related by other families.

Obviously, making friends is not a simple matter in an urban area with a transitory population. Nevertheless, even those who complain-

ed of feeling isolated showed little desire to have their work organization fill the void in their social lives.

SUMMARY

Of the features of work organizations that most appear to affect
family life, long working hours certainly do seem to have a constraining effect on family interaction. It seems that families where wives
are not employed are particularly likely to split into two activity
patterns, one for the mother and children and one for the father.
Flexible work hours permit some individual discretion in establishing
a daily schedule but in no way break what Young and Willmott call
the "locksteps" that organizational schedules impose on families
(1973, p. 283). And finally, in spite of the fact that most employed
people value their jobs as a source of both monetary and nonmonetary rewards, there is a widely expressed desire for there to be limits
on the employer's intrusion into family time and activities.

The case of Jean and Larry illustrated one kind of response to
the constraints on time that occur when both husband and wife are
employed full-time. This is to *organize* one's time. This organizing
activity is the subject of the next chapter.

CHAPTER **V**

Rationalization of
Family Work

One consequence of modernization is what some describe as the privatization of the family. At one time, home and workplace were for most people one and the same place. As the economic workplace has moved away from the home to its own separate setting, the tendency has been to think about the tasks that continue to be performed in the home—that is, housework—as "not work." Admittedly, economists today have refined their earlier theories of work and leisure to include an extra category called "home work"—that is, work for which one is not paid but that is, nevertheless, distinct from leisure (Gronau, 1977). Nevertheless, largely because people tend to think of work as an activity for which one is paid, housewives have had something of an uphill battle in getting housework acknowledged as real work.

Largely because of this reluctance to define housework as real work, the norms, and even the scientific theories, that are applied to activity in an organizational setting are generally assumed not to apply to activity in the home. Glazer, for example, claims there is a "resistance of housework to rationalization," suggesting that the reason for this resistance is that some domestic duties are socioemotional in nature (1980, p. 259). However, she admits that many services with a "socioemotional core" are performed by quite rational actors outside the family—notably, counselors of all kinds. I would go one step further to suggest that there is no family activity that is not some-

61

times performed by rational institutions and instrumental actors outside the family.

Rationalization itself, even in an organizational setting, presup-
poses a view of the world that looks on *time* as a scarce commodity.
An employer buys an employee's time, as well as the latter's skill,
experience, and so forth. Thus time in such a setting is something
to be used efficiently, not to be squandered. By contrast, when one
has so much time that the problem becomes how to "kill time," it
does not make as much sense to worry about the efficient usage of it.

Families vary in the extent to which time is seen as a scarce commodity, and, as I have already argued, this variation is likely to be a
result of variations in the constraints placed on them by their institutional affiliations. Recall how important "being organized" was to
Jean, an employed wife. The same theme is echoed in the story of
Bob and Nancy.

Bob and Nancy have been married for about eight years. Bob is a
doctoral candidate at a leading West Coast university. He is now ac-
tively working on his dissertation and holds a part-time job as a research assistant at the university. Nancy works full-time as an elementary school teacher. Their only child is a ten-month old baby boy.

Bob and Nancy's story is interesting because it underscores a facet
of current U.S. life that foreign observers often think of as peculiar
to this country. This is the seeming compulsion of so many people
to impose on themselves incredibly complex and harried lives. In
Bob and Nancy's case at least, this need for constant busyness is accompanied by deliberate efforts to organize and plan activities so
that their frantic schedule can be carried out.

Bob and Nancy (Interview #8)

Bob and Nancy live in married students' housing at the university.
Their housing unit consists of a very small living room with kitchen
and adjoining eating area downstairs, and two bedrooms and bathroom upstairs.

I arrived in the evening after dinner. The baby was asleep upstairs.
Bob and Nancy greeted me warmly. They seemed genuinely interested in discussing the problems of busy modern married couples and
were eager to share their experiences with me. Our conversation
started by their telling me they had recently lived in New Zealand

for two years. Bob and Nancy were enthusiastic about New Zealand and said they would love to return some day. The pace of life there was so relaxed and casual. Bob said, "People just sit around all afternoon and sip tea." The frantic, high-pressure schedule so typical of U.S. life is just not to be found. In New Zealand, they explained, if you feel like visiting someone, you just drop in anytime, and vice versa. Their main reason for living in the United States now, they told me, is that both sets of grandparents are here and they are reluctant to separate their baby from all family ties.

This discussion was followed by a description of the hectic daily schedule they follow now. Nancy teaches sixth grade. She estimates she spends ten and one-half hours a day working and commuting. This includes an hour a day in taking the baby to a sitter's house and picking him up again. They are hoping that they will be able to find a sitter closer to home so that much of this time will be eliminated. Nancy spends an additional five to eight hours a week in preparing for her classes, "but I really should do more," she says. About once a month she has to stay at the school till about 9:00 p.m. because of school events, such as open house. One evening a month she contributes two hours of time to working in a university "trading post" where they rent out children's furniture, camping equipment, and so on. People who contribute time get a 75 percent discount on anything they rent.

Nancy and Bob also belong to a babysitting pool. There is no pay involved. People earn points for sitting. They usually sit one evening every couple of weeks. Right now, Nancy is the secretary of the babysitting pool. This ties up another hour or so a week of her time. She has also recently joined a health spa. There are, of course, no set hours associated with this, but Nancy says she plans to go two or three times a week for a couple of hours at a time. Whether or not she can do this depends largely on Bob's schedule, because he will have to take care of the baby when she is away.

Bob is officially a half-time research assistant. This implies a 20-hour per week commitment. However, his present job is very demanding, and last quarter he was putting in as many as 60 hours a week on his job, returning to school most evenings after dinner and usually working every Saturday morning too.

Bob: Often I'd leave without even seeing Nancy and the baby, get home by 6:00 for dinner, and then leave at 7:00 till 10:30 or 11:00. Even in

the evenings when I was home, like on a Friday or Saturday night, people would call me all the time about work.

This quarter, his schedule is a little easier; however, he still works
from 8:00 until about 5:30 five days a week and goes into work on
Saturday morning. He is also active in student affairs. He is at present
student representative for his department at the university. This involves various time-consuming activities, including attending regular
meetings, conducting special surveys, and writing reports.

> Bob: I really enjoy it [these commitments], but I would like to give up
> some of it and work on my dissertation. The trouble is it's difficult to
> get out of this student rep. commitment. I was voted into office.

Bob's chief activity is *supposed* to be doing the research for his dissertation, but his frantic schedule leaves him little time for it. He is
engaged in a constant struggle to try to find time for the dissertation.

> Q: Why do you work at such a time-consuming job? Is it principally for
> the money?
>
> Bob: Yes, it's principally for the money. If I really wanted to get finish-
> ed up quickly, I could cut my stay [at university] by at least a year by
> giving up my R.A. You see, I've applied for a grant to enable me to go
> back to New Zealand and do my dissertation there. In case the New
> Zealand grant doesn't come through I'll have an alternative.
>
> Q: If you go back to New Zealand, will it just be for a short time, to
> get your dissertation done?
>
> Bob: Yes, it would just be for six to nine months. I'd mainly be doing
> it just because we'd like to go back there again.

As we talked more, it became evident that Bob didn't stick with
this job *just* for the money.

> Bob: All my heavy work experience last quarter made me rather angry,
> but it wasn't so much the long hours that were making me feel resentful.
> It was more the fact that I was getting only half-time pay and little or
> no credit from the project supervisor. Basically, it was a wonderful ex-
> perience for me, having so much autonomy and discretion in running
> the project. I was really in full charge of 20 assistants.

It seemed that the project supervisor, and some of his colleagues also, were slow to praise him for what he felt was a truly worthy effort on his part but were quite willing to simply assume that he would handle all the work that needed to be done. He felt he was being "taken for granted," in other words. Nevertheless, he felt the experience he was acquiring was extremely valuable to him in his career, and this feeling partly compensated for his feelings of resentment at being overworked and underpaid.

Bob, like his wife, was a schoolteacher before entering the university to work on his doctorate.

> **Q:** Being at school really makes life hectic for you. Were things quieter before you went back to school?

They exchanged glances and Bob gave a rueful little laugh as they both said, "No."

> **Nancy:** He's a workaholic of sorts. He's always been incredibly involved in things. He would take on projects left and right. He was always tied up evenings and weekends.

Although "workaholic" is not necessarily the right word to describe either of them, both Nancy and Bob do seem to have a driving need to fill all their hours with activity, *but,* at the same time, to speak wistfully of the leisurely life they found in New Zealand and their own desire to slow down. For example, Bob's schedule last quarter was admittedly too much for them to handle. Because he was so tied up with his job, Nancy was left to handle her own job, the baby, and household arrangements as best she could. Before that quarter started, Bob had taken the baby to school with him every day.

> **Nancy:** We both felt very good about that. I felt the baby was in good hands and developing a good relationship with his father. And Bob enjoyed having him around. Then his R.A. job got very hectic and this wasn't possible any longer. So then I had to start taking him to the sitter on my way to work. That adds an extra hour a day to my commute time—the sitter is a bit out of the way. Then if I'm held up at school for any reason, this causes a real hassle because the sitter gets annoyed. I feel really constrained by the sitting arrangements.

The strain caused by the time pressures and hassles with the sitter had, Nancy felt, most like been responsible for her low state of physical health the previous quarter.

> Nancy: I felt tired and rundown all last fall. I was feeling nauseated and depressed. Finally, I went to a doctor, and he gave me antibiotics. I probably did have a low-grade infection because I got much better, although I generally think it was probably because of all the guilt I felt at leaving the baby with the sitter every day and all the strain of having to take him there and everything.
>
> Q: Did the doctor find anything specific wrong with you?
>
> Nancy: No, he didn't, but he gave me the medicine anyway.

She feels other factors besides the medicine may have aided her in her rapid recovery at the end of that quarter.

> Nancy: Christmas was coming and we were looking forward to going home [Washington state] for a couple of weeks. Then we had a big Christmas party and a tree. My spirits really soared.

She described their delight at seeing their little son's reaction to the tree and his first Christmas.

Although their schedule this quarter is more relaxed than last quarter, Nancy said:

> Really last quarter is more *normal* for us. That is really more often the state of affairs than *now*. Now we're having an unusual amount of time together. I just hope it continues.

Last quarter, she explained, they were lucky to see each other for as much as one hour a week in the evenings. Now they have a brief time together in the mornings, a longer period each evening, and most of the weekends. However, I could not help noting silently that Nancy is planning to take advantage of much of Bob's extra available time in the evenings by leaving him to take care of the baby while she visits the health spa. Nancy has, in fact, a whole list of projects lined up that she plans to engage in if Bob can find extra time to sit for her. These include a pottery class and a number of adult education classes. Bob also would like to spend more time on *his* hobbies. He belongs to a photography club on campus but hardly ever uses the facilities.

He says he would love to become more involved if he can ever find the time.

Nancy has a number of other hobbies—such as sewing and various handicrafts—that she does at home. Also, she and Bob have friends who own a large piece of land in the Santa Cruz Mountains. Nancy and Bob farm a small part of this ground and keep a pig there. Every couple of weeks in the summertime, they spend a day up there working on their land—or, if Nancy is busy with schoolwork, Bob works the land while she prepares her lessons. In the winter, they drive up about once every three weeks or so.

In addition to their jobs, educational commitments, and hobbies, Bob and Nancy lead a fairly active social life. They have friends over for dinner or go out with friends at least once a week. They often go to the movies on Sundays. They love entertaining and regret the fact that Californians don't do more casual dropping in for snacks and meals rather than waiting for formal invitations.

> Q: Nancy, when Bob graduates and gets a full-time job, will you still go out to work?
>
> Nancy: We've talked a lot about that. It would partially depend on whether we'd committed ourselves to buying a house, which we'd like to do. If he were to get a job, we'd probably get a house right away. Then I might have to keep on working to pay for things.

She added:

> If I didn't have to work right now, I think I'd have taken off this year to be with the baby.
>
> Bob: It would also depend on what sort of a job it was, how close to home, how well it paid.

Nancy was thoughtful at this point. Obviously, her work decision is dependent on a number of factors and she feels competing pulls on her.

> Nancy: I just got my master's degree last summer. My school district really pays well, and really I enjoy my job very much. A beginning professor [i.e., the sort of job Bob would probably get when he graduates] doesn't pay too well, and even if he gets a job it will probably be a few years before his salary would support us by itself.

Q: Do you think you would enjoy staying home?

She was plainly hesitant.

> **Nancy:** Well, I'd like to try it. *I think.* When the baby came, I took eight weeks off work and I was quite happy to go back. You know, the best time to take off is the first year of a new baby, and now I've missed that. I'd like to have more time for hobbies. I like to crochet, make things around the house. I have trouble finding the time at present.

She talked more about being with the baby. She really feels it would be good for him if she were at home with him during the day:

> It would benefit my peace of mind, ease just that wee bit of guilt at leaving him every day.

One problem with their present lives, she feels—echoing the attitude that Larry expressed in our first case study—is that they feel guilty leaving him with a sitter in the evening or weekends because they already leave him with a sitter so often.

> **Q:** Bob, how do you feel about Nancy working? Do you think it would be better if she stayed home?

Bob had listened intently, though silently, to our discussion till now.

> **Bob:** It just doesn't worry me whether she works or stays home. I feel sure she'll be happy once we manage to change our sitting arrangements [i.e., to find a sitter closer to home].

His tone was sympathetic, and I got the impression that *he* felt Nancy would really rather work if only they could find good sitting arrangements.

Bob and Nancy described what each would consider a "perfect" daily schedule.

> **Nancy:** I'd like a time schedule with free evenings. Also I'd like a later start to the day. Now I get up at 6:00. I'd like to make this 7:00. Oh, let's be honest, 8:00 or 9:00 would be perfect! I'd also like to reduce my commute time, but I think this will be done shortly when we find a babysitter locally.

Nancy says she has considered sharing a contract with a friend, so that one week she will work three days and the friend two days, and the following week she will work two and the friend three days.

> **Nancy:** That sounds heavenly. I have an interest, professionally, in kids and would like to keep up my job. San Jose is doing a lot of this job-sharing now. I couldn't do it right now, of course, financially.

We went on to discuss the way they divide domestic tasks between the two of them. Unlike Jean and Larry, Bob and Nancy appear to have an egalitarian division of labor that is satisfying to both of them. They share all child-care responsibilities—feeding, bathing, diapering, taking the baby to the doctor, and so on. Each gets his or her own breakfast, Nancy always cooks dinner, and Bob always does the dishes. Nancy does most of the laundry now that they have an automatic washer and dryer. Before, Bob used to take the clothes to the laundromat. Bob said that he does most of the mending and fixing, but Nancy interjected that this is a shared responsibility also because she is the one who sews on buttons, hangs pictures, and so on. They do a major grocery shopping once a month and buy fresh milk and vegetables every two weeks. They laughed when I asked who does the cleaning and said, "We gave that up." Then Nancy explained that at one time they had shared the cleaning—Bob would vacuum and she would dust and clean the bathroom. But the place seemed to be constantly dirty. So now they have a cleaning woman who comes in two to three hours a week, and "whatever she doesn't do doesn't get done."

Bob comes from a very traditional family. He was one of three boys, and none of the men in their family was ever expected to do "female" work. His mother, however, is delighted at how much Bob helps Nancy in the house and with the baby. Bob gives his wife credit for having taught him to do so much around the house.

> **Bob:** I think I do so much because Nancy expects me to. Also, it's just not fair to expect her to work and then *not* to help her at home.

However, he added that if Nancy had not had such high expectations of him, he probably wouldn't have volunteered his services. Nancy said, "If he wasn't willing to help, I probably wouldn't have stuck it out."

Bob and Nancy provide a good example of the way that people perceive that rationalizing housework enables them to cope with busy schedules. On several occasions, Nancy spontaneously volunteered the information that they deal with their lives most effectively by being organized.

> **Nancy:** We're very organized people. This morning I was three minutes off in my timing, waking my husband three minutes early, so he had baby ready three minutes before I was due to walk out the door. [She chuckled.] He angrily said, "Why on earth are we so early this morning?" Our timing is split second. I get ready to leave for work, prepare baby's bottles and food for the day. He gets up and dresses baby, then walks down the stairs and hands me the baby just as I'm ready to walk out the door.

At another point, she said in similar vein:

> I'm really organized in the kitchen. I can plan ahead and stock up for a month. I make desserts ahead and do all of the baby's foods. Grind up our meats and put them in ice cube trays and freeze them for him. We don't buy any of these bottles of baby food at all.
>
> **Q:** You often mention being organized. I take it you feel this makes a big difference in being able to cope with such a hectic schedule?
>
> **Nancy:** Oh, yes. It helps you cope enormously. It would be terrible not to be organized. [Bob was making murmurs of agreement.] The night before you can think what you need to do the next day, the food you're going to eat, and everything. It makes such a tremendous difference.

Recall that for Jean being highly organized seemed to be accompanied by a certain lack of flexibility. Jean had reported how much it upset her day to have an unexpected event, like last-minute company for dinner, occur. However, Bob and Nancy were firm about the fact that being organized gave them the ability to be spontaneous and adaptable. Because they have a freezer full of dishes of various kinds, "it's no big deal to pull something out of the freezer" when unexpected company arrives.

Paradoxically, their one complaint about their present *social* life is that it is "too planned." People usually phone before coming over; they, in turn, are expected *not* to drop in on friends without giving prior warning. They would like things to be more spontaneous than this. To them, being organized is a highly desirable way to be, but it is not synonymous with having a totally predictable day or week. The consequences of a carefully planned life are thus slightly different than is the case with Jean. For both families, being organized implies not wasting time, planning carefully so that all routine activities are properly performed; however, Bob and Nancy's "organization" builds in the contingency plans to cover those (generally rather few) hours in the evening or weekend when the unexpected is allowed to occur. One big difference, of course, between the two couples is that Bob tries to contribute equally with Nancy to the running of their home, in contrast to Larry who admitted trying to "get away with" as little as possible.

Nevertheless, Bob, like Larry, seems to feel he is more relaxed about housework than his wife. He remarked:

> Normally, Nancy does bitch about things like undone dishes. But not me.
>
> **Nancy:** Yes, that's true. Last quarter, when I was so tired and tense, I often screamed at him for leaving dishes undone.
>
> **Bob:** I usually don't notice undone things, and if I did notice, it wouldn't bother me.

Bob's manner was relaxed, and this discussion did not provoke any tension between them. Undoubtedly, for this couple, housework is one of the realities of life that must be dealt with in as efficient and matter-of-fact a manner as possible. It is not an arena for a battle between the sexes.

Bob and Nancy had been married seven years before their baby arrived. As yet, they have not formulated a philosophy of family togetherness. They feel their friends are important to them, and they enjoy joint activities with other people. However, so far, their son is too young to be perceived as a real companion, and possibly when he grows older they'll give more consideration to the idea of family outings. So far, they've managed to take him with them when they go out with friends.

> **Q:** Do you think it's important for the two of you to save time for yourselves, apart from the baby?
>
> **Nancy:** That's the problem with being so far from grandparents. You just can't leave a baby for a weekend with a sitter. We're really feeling the need to do this, especially last fall when things were so hectic. But

we feel guilty as he's with a sitter all week. If we could leave him with his grandparents, that would be okay.

Recently, they had left the baby with a sitter for a whole day while the two of them took a trip to San Francisco. They had enjoyed that day immensely, and both glowingly reminisced about the day. But they repeated that they just wouldn't feel right taking off like that too often.

> **Nancy:** We would love to have as many kids as we could financially afford; we would love to give Rich [the baby] as many brothers and sisters as possible. [Bob indicated his agreement with this.] Of course, social pressures limit our aspirations somewhat.

I asked what these social pressures were, and they both said vaguely "zero population growth, things like that." They indicated that they feel these pressures quite keenly, not just in the sense of wanting to avoid approbation from others but also in the sense of feeling a real responsibility to limit their family size.

> **Nancy:** I don't know. We've enjoyed having the baby so much more than we ever thought possible. Who knows, maybe we'll just go ahead anyway, social pressures or not.

Bob looked sympathetic but also somewhat dubious as she said this, as if he is not quite so willing to consider ignoring the "pressures" as she is.

Bob and Nancy were one of several couples I talked to whose behavior and expressed opinions showed a strong commitment to the idea of husband and wife sharing family roles. Both feel their careers are important to them, and they are sympathetic to each other's needs in this regard. Both feel it is essential for husband and wife to share household and parenting tasks and responsibilities if each is to pursue a career with any success. Thus, I was a little surprised when we talked about their plans for the future to find that they have not ruled out the possibility that Nancy will stay home to raise their child when Bob earns enough money to permit this.

This became clear in the following exchange.

> **Q:** Where do you think you'll live when Bob graduates?

> **Nancy:** It depends on where Bob gets a job.

Q: You mean it is Bob's job, rather than yours [Nancy's] that would determine where you live?

They both hesitated and looked at each other, as if they were wondering how to answer this question without compromising their stated commitment to equality between them. Finally, Bob produced a rather roundabout response.

Bob: Well, eventually, Nancy would like to get a different kind of job, one where she might be supervising teachers at a university level. I'd want to get an academic job of some kind—teaching plus research—so, hopefully, wherever I'd go she'd be able to find what she wanted too.

Nancy: Oh, I can get a job anywhere. That won't be a problem.

So for Bob and Nancy, implicitly at least his career is more important than hers. Also, in spite of the fact that he loves taking care of the baby and is a good father, the option of staying home with the baby is apparently one that they feel is available to *her* but not really to him. When I summarized these conclusions aloud to them, they rather sheepishly agreed that in spite of their sharing behavior and egalitarian ideology, they could not divest themselves of underlying traditional images of family life and were not completely certain that they wanted to abandon them entirely.

We ended our interview by talking a little more about another seeming anomaly in their lifestyle—that is, the way they regularly undertake what seems like more commitments than they can comfortably fill but, at the same time, express yearnings for the quiet and more spontaneous life they knew in New Zealand. They laughingly agreed that as soon as their schedules relaxed at all, they quickly sought some way to fill the extra time—with yet more classes, voluntary work, or something. Bob and Nancy, it seems, have no intention of changing. They are living the kind of life they want to live.

The issue to be discussed in this chapter is the extent to which, and the conditions under which, organizational norms become salient in family life. Recall that my argument is that as time pressures increase for a family, they will increasingly tend to rationalize domestic activity. This tendency will be enhanced to the extent that the people involved work for bureaucratic organizations and are directly exposed in their workaday lives to norms of organizational rationality. By and large, a wife's employment will constrain the time available for housework; thus, families with employed wives will be more likely to organize housework than will families where wives are not employed.

The interviews with Jean and Larry and with Bob and Nancy, both dual-worker families, provided examples of a rational orientation to domestic work. As we shall see, when findings from the 30 families are aggregated, there is the predicted association between the wife's employment status and the rationalization of housework. However, this is not a perfect association: there are some nonorganized employed wives and some organized nonemployed wives. As in any qualitative study, an exploration of cases that are exceptions to the hypothesized rule is critical to our understanding of the underlying associations.

Information concerning organization of housework was obtained as follows. If the issue did not arise spontaneously, and it frequently did, respondents were asked, "Do you try to organize your housework at all?" Further questions would then be asked to uncover definitions of "organization," attitudes toward it, ways in which it is applied to family work, and conditions that affect it.

Two rather obvious points were quickly brought home to me. First, the propensity to "be organized" may be an individual rather than a family trait, so there are families where the wives are organized and the husbands are not, or vice versa. Second, people may *want* to organize their housework but are not necessarily successful. It seems that they are most likely to be successful when they have had training and experience in the rational scheduling of time and activity—and a work setting is a good place to acquire such training and experience.

Table 5.1 summarizes reports from 27 of the wives interviewed. The left-hand columns of this table indicate that most of the employed wives report attempts to organize housework and most of the nonemployed wives do not. As indicated in the right-hand columns of the table, four of the 15 women who report making attempts to organize do not feel they succeed in doing so. (See the difference in totals of the first and third columns, and the second and fourth columns.) Six of the nine full-time employed wives and two of the three nonemployed wives feel they have well-organized households.

We now examine in more detail what "organization" means in a family context, how it is achieved, and the factors affecting the success or failure of rational attempts to deal with housework. In order

Table 5.1.
Wives' Reports on Attempts to Organize and Success
at Organizing Household Work by Wife's Employment
Status (N = 27)

Wife's Employment Status	Attempts to Organize		Succeeds in Organizing	
	Yes	No	Yes	No
Full-time	9	2	6	5
Part-time/student	3	3	3	3
Nonworking	3	7	2	8
	15	12	11	16

to do this, responses will be explored in three clusters: successfully-organized employed wives, unorganized employed wives, and nonemployed wives. (For the present purpose, responses of part-time employed wives will be included with those of full-time workers.)

ORGANIZED EMPLOYED WIVES

We shall first try to determine what "organization" means in a working-wife family by sampling some comments from the total of nine women who are employed at least part-time and who feel they are successful at organizing housework.

Bob and Nancy, as we have already described, are "very organized people," who feel the high degree of rational planning in their daily lives is essential to enable them to cope with busy schedules. In the case of Jean and Larry, Jean feels that *she* is primarily responsible for running the house and her discussion stresses how organized *she* is. Jean is one of several wives who claim that going out to work is a factor that dramatically increases the amount she organizes her time. In fact, she claims as much gets done in the house whether she works or not.

> **Jean:** I just don't do any more when I'm home all the time. When I'm working, I just get more organized and more efficient.

In a third well-organized family, Ron and Lucy (Interview #20), the wife is a schoolteacher who stays home every summer. She claims to be a "different person" during the working and nonworking periods of the year.

> Lucy: I can accomplish so much more when I work because then I'm more organized. I can keep the house clean, do so many more activities, and really accomplish a lot.

I asked Lucy what "being organized" means.

> Lucy: It means getting up early in the morning. Making sure my hair is done and I'm dressed puts me in the right mood to do things. I get into gear. I know a lot has to be done, and I go ahead and see that it is done. In the summer, I'm just not geared up—I procrastinate. If I'm on a schedule, there are deadlines. I know it has to be done. I'm not the world's best housekeeper, but I can get things cleaned and manage my job very easily because I work at a faster pace—I'm more efficient— when I work.

Ron and Lucy highly praised the virtues of being organized both at home and at work. She claims that everyone at work is always commenting on how "super organized" she is. This, she says, is why teaching is so easy and comfortable for her: she manages her time well, assigns priorities to activities, and sees that everything is done at the right time. Her husband also claims that his ability to organize his work life enables him to leave work early every day and have more time to spend with his family.

A final example is that of Gloria (Interview #25), who works only periodically as a substitute school nurse. She, like Lucy, describes moving into a different frame of mind when she is called into work.

> Gloria: When I have to be at school at 8:00, I really have to get up at 6:30. Obviously, it forces you to plan ahead. I would make the lunches the day before, plan the meals ahead. I'm not a scheduled person. I find that if I have an externally imposed schedule, like substituting at the school, then things get done more efficiently—in more sequential order. If I have a free day without anyone else's schedule imposing on me, things are much more casual. I might make a bed after lunch, for instance.

From these remarks, we can make some inferences about what organization means in these families. It means preplanning, scheduling, and coordinating activities. It also means getting into a certain frame of mind in which time is to be treated as a valuable commodity to be utilized as efficiently as possible. The wife's employment is a factor that places constraints on time, and being organized is seen as one way to conserve it.

NONORGANIZED EMPLOYED WIVES

We shall turn next to the eight women who are employed at least part-time but who either make no attempt to organize housework or who report making unsuccessful attempts. Chris (Interview #24) is one such person. (The case study in Chapter 8 is of Chris and her husband, Mike.) She and her husband have been married only a short while. His ten-year-old daughter from a previous marriage lives with them. Although she was previously married for a brief time many years ago, she has lived as a single woman for most of her adult life. She works full-time as a secretary in a large corporation; her husband has a management position in the same company. With the sudden acquisition of a full-fledged family, Chris finds the burden very heavy, even though the other family members share in the housework. She desperately feels the key to handling her many duties is good organization, which she feels she has not achieved. She says:

> The only thing I really have control over now is the grocery shopping. The laundry is pretty under control too. The rest of it is out of control, I would say.

As it happens, the tasks she feels are "under control"—shopping and laundry—are those for which *she* is responsible. Her husband and stepchild are responsible for the vacuuming and cleaning, and these she reports to be "out of control." In the past, Chris had a rather casual attitude towards housework. Her new husband, however, has always been quite particular about keeping a clean and neat house, and she finds his high standards adding considerably to her tension. Unlike other employed wives like Jean and Nancy, Chris has little faith in her ability to eventually solve her problems through good organization. Both she and her husband feel the only good solution is for her to leave her job, which she plans to do as soon as they can afford it.

The remaining working-wife families in which housework is not organized, at least not with any success, have in common the fact that interviewees are all of a working-class background. Two of these families report making no attempt to organize housework; the other two say they try but do not succeed. One women, an assembly worker with two teenagers (Interview #17), says:

> I try to be organized. I come up with a real grand plan and present it to everybody. But it ends up I just get mad and start screaming and yelling.

She explained that she "screams and yells" because the rest of the family will not cooperate. I suspect from other discussions with this respondent that her attempts to "organize" consist largely of attempts to allocate housework to other family members. She says she does not try to impose any schedule on herself:

> What needs to be done I try to do. I don't have a schedule. A schedule would give me even more time pressure.

Another assembly worker, a young woman with two preschool children (Interview #27), says she is always trying to be organized but finds it difficult because her husband is often at home during her housework hours. (She works evening shift.) He works for the U.S. Navy and they live on base. He has a lot of time off because he is permitted to go home whenever things are slack at work, and this occurs frequently. Because they work different shifts, there is undoubtedly the temptation to relax together in the daytime when they get the chance. She says:

> I decide to do something [in the house], and then he comes home, and we'll go to the park or something.

From discussions with these nonorganized families, it seemed to me that there is not a very clear idea of what "being organized" means. Respondents have a vague idea of it being something good that will help one handle work, but they seem to lack knowledge of what might be an appropriate way to organize housework.

NONEMPLOYED WIVES

Three nonemployed wives reported making attempts to organize their housework. In the cases of Betty and Mimi (Interviews #15 and

#31), the attempts were highly successful. Betty and Mimi both have husbands who work long hours and children who are engaged in many extracurricular activities. Both women have high standards of housework and set exacting schedules for themselves. Betty, the wife of a corporation executive, says:

> I have a weekly schedule or I'd never get through a house this big. On Monday, I change the beds and clean the brown wing—that has three bedrooms and one bath. On Tuesday, I have volunteer work part of the day; then I clean the green wing—that has three bedrooms and two and a half baths. Wednesday, I clean the laundry room, breakfast room, kitchen, and family room. On Thursdays, I shop and also sometimes work in the school library. On Fridays, I clean the living room. Then there is ironing and washing that gets done all the time. I really do nothing at the weekends—except for gardening or entertaining.
>
> Q: And do you stick pretty closely to this schedule?
>
> Betty: With too great a passion!

I asked if things had been easier for her before they had moved to their present large house. She smiled and said she had routinely cleaned their former, smaller house *twice* a week.

Mimi, whose husband owns an automobile dealership, reports a similar story. She says she feels extremely uncomfortable with what she calls "unstructured" time. If, for example, she anticipates a free block of time for the next day, she will deliberately schedule some activity to fill that space. She cleans house almost every day. I asked why she felt this need to structure her time.

> Mimi: I've been organized all my life. I'm happier and more comfortable [this way]. Probably because my mother was, and I was raised in it. My children will have a structured life because they have one as kids.

Mimi's two sons are in elementary school, and she is seriously considering taking up a career. She admits that if she were to get a job, she would have to greatly relax her standards for housework. But, she explained, it wouldn't matter because she'd have her job to provide her with the structured activity she needs.

Note the sharp difference between the reports of these two organized housewives and the earlier reports of organized employed women. The employed women have difficulty finding enough time to do all that has to be done. By being organized, they are trying to make more efficient use of their limited time. Betty and Mimi, by contrast, have a lot of potentially "unstructured" time, feel uncomfortable with this, and sufficiently inflate housework standards so that a time shortage is created—which they then deal with by being well organized!

Betty and Mimi were the exceptions among the nonemployed wives I spoke to. Most housewives did not make attempts to rationalize their domestic activities. Fran (Interview #7), the mother of a baby boy, claimed she made sporadic attempts to do so. However, the chaotic condition of the house suggested to the outside observer that any such attempt was probably a failure. Fran had worked up until the time her baby was born a few months before. Her husband has a long commute to his job in an advertising agency. They both admit that certain chores like yardwork never get done at any time and that nonessential activity—in which they included housecleaning —gets done only sporadically.

I asked Fran why she tries to organize her housework. She answered hesitatingly:

> I've really felt the need to organize *more* since I left work. [Pause] When you go to work, even as a secretary, you can always say, "Well, I was at work today." When you're at home . . .

She struggled to find words and then said:

> Well, anyway, I try to be really organized and then that makes me feel good about myself.

We discussed this for a while, and she explained that even though she and her husband feel staying home to raise children is important, this kind of activity is distressingly undervalued by friends and acquaintances who don't regard it as "real" work. Thus, for Fran, organizing her housework makes it seem a more worthy activity, enhancing her own feelings of self-worth by engaging in such an activity. This, of course, is the argument proposed by Oakley (1974) to explain why many of the British housewives she interviewed attempted to develop "worklike" (that is, rationally organized) schedules and routines for performing their housework. Similarly, Mimi (discussed earlier in this chapter) appears to feel that being an efficient and organized housewife is a partial substitute for having a real job (that is, paid employment).

Unlike Betty and Mimi, Fran is ambivalent about tightening up her relaxed standards for housework. Note her contradictory statements.

> Fran: Often *I feel irritated* at the fact that the place isn't vacuumed or something. I'm real aware that I don't utilize my time as I should. Like in the morning, if I don't have to go to my exercise class, I often hop back into bed after David leaves and read the paper. *It doesn't bother me though* (Emphasis mine).

It seems then it is difficult to be well organized if there are no time pressures, for these appear to implicitly underlie the necessity for organization in these families.

The majority of housewives interviewed say they make little or no attempt to organize housework. Some generalizations can be made about this group of women. First, on the whole, their housework standards are probably rather low. The following quotations are typical of those received in these seven interviews.

> I don't do it [housework] all every week. I'll save it. One week, I'll spend that week cleaning, then let it go for a couple of weeks. I get in here [living room] once a month (Interview #29).

> I'm very disorganized. My cupboards—things fall out of them when I open them. Certain days I clean more. Certain days I just leave for the day (Interview #30).

> The housework isn't scheduled. I do it when people are going to come or when I can't stand it any longer (Interview #25).

Second, these women say they experience no shortage of time to do whatever they need to do. Some explicitly describe having plenty of time and a relaxed schedule as advantages of not going out to work. Many do have to handle complex after-school schedules for their children, and, as a result, commonly the later afternoon hours are regarded as more constrained than the earlier part of the day.

Third, there is a routine of sorts for the performance of housework in most of these homes. Many women say, for instance, "I usually clean on Fridays," or state another day of the week for shopping or laundry. But this schedule is not taken too seriously in that almost any other activity is permitted to interfere.

> Last Friday, I was going to clean the living room, but then my girlfriend
> stopped by, so I went shopping with her instead (Interview #29).

Fourth, in these families husbands are frequently well organized
in performing *their* household duties even though the wives are not.
In some families, this difference is accepted philosophically; in others,
it is a source of conflict. Paul and Josie (Interview #22) have four
young children, with another one expected soon. Although she is
not employed, Josie spends a number of hours a week on voluntary
work connected with their church and the children's schools. She also
reports the highest number of hours spent on housework for any of
the women I interviewed (70 hours per week). If "organization" is a
way to handle time shortage, it would seem she could benefit from it.

> Josie: I heard a saying somewhere: I'm so busy I don't have time to get
> organized. That's how it is with me.

Her husband, a corporation executive who prides himself on his efficient management of time at work and at home, expressed open irri-
tation at this comment:

> The more organized she is, the better able she'll be to get things done.
> *We have talked about this many times.* By planning her time better, she
> will be able to get more done and have more free time too. (Emphasis
> mine).

Josie apologetically explained she was going to make a concentrated
effort to manage her time better in the future. Her husband has just
bought her a desk in which to file papers and bills to help her get
started on her goal.

Ben and Irene (Interview #32) provide another example. Ben is
an operations manager. Irene works as a substitute schoolteacher.
She doesn't try to organize her housework.

> Irene: He's an organizer. That's why we get upset with each other. I'm
> not an organizer. If it doesn't get done, it doesn't.

In this family, there was an interesting debate between husband and
wife that uncovered a conflict, but also ambivalence on both their
parts, concerning family values. They both agreed that *he* was far

better skilled than she at managing his time and that of the children; that he would, in fact, make a far better housekeeper than she were their roles reversed. Ben spoke with pride at the tremendous amount of household work he gets accomplished in the limited time he has available at weekends. He says he forms his children into an efficient work force to help him and there are no problems as long as Irene is not around.

> **Ben:** I can get all the kids up and get them doing things. No conflict. But if Irene is here, they'll be sitting on her lap telling her things.

To Irene, having the children "tell her things" is an essential part of being a good parent. She says, "What else are mothers for?" She feels that if too much stress is placed on performing household work efficiently, the crucial factor of having time available for warm and spontaneous interaction is likely to be lost. The discussion between them uncovered a certain ambivalence in that both felt to some degree it is important *both* to have a well-run (organized) house *and* to find room for the family's expressive functions. However, the emphasis each placed on the relative importance of the instrumental as opposed to the expressive activities of the family differed sharply.

I shall end this chapter with a few general observations on differences in the structuring of domestic work that regularly appeared between dual- and single-worker households. One of these, as already discussed, is the greater tendency of dual-worker families to rationalize housework—to preplan domestic activities, to approach housework in a calculated manner aimed to maximize the efficient usage of time.

Another quite consistent difference between dual- and single-worker families is the way they distribute housework throughout the week. Of the nonemployed women, all but two said they do the bulk of housework during the week (Monday through Friday)—sometimes spreading it evenly throughout the five days, sometimes setting aside one or two days for a "big clean," another for the shopping, another for the laundry, and so on. But always the aim is to keep the weekends clear of all but essential daily tasks, such as fixing meals and doing dishes. The two exceptions claimed to spread the work throughout the seven days of the week.

The reverse process applies for most of the full-time employed wives. Their aim is apparently to keep the weekdays clear of all but essential tasks and to save the bulk of the household work (cleaning, shopping, laundry) for the weekends, generally Saturdays. The two exceptions here were wives who had paid help to clean the house.

DECENTRALIZATION

Decentralization, the process of replacing a centralized structure with a set of relatively autonomous subunits, is one option available to complex organizations when the costs of coordination become too high. In families where members are subject to the different schedules of various organizations, it is likely that the scheduling and coordinating of domestic activities might frequently be difficult. Family decentralization is one possible solution—with every individual being responsible for his or her own food preparation and cleaning, laundry, room cleaning, and so on. This is presumably a workable option for the children only when they are old enough to handle the tasks involved.

In many of the families interviewed, children do take over certain personal tasks, such as cleaning their own rooms and doing their own laundry, as they grow older. This is not necessarily related to time pressures or coordination problems, however. Often, it simply reflects the general philosophy that children ought to contribute something to the running of a home. (This issue will be discussed further in Chapter 7.)

There was evidence, however, that in some of these families increasing time pressures have led to the situation where, for many domestic functions, each individual operates as a relatively autonomous unit. For instance, five families specifically mentioned the wife's going out to work as a factor that led to the husband and the children becoming responsible for fixing their own breakfasts and lunches, doing their own laundry and ironing, and even tidying up the areas of the living room and kitchen that they had untidied.

This was the case with Rose and Kelly (Interview #10). They both work full-time. His two daughters by a previous marriage live with them. Although both Rose and Kelly feel strongly the children should contribute to the housework, there is a fair amount of friction between the children and their stepmother over this issue, and she has found it difficult in the past to insist on their help. As a result, standards for housework have been extremely low, with the house remaining dirty and untidy for long periods of time.

A few months before the interview, this family put their house up for sale. It then became important to have the house clean and tidy at all times for prospective buyers. The rule was established that every person in the family had "to clean up their own mess"—that is, each person had to do his or her own laundry, fix his or her own meals except for dinner, clean up his or her own dishes, tidy every area of the house he or she had untidied. It was apparently easier for the parents to rationalize their demands to have the daughters wipe the kitchen table or tidy the living room if the daughters had created the mess in the first place—as compared with asking one child to vacuum the whole living room or be responsible for all the dinner dishes, mess that had been created by the whole family. In fact, the parents confided that they so love the clean and tidy house that has resulted from this new "decentralization" policy they are planning to continue it even after they move to their new house.

A rational approach to planning one's own time is one way the world of organizations can influence domestic activities. In addition, quite specific procedures to deal with various situations can sometimes be learned at work and then transferred to a domestic setting. One example of the latter arose in the interview with Ted and Marsha (Interview #13). They have a fairly unusual way of dealing with complex domestic schedules, and the method they use was one that Marsha learned in her job and then adapted to her family situation.

Marsha is a personnel clerk. It became necessary for her to go to work several years ago, when Ted had a serious heart attack and had to "take things easy" for some time. His present job as a real estate salesman is less strenuous apparently than his former job in a manufacturing plant.

This family has an extremely complicated scheduling problem. Ted's hours are most irregular. Some days he doesn't have any work at all, but when is he trying to close a deal with a customer he might work "around the clock." The children all have part-time jobs that require their services on an irregular and frequently last-minute basis. Added to this, the family enjoys entertaining friends and relatives. Thus the workload is heavy, and, although there are many hands available to help out, the help that they can provide is unpredictable from day to day.

When Marsha first went to work, they attempted to handle their household work by assigning certain chores to certain family members. This didn't work well. Not only were some individuals unhappy with the particular duties assigned them, but frequently the "right" person was not available to do a job when it needed to be done (due to their unpredictable work schedules). Marsha then realized the similarity between the family's scheduling problem and the personnel scheduling problem that she dealt with every day at work. Her job in a large department store included the daily scheduling of employees, some of whom were part-time and some full-time, and who had a fair amount of discretion in picking their work hours. In order to insure that sufficient employees were available at all times, a sheet was posted allowing employees to sign up for preferred work times—with the company reserving the right to switch assignments if necessary to obtain full coverage.

Marsha says it just "hit upon her" one day that the family's housework scheduling could be dealt with in a similar way. The family now has a sheet posted by the refrigerator calling for signups for all tasks that need to be done on a particular day or week. Usually Ted or Marsha list the tasks, and the list can be amended at any time. If coverage of all tasks is not obtained by voluntary signups, then husband or wife make arbitrary assignments. The whole family feels this system has worked extremely well—providing the most efficient utilization of available workers while allowing the maximum degree possible of individual self-determination and flexibility.

SUMMARY

Most of the families interviewed gave the impression that they believed rational, "organization-like" procedures to be the best way to deal with the problem of time pressures. As would be expected, working wives are more likely on the whole to have these time pressures and, thus, to attempt to organize their housework than are housewives. Indeed, several wives described switching from an unorganized to an organized mode, or state of mind, when they became employed. Some women who are not employed but who like to be organized appear simply to inflate housework standards so as to create extra workload, which, in turn, creates the time pressures that warrant organization. In addition, for some women, approaching household work in a rational or bureaucratic way makes it seem more like "real work" rather than "just housework"—a finding that supports Oakley's thesis.

It is clear, however, that not all people know *how* to organize their time. In keeping with the spirit of "generalization theory," discussed earlier, there does seem to be some tendency for those people whose occupations call for the appropriate time-management skills to be more successful in scheduling and coordinating domestic activities than those people whose occupations do not afford them such opportunities. Thus, respondents in managerial or supervisorial positions are more likely to report successful domestic organization than are respondents in lower level, blue-collar jobs. However, the case of Ted and Marsha, described above, suggests that even at lower occupational levels people can and do successfully transfer work practices to a family setting.

CHAPTER **VI**

Family Functions

Have family functions changed much over the past century? And, if so, how? Before embarking on a discussion of this issue in general and the findings of my study in particular, I will describe an interview with a suburban housewife, whom I shall call Debbie.

In recent years, the lifestyle, joys, sorrows, and needs of employed wives have tended to capture public interest and concern. We should not forget, however, that even though half the married women in this country today are employed, this still leaves half of them who are not. Many of these nonemployed women would not describe themselves as idle. In the suburban areas around San Francisco, it is difficult to find a full-time housewife whose time is not largely occupied with some form of structured activity—college classes, voluntary work, supervision of her children's extracurricular sports and other activities. Debbie is one such woman. She attends college classes from September through June and spends a lot of time on her children's school and recreational activities. Her story illustrates an extremely casual—bordering on the indifferent—concern with many of the traditional domestic functions.

Debbie and John (Interview #18)

John had volunteered the name of his wife, Debbie, to be interviewed. When I telephoned her, she asked that I come over during the workday rather than in the evening. It is a common misconception that "research on families" is a matter for women (undoubtedly enhanced in this case by the interviewer's being female also). However, it is not my policy to insist on seeing the husband if the wife claimed he is "too busy" to be interviewed.

It was ten o'clock on a warm summer morning when I arrived at Debbie's house. It is a fairly large house, in a well-established and heavily treed neighborhood. Very quiet and pleasant. With its mature trees and shrubs, the area has a tone of quiet elegance, and it undoubtedly is one of the more expensive areas in that part of the city. Debbie commented at one point that most of their neighbors are "older," as had been the original owners of their house. She said, "They still call our house the Parkers', after the people who used to live here before us."

Debbie and I talked, with accompanying cups of coffee, in a family room off the kitchen. She has two sons, aged nine and seven, and they were on the patio with Debbie's mother, who was visiting them for a month. They also have a pool, and the grandmother appeared to be watching the children while Debbie and I talked.

The answer to my first question, which I had thought would be a rather straightforward one, illustrates the rather large gulf that exists between the lives of husband and wife in many a household.

Q: What does your husband do? That is, what is his job title?

This proved to be a tough question for Debbie. She mused aloud that she thought he had multiple job titles. This seemed a little unlikely to me in view of the fact that he worked for an extremely large corporation.

Debbie: Labor Relations Manager, Safety Manager. He's in charge of Workmen's Compensation Benefits and EEO.

I asked what "EEO" was. She thought, "It's to do with equality." I suggested "Equal Employment Opportunity," and she agreed that was it. She went on to explain that his responsibilities are rather far-ranging and shifting, and recently the company has attempted to consolidate his duties into one official position. She was not too clear about it, however.

Debbie said that John leaves home between 7:30 and 8:00 a.m., and gets home between 6:00 and 7:00 p.m. I asked if his working hours were flexible.

Debbie: No, he's supposed to get there at a certain time. [Pause] I think he is. I think he's supposed to start at 8:00. It depends on the traffic really how long it takes him to get there. It only really takes a few minutes if the traffic isn't bad. I'm sure he does have a specific starting time though.

Her husband has worked for the same company for 15 or 16 years, practically all the time they've been married (which is 17 years). Debbie herself worked briefly before marriage and then for an additional eight years after they were married. I asked what kind of work she had done.

Debbie: I worked in insurance. Clerical work. Yes, I guess you would call it clerical. It wasn't secretarial or anything like that.

Her tone indicated that "secretarial" was far above what she did.

Debbie: I gave up work when I became pregnant. We had been so looking forward to having a baby. We'd been trying for a baby for many years. When it finally happened, we were thrilled. I was kind of happy to give up work; it was kind of boring.

She hasn't worked since, but for the last two years she has been attending community college to study art.

Debbie: When my younger one was born, I was still really tied down. So John went out and bought me an oil painting set. I really loved it. So I decided to take a couple of classes. And then I took it up more seriously.

About college, she says:

I really enjoy it. I enjoy the people a lot. There are so many people exactly like me—never had any college before, young kids at home, just like me. I really enjoy meeting them.

Q: Have you ever considered going back to work?

She gave a half-mocking burst of laughter.

Debbie: I want to be an artist! [Then, more seriously] No, really, it's fun to do. I certainly would never want to go back to what I was doing before—the insurance.

She does not attend classes during the summer months when the children are home from school. But while the semester is in progress, a typical college schedule for her is 9:30 a.m. to 3:00 p.m. two days a week and from 9:30 until 11:30 a.m. three days a week. She seemed indifferent when I asked if she'd eventually like to get a degree.

> Debbie: I'd like to transfer to another school sometime, I guess. It depends really on what the kids' hours are and what's happening with them.
>
> Q: Do you have much homework to do when you're in school?
>
> Debbie: Not for the art classes. But I take other classes. There was one history class that was really ridiculous. It was way out of line. But, you know, I enjoyed it. I got an A, and then looking back I enjoyed it. I really worked hard and I knew I deserved that.

Both Debbie and John are involved with their sons' sports activities. John has been soccer coach for three seasons now. This involves three full evenings a week, two of practice and one for the game itself. There's also a Saturday game sometimes. Debbie said, "He's even switched his golf morning to Sunday because of the soccer." He also participates in the YMCA Indian Guides. When the boys were younger, John and Debbie were part of a cooperative nursery school.

> Debbie: I was maintenance chairman once, and that meant a lot of work for John. We had to spend a couple of hours per weekend mowing the lawn and doing cleanup at the school. Also, there were meetings to attend, and he spent a lot of time helping me set up schedules, telephoning people to remind them of jobs they had to do, things like that.

Currently, Debbie works with the local Welcome Wagon, and this involves social activities such as a barbecue once a month. She was also recently president of her bowling league.

> Debbie: There was nothing involved in that. Just sometimes we'd have a lunch that required a few arrangements, but nothing much.

Apparently, for most of their married life, John has been a part-time student, and this has occupied a lot of his free time. John did not finish high school. The first year they were married, he started night school in order to get his high school diploma.

Debbie: That took a year or two. Then he went on to get his B.S. in Engineering. That took eight or nine years. Then he went for his M.B.A., which took four or five years. He used to go straight from work to school and not get home until about 11:00, four nights a week. Then he would study from 11:00 till about 1:00 in the morning. He never studied much at weekends unless he had to for an exam or something. One thing that really helped him a lot when he was in graduate school was that a friend who worked with him started going to college with him also. They gave each other quite a bit of support. And that way the wives had each other too.

There has been no school for John the last couple of years, and Debbie says he feels his schedule is extremely light in comparison to the earlier years. However, John's boss has a law degree, and now John has started to talk about maybe going back to night school to work on a law degree himself.

Q: Has all this schooling helped him advance in his career?

Debbie seemed dubious, and thought about this for a moment. She finally replied, "I'm sure it has figured in some way." She went on after a moment:

Probably. I don't really know. Mainly it's just that he wanted it. At least when he started out.

She chuckled as she confided that she personally thinks his current desire to go to law school has come about only because his current boss has a law degree.

Our conversation moved into the area of housework, and it quickly became evident that this was "no big deal" (her words) for Debbie. We went through a list of routine tasks, and she claimed to be responsible for most of them: housework, laundry, grocery shopping, and shopping for everything else.

Debbie: You want to know the only time he ever shops? That's Christmas. The only time.

He shops not only for her presents, but also for the children.

Q: That must be nice. To have a husband who's willing to do the kids' Christmas shopping.

Debbie looked doubtful.

Debbie: Well, maybe. We usually end up fighting about what to get.

Debbie does all the cooking. She doesn't fix breakfast for her husband on weekdays, but does for the kids. She always cooks dinner. She said: "John doesn't like to barbecue, so I have to do that too." I commented that even husbands who dislike cooking often do agree to barbecue. She said, "I *know*," as if she found this very amusing, and added firmly, "But John won't." She always does the dishes. She pays the bills.

Q: Who decides on allocating money for various purchases?

Debbie: We both do the deciding—like for our vacations.

The issue of money arose again later in our discussion when I asked if she ever missed having her own paycheck. She answered promptly, with amusement.

Debbie: It bothers John not to have *his* own paycheck. He puts it in the bank and I handle it.

Debbie doesn't do any work in the yard. This is John's responsibility. He spends "45 minutes at most" per week doing this.

Debbie: He does things like the car washing. He takes care of the pool.

Q: How about fixing and repairing?

Debbie: Oh yes, definitely, he does all that. He finished off that room back there [waving to a rumpus room that led off the family room through a brick arch]. I do all the painting and wallpapering. He won't paint. Also, I built that brick wall that you can see in the back room. And I laid a brick patio.

Debbie said she really enjoys working on such projects.

Q: How much time do you estimate you spend on housework?

Debbie thought about this for a few moments. At first, she said she just couldn't estimate this, but then abruptly changed her mind and said firmly, "about one hour every morning." I initially interpreted this to mean time spent on breakfast and early morning cleanup, but as I questioned her further it turned out this was her total housework time for the day, apart from dinnertime activities.

> **Debbie:** I clean one room a day. I don't have any day for a big cleanup, although when someone's coming—like you today—I go around and pick up, sure. It doesn't take much.

One day's chores might consist of cleaning the bathrooms, another of cleaning the living room, and so on. The kitchen floor is washed every day because they have three dogs (none in evidence during our talk) and the doghair spreads around.

> **Q:** But then you also have to spend time fixing dinner?
>
> **Debbie:** Oh, so what's that? About half an hour.

And dishes? "15 minutes." Laundry and grocery shopping?

> **Debbie:** I do things like that in combination with other things. Like I grocery shop while the kids are taking tennis lessons. Not now, of course, because it's summer.

She does not spend any more time on housework in the summer than during school months. In fact, she probably spends less.

> **Debbie:** Unless someone's going to come over, we don't do the things we normally do. We just pick up for company.
>
> **Q:** Do the kids take a lot of lessons?
>
> **Debbie:** Between them, there's guitar, tennis, Little League, soccer, Kung Fu.

During the school year, she spends a lot of time driving them to these activities, waiting for them, and so on.

> **Debbie:** It takes up every afternoon between 3:00 and 8:00. We very seldom eat before eight o'clock. Sometimes my husband is coaching, or sometimes he just goes to watch the Little League.

It seems they save time on dinner preparation by using fast foods.

> **Debbie:** We eat at McDonalds a lot. Usually at least once a week, maybe more. Then with the kids' ball games, we often eat hot dogs at the ballpark or sometimes have hot dogs at home . . . or bring home a pizza.

Debbie had worked for eight years before the children came, and I asked her how different her household load and domestic duties were in those early years from the present.

> **Debbie:** We just left everything until Saturday then. We did a lot more together [i.e., she and John]. We did the shopping together. Then we didn't have a washing machine, so we went to the laundromat together when we did the shopping. We didn't have a lawn to be mowed. It was just a tiny apartment.

John had never done any housework, however. Debbie didn't think he did any domestic chores at all.

> **Debbie:** I just don't remember. All I can remember is him being slumped in front of the TV at the weekend. It was just a tiny apartment. There just wasn't that much to do.
>
> **Q:** Who cooked the dinner on weekday evenings?
>
> **Debbie:** It wasn't that difficult. We had a lot of TV dinners. I just let the dishes pile up and did them all on Saturday. I really worked all day Saturdays.

A little later in the interview, when we were discussing John's schooling again and the fact that he had until recent years gone straight from work to school four nights a week, Debbie said, as if this had just occurred to her:

> That was why he didn't help out around the apartment much. That was why he just watched TV at the weekend. He was just tired out.
>
> **Q:** Did John help you with the kids when they were little?
>
> **Debbie:** Yes, he'd do anything I asked except change the diapers. Once, he even called up my sister-in-law and asked her to come over to change a messy diaper. He just wouldn't do that. But he'd do anything else. He really enjoys the kids.

Q: What do your children do to help around the house?

She smiled patiently as though she understood that I had to ask such a question for the purpose of my project, but that I must understand it was rather a ridiculous one.

Debbie: Well, they take out the garbage. Get the mail. They have to earn 10¢ to contribute to their Indian Guides, so sometimes they'll try to do something to earn that. [pause] They straighten up their rooms.

Q: Make their beds?

Debbie: [Abruptly] If they do, they only have to be remade. They feed the dogs and play with them. The big one gets groomed every four months. The others are only small. They're pretty easy to take care of.

Her tone implied that politeness obliged her to think of answers to my trivial question. But that I must know what the real answer was: children basically do nothing around the house. She expounded her philosophy on this:

I kind of believe they're only children. They'll have plenty of time later to help out.

But then she became pensive, as a new train of thought ran through her mind.

Debbie: It's funny though. There's a janitor at school, and as soon as they get to school they go and try to help him with the chores. Maybe it's because they get recognition there that they don't get at home. [She added, as though she felt it was unreasonable of them to feel this way.] When I was little, I had to do the dishes every night from the time I was eight years old, and I really hated it.

Debbie was the oldest of three children. She has a brother and a sister. Her mother was divorced and has been ever since Debbie can remember. Her mother worked full-time. The only household chore Debbie was asked to do was the dishwashing. She doesn't remember her brother and sister being asked to help in the home. Except for the hated job of doing the dishes, it seems that Debbie has neither positive nor negative memories of housework from her childhood days. It seems likely her mother handled most of it. John was an only child.

> Debbie: His mother worked on and off while he was young. She still works now. My mother-in-law doesn't drive, so my father-in-law has always done all the grocery shopping, the errands. Also, he does the dishes every night and takes care of his own laundry. Sometimes he cooks too.
>
> Q: They seem to have a pretty egalitarian division of labor? Do you know how this came about?
>
> Debbie: I don't know how they started doing things like that. I think it's because she doesn't drive, so he had to do the shopping. Then also he's always got home earlier than she has. He's a salesman and often didn't have to work that long hours. She works nights a couple of times a week too. So I guess *that's* how he got started with the dishes.

She said this last sentence almost with relief, as if she'd finally solved *that* mystery.

Debbie really has not spent much time thinking about the future when the children grow older. She is sure she does not want to take a job like the one she had before. "I'd just like to paint—at my own leisure and my own pace." This is not a subject she and John discuss.

> Debbie: We've never really talked about me going back to work. He doesn't mind my going to school. That doesn't bother him a bit. I'm sure he wouldn't mind if I got a part-time job.
>
> Q: How do you feel about mothers having careers and leaving their children with sitters?
>
> Debbie: I think mothers should be home with the kids. *The mothers need it* [emphasis mine]. You're just too tired out at night, never have enough time to spend with the kids, when you work. I really enjoy them. Time goes so fast. They grow up so soon.
>
> Q: How do you think it affects the kids, having their mothers work?
>
> Debbie: I don't think it hurts the kids. Sometimes we go away for a couple of weeks and leave them with their grandmother. They're just as happy. They don't miss us at all.
>
> Q: Do you and John ever discuss things like the woman's movement or any of the issues they raise like sexual equality?
>
> Debbie: No, we never have.

Her tone indicated that this was an issue of complete indifference to them.

> Q: How do *you* feel about it?
>
> Debbie: If I was to go out to work...I just don't know if John would help out around here. Of course, if I had a paycheck, I would have someone in to clean, send the laundry out, things like that. But what I'd be doing is trading my time for the paycheck. I just don't think it would work. I really don't think John would change that much. It's been too long. It's too late to change him I think.
>
> Q: Do you feel that it is really John's responsibility to provide money for the family?

Debbie shook her head very emphatically!

> No. I don't agree with that at all. See, my mother had to work to take care of us. Sure, my father sent child support, but it wasn't enough. She had to work. It's just that if I went to work, John wouldn't help.

She added, "We can afford all we need anyway."

Many nonworking women, even though their lives are comfortable, seem to show signs of guilt if they aspire to no more than runing a home. This was not the case with Debbie. She appears to thoroughly enjoy her present lifestyle and is not the least bit apologetic about her feelings. About the housework, she said:

> Well, it's okay. It's just something that has to be done. It's no big deal anyway. It doesn't take much time.
>
> Q: What do you do in the summertime if your housework only takes an hour or so a day? What do you do the rest of the time?
>
> Debbie: I sit out by the pool. Read a couple of books. Go to the movies. Normally, we hardly ever go to the movies. In the past week, I've been to three.
>
> Q: Is this because your mother is visiting you now?
>
> Debbie: Well, my mother wanted to go one time. But the other times it was because the kids wanted to go.
>
> Q: What changes would you make in your life, if any, if you suddenly inherited unlimited wealth?

From her expression, she didn't find such a prospect interesting and answered rather indifferently:

> Well, I certainly wouldn't think of hiring a maid unless I had a house to go with it. I think I'd probably just invest the money.
>
> Q: Then you feel your present life and schedule are pretty comfortable?
>
> Debbie: Yes, I really do. I have enough time left over to do anything I want. I can read a book anytime.

She says there is more time pressure during the school year with her art classes and the children's activities.

> Debbie: But it all works out. Everything gets done eventually. You know, Johnny doesn't do anything, but then he's not the type of husband who says "This is dirty. How come you didn't clean this?" He's real easygoing.

Debbie feels the four of them have a good family life together. They go on many picnics, little one-day trips, drives on Sundays, bowling on Sunday mornings sometimes.

> Debbie: The boys' sports, like the soccer and Little League, are family activities we all join in. John is soccer coach, and I'm his assistant. We try to do as much with the kids as we can. We really enjoy being with them. But every couple of months, we manage to have a weekend without them too.

She feels her casual approach to housekeeping makes her easily able to adapt to the unexpected.

> Debbie: We've had a couple from back East who came to stay on just one day's notice. It really didn't bother us. I just pick up a little.

Thus Debbie seems to be a woman who knows what she wants from life and is lucky or clever enough to have found it. There was only one instant when she revealed any uncertainty. I had asked her what she felt was most important in a marriage. We discussed those factors suggested by Blood and Wolfe: husband's love, companionship, understanding, standard of living, the chance to have children. Debbie was thoughtful as she tried to think of additions to the list.

> **Debbie:** I can't think of anything else. I'm trying to think... [Long pause] I'm just trying to think of *what my needs really are,* but that would take me a long time to figure it out [Emphasis mine].

It would have been intriguing to have pursued this further, but, unfortunately, we had run out of time.

Clearly, institutions outside the home perform many functions that once took place in a domestic setting. The economic production of goods and services for the market has moved out of the home and into offices and factories. Bureaucratic institutions educate our children, care for our sick and disabled and elderly, and even arrange many of our recreational and leisure activities. Although this steady institutionalization of activities formerly occurring in a family setting has been described as a "loss of family functions" (see Chapter 1), it is not clear that this is an accurate description of what has happened. The family still remains responsible for meeting the basic needs of individual members—providing food, shelter, clothing, physical attention, and socialization of children—but how it does this varies over time with changes in technology and the marketplace.

There are several factors that affect the kinds of instrumental activities families perform and the amount of time they spend on these. Family workload—that is, the total amount of work there is to do—is obviously affected by the number of people in the household and the presence of very young children.[1] Evidence for this is provided by findings that show a strong positive relationship between the amount of time that is spent on housework, the size of the family, and the presence of a young child (Walker and Gauger, 1972; Robinson, 1980). The author's study of 863 families (see Appendix) provides similar evidence. In that study, each additional family member resulted on the average in an extra one and a third hours per week of housework time for the wife.

A glance at Table 3.2 will confirm that for the 30 families interviewed, by and large, the younger the children and the more of them

---

[1] Size of residence is another obvious factor that is not dealt with here. A study by Hall and Schroeder (1970) found that the time spent on housework is positively affected by size of dwelling space.

there are, the greater the number of hours reported for housework. However, this table cannot give us definitive answers because the children's ages are strongly confounded in this sample with the wife's working status.

Other important factors that affect family functions and the time spent on household work include changes in technology, the nature of the tasks performed, employment status of husband and wife, individual standards of performance, and individual preferences and skills. These are not independent factors. For example, whether or not a wife is employed will depend on such "workload" factors as the number and ages of her children. Similarly, the family's standards for domestic cleanliness and order are likely to rise and fall with the availability of time, especially the wife's time, and this is affected by her employment status.

CHANGES IN TECHNOLOGY

The past century has seen the development and diffusion of a large number of technological innovations that directly bear on domestic functions: clothes washers and dryers, dishwashers, vacuum cleaners and carpet shampooers, food choppers and grinders, microwave ovens, to name only a few. Obviously, these have changed what the homemaker does and, because technological innovations penetrate the marketplace also, have changed the range of options available to the homemaker.

For example, by the turn of the century, the homemaker could not only buy a sewing machine for home use, but the diffusion of sewing machines in commercial establishments meant that ready-made clothes became cheaper and more plentiful. Which option was chosen —to buy a machine or to buy ready-made clothes—depended on a number of factors, including the relative costs to the individual of picking one option over another.

Another example is the case of laundry. Commercial laundries did a substantial business in the early part of this century. Strasser (1980) describes one study of urban working-class families that found that 44 percent of even the poorest group spent at least some money on laundry. As domestic washing machines became easier to use (the earliest ones made washing an onerous chore barely preferable to hand washing) and lower in cost, increasingly families acquired them, and over the last few decades laundry has moved back into the home.

A fascinating "nonfinding" is uncovered when we examine the relationship between technological change and the time spent on household work. Studies show that the amount of time women report spending on housework has changed remarkably little from the 1920s to the present in spite of the increased availability of domestic appliances (Robinson, 1980). Incidentally, a similar phenomenon has occurred in the workplace, with workers appearing to "compensate" for shorter workweeks by working overtime or moonlighting (ibid., p. 55).

Goldberg (1977) suggests that an explanation for this phenomenon is that a rise in people's standards has accompanied technological change. With a home washing machine, a man comes to expect a clean shirt every day; in the days when doing laundry was difficult or costly, he was satisfied with a clean shirt every week.

NATURE OF HOUSEWORK

Goldberg makes a useful distinction between "production" functions and "maintenance" functions in the home. Maintenance functions include cleaning, tidying, and repairing activities. Production functions involve transforming raw materials into finished products, such as making clothing and furniture, baking bread, growing and canning vegetables, and so on. Cooking is one activity where the amount of "production" involved can vary considerably—depending on whether a meal is being prepared from basic ingredients or consists of opening a can and heating the contents.

Goldberg argues that although the amount of time spent on housework has been fairly constant over the past few decades, there has been a shift in the nature of housework from primarily production to primarily maintenance functions. I am not sure how much good evidence there is for this assertion, especially in the case of urban households. Although farm families in the past undoubtedly produced much of their own food, it is unlikely that city dwellers were able to do so. Strasser writes that many domestic activities that we commonly associate with families in times past may not have been as commonly performed as we think. For example, she cites a writer of the 1880s as describing home canning as "so troublesome that one can not wonder that it is not attempted oftener" (p. 34).

Then also it is true that the production function has not entirely vanished from today's families either. The post-World War II "do it yourself" boom resulted in a proliferation of home production projects. The popularity of home arts and crafts can be seen in a similar light.

Undoubtedly, the domestic activities that took most time in the past were such routine maintenance chores as washing dishes and clothes and cleaning the house. It is possible that the time spent on these has decreased in recent years. For example, a study by Robinson using a 1975 survey showed a decline in housework between 1965 and 1975, concentrated mainly in routine cleaning and maintenance activities. As Robinson says, this period of time saw sweeping changes that might account for this reduction: such as, the increase in the proportions of wives working, increases in the numbers of childless couples, smaller housing units requiring less care, significant increases in ownership of such household appliances as washers, dryers, dishwashers, disposals, and freezers, undoubtedly at least partly accounted for by the growth in average family income (1980, pp. 55–56).

It is reasonable to suppose that those families that do perform production functions today probably spend more time on total household work than those families who do maintenance work only.[2] This certainly is the case with Josie (Interview #22), the mother of four with a fifth on the way, who reports spending 70 hours per week on household work. In her family, standards regarding "maintenance" (cleanliness and tidiness) are very high; at the same time, the family grows and cans its own food, and Josie bakes bread and makes clothing. Thus they place a strong emphasis on both production and maintenance functions, and this is reflected in the total time spent.

On the other hand, some families emphasize production to the relative neglect of maintenance. Bob and Nancy, for instance, have little time available for household work owing to their heavy external time commitments. Yet the couple report that much of the seven and one-half to ten and one-half hours per week they each spend in the home is involved with "production" activities. They enjoy cooking elaborate meals and freezing them; they spend several hours a month growing and freezing their own fruits and vegetables and tending a pig

---

[2] Some evidence for this was provided during the Foundation for Child Development Seminar held at Stanford University in November 1978 when Melvin Kohn verbally described some preliminary findings of a study he and his associates are conducting. These findings show that complexity of housework is positively associated with time spent, and Kohn's idea of complexity is consonant with Goldberg's notion of production functions.

on a friend's farm. They would like to do even more work of this kind if they had more time. Recall that, as far as maintenance is concerned, Bob and Nancy hire a cleaning woman to clean once a week, and what she leaves undone doesn't get done. Before they hired her, the house was hardly ever clean or tidy.

EMPLOYMENT OF HUSBAND AND WIFE

We will consider the wife's employment first. The very fact of a wife going out to work seems to be strongly negatively related to the amount of time spent on housework. In the author's study of PSID data, for instance, every hour of the wife's employment was accompanied by a 23-minute decrease in the amount of time she spent on housework. Among the 30 women interviewed, the working wives report on the average considerably fewer hours per week than the housewives. And even though their husbands and children spend more time on housework, this does not make up the deficit. (The issue of time spent on housework by the family members interviewed will be discussed in greater detail in Chapter 7.) There is, however, considerable variability among individual families. (See Table 3.2, which shows that some employed wives spend more time on housework than do some nonemployed wives.)

It should also be noted that this finding may be misleading to some degree because many women report that, in terms of outcomes, the actual housework tasks done, they can accomplish as much or almost as much when going out to work as when staying home. They claim that "Parkinson's Law" operates when they are home: when the time is available, the work expands to fill it.

All families were asked how the wife's employment affected *what* gets done in the household. Where the status of wives has changed (from employed to nonemployed, or vice versa), this question was asked in terms of actual results noted. Where the wife's employment status has not changed, respondents were asked to predict the consequences of a change.

The most common effect noted or predicted amongst all families was that "eating out" increased considerably when the wife became employed. This is reasonable in view of the fact that a meal eaten in a restaurant saves time spent on grocery shopping, meal preparation, and cleanup. Another factor mentioned by many families was that the wife's employment would or does lead to a sharp reduction in time spent on children's organized activities by the mother. This was seen by several full-time housewives as actually inhibiting them from even considering employment. One of these women commented that employment would just interfere overall with "being a good mother."

Apart from these two factors—eating out and children's activities—it seems that a woman's employment does not or is not expected to eliminate or affect in any dramatic way any other family functions among the families I interviewed.[3]

The effects of the husband's employment on the time he spends on domestic tasks has received considerably less attention in the research literature than the analogous issue for wives. The time budget study by Walker and Gauger (1973) found a negative relationship between men's working hours and time spent on household tasks: men working less than 40 hours per week spent an average of 2.1 hours per day on housework; those working 40 to 49 hours per week did 1.7 hours of housework daily; those working 50 or more hours per week did an average of 1.3 hours daily of housework.

There was a similar finding in the author's analysis of PSID data (Appendix): for every hour the husband worked outside the home, time spent on domestic work was reduced by an average of three to five minutes. Thus, in absolute terms, effects were very small.[4]

INDIVIDUAL SKILLS AND PREFERENCES

It is clear that people's standards vary considerably, even when we take account of the wife's employment status. Mimi, one of our self-reported organized housewives, reports that she always makes meals "from scratch": she doesn't use frozen or canned goods if at all possible. This is in direct contrast to Debbie, another full-time

---

[3] Only three working women said they had utilized more paid help with the housework since starting work. Several other working women do not have paid help because they cannot afford it, but they said they see this as a potential solution to many of their domestic work problems.

[4] Another recent study (Clark, Nye, and Gecas, 1978) reported no effect of the husband's working hours on the housekeeping role. However, these researchers did not use a measure of actual time spent on housework; instead, they asked respondents whether the husband or the wife usually performed the housework. Thus, their indicator may not have been sufficiently sensitive to capture small absolute differences.

housewife, who allocates no more than 30 minutes a day to dinner preparation and says their meals consist of hot dogs or "TV dinners" several days a week. Mimi does some housecleaning almost every day and is rather proud of her housewifely abilities. Debbie speaks of housework as a trivial activity on which she spends minimum time. Mimi feels the need to schedule her entire day in some systematic way; she does not mind whether the activity consists of housework or a paid job. Debbie, on the other hand, is reluctant to get a job because it would be boring and constricting to her to have her time scheduled; she enjoys the flexibility that being a housewife permits. Debbie's comments were, incidentally, echoed by several other housewives, who described themselves as basically "lazy" and "disorganized" and who feel that going out to work is something that would require them to be more hardworking and efficient (an undesirable consequence, in their eyes).

It seems that the way time is allocated among different family activities is a function to some extent of individual skill, competence, or upbringing. (As already discussed, this is true also of the tendency to rationalize housework.) For example, there are three families who report much food growing, canning, freezing, and bread baking—and these husbands and wives all grew up on farms. (On the other hand, Bob and Nancy, who also enjoy such activities, did not have a rural background.)

Similarly, men who manage finances as part of their occupation tend to report time spent on managing family finances as an important part of their household contribution. A good example is a division controller for a large corporation (Interview #25) who spends several hours a week on his family's financial management. Furthermore, his two children, aged ten and eight, are instructed to keep records of all money they earn and spend, and every weekend the father spends about 20 minutes going over their "accounts" with them in detail.

In order to ascertain fully the effects of background and occupation on a family's activities, far more detailed interviews would be required. There do, however, seem to be some hints here of the likelihood of any particular family's activities being reflective of more general skills and aptitudes of members, which they display in other settings too.

Having discussed what these families do and how they do it, we now move to the issue of who does the housework.

CHAPTER **VII**

Who Does the
Housework?

The issue of who does the housework is all too often an emotion-ally-charged one. And little wonder! For the whole question of family roles—who does what and who is responsible for what—is intertwined with complex social, economic, political, and legal issues. Many writers claim that sexual inequality is so deeply rooted within our social structure *because of* the normative endorsement of a sharply drawn division of labor in the home (e.g., Chafe, 1972).

Through the years, it has been the expressed belief of many cham-pions of female equality that if women succeed in gaining a foothold in the economic sphere, they will then be able to negotiate an equal sharing of domestic duties. The working wife phenomenon of the post-World War II years is surely evidence that such a foothold has been gained (leaving aside, of course, the thorny issue of actual equal-ity in employment). Yet the numerous studies that have examined the effects of a wife's employment on the family division of labor lead us to the conclusion that no dramatic shift in domestic roles has occurred. Or, to take the most optimistic viewpoint, if such a shift is occurring, it is happening *very* slowly. (See Chapter 2 for a discussion of this literature.)

One aim of presenting some relatively detailed case studies here is to try to bring to life some of the families represented by the statistics in the research literature. We have already looked at three such famil-ies. The bantering, bordering sometimes on the bitter, dialog of a couple like Jean and Larry is typical of many couples I spoke with. For such couples, who does the housework is a topic for frequent and heated discussion. There are innumerable homes, however, where the issue is not openly debated and where the working wife simply carries her dual burden with seemingly total acquiescence. Such is apparently the case with Beth, whose story follows. Beth is an assembly worker. Her husband, Bill, is a maintenance machinist in a large plant. Their two oldest children have married and left home; the two younger teenage sons still live with them.

Beth and Bill (Interview #23)

My appointment with Beth was for a weekday evening. She had explained to me on the phone that she usually went to bed by 9:30 and would appreciate not having our interview run any later than that.

Beth and Bill and their two sons live in a low-priced housing tract. The small houses are crowded together. Cars and trucks line the streets. The tract is fairly old, having been built perhaps 30 to 40 years ago. Their tiny front yard was full of bright flowers and shrubs. Beth was adjusting the sprinkers when I arrived. She greeted me a little shyly and led me into a small living room that faced the backyard. I could see through an open archway into what was apparently a kitchen with attached eating area. Beyond that, there was a former garage that had been converted into a game room with pool table. The rooms were small and crowded with furniture.

Like some of the other respondents, Beth was stiff in her responses to start with, as if she felt she were on trial somehow. However, she relaxed as our conversation progressed. She told me that her husband was out on a job that evening and would be unable to talk with us. When he came home later in the evening, I asked her if he'd mind joining us for a while, but she was reluctant to ask him. I think, in retrospect, her unwillingness was probably because she feared that his participation might prolong the interview until past her bedtime, rather than because of any reluctance to have me talk to him.

The couple's two oldest children, a boy and girl, are married and live away from home. The two younger sons, aged 16 and 17, are high school students. They did not come into the living room where we sat but popped in and out of the adjoining kitchen, occasionally grinned at me from the doorway, or called out ad hoc comments when they overheard parts of our conversation.

Beth has worked full-time for six years. Until a week or so ago, she worked on an assembly line at an electronics company. Now she has a new job in a different company and is very enthusiastic about it.

> Beth: I'm training to be an instructor. I'll teach new people how to run the equipment—the methods and processes. We aren't ready to train anyone [yet]. This is a new program. We might be ready by September.

Previously, she had worked at the same company as her husband, Bill. They had liked that as they were able to commute together. Now they travel separately. She leaves home at 7:00 a.m. to start work at 8:00. She leaves work at 4:30 and usually gets home at 5:00 or 5:15. In her former job, both she and her husband usually arrived home by 4:00. She had, however, been very dissatisfied with her previous job and says, "I felt like I was in a rut." (Later in the interview, she talked more about this, and it was clear that she was not only bored but extremely unhappy with her previous job.)

Before her marriage 26 years ago, Beth had worked as a telephone operator in Oakland. She had met her husband while he was in the San Francisco Bay Area with the military. After they married, they moved to his home state of Montana and lived on his father's ranch for about five years.

> Beth: There was no call for telephone operators in the small town there. So I didn't work at all then, except on and off on the ranch. I helped out a bit.

They then moved into the small nearby town and her husband worked in the hardware store. He was there about 15 years while they were raising their young family. When her youngest child turned three (13 years ago), she went to work at the hardware store part-time. She was a bookkeeper clerk, helped with the inventory, and filled in for regular employees in the store who were sick or on vacation.

> Beth: Then the hardware store was sold to an eastern company. They turned out to be a liquidating company, so they closed it down. So then suddenly we were without any income. There weren't many sources of jobs in that small town.

So the family moved to the Bay Area where Beth had grown up, and a relative found a job for Bill. Bill has changed jobs several times in the six years they have lived here and has been unemployed for periods of time. At present, he is a line mechanic, repairing and maintaining the equipment that "the girls work on to make the integrated circuits." He leaves home at 6:00 a.m. He doesn't have to start work till 6:45, and it's only a 20-minute commute; but, as his wife explained, he likes to spend the extra time drinking coffee with the other mechanics, and "they talk over what has to be done that day." Similarly, although his regular quitting time is 3:15, Beth says:

> He sometimes doesn't leave till 3:30 because if he's busy on something, trying to get it up, he just keeps going until someone comes to relieve him.

He is home by four o'clock. However, in addition to his regular job, he has what his wife describes as a "handyman business." I asked what he did in this.

> Beth: Everything from plumbing to laying cement. He used to do this in Montana before we moved here. It was only a small town, and word got out that he was a good fixer. Then shortly after we moved to California, someone asked him to help with a swimming pool, then another job came and another. Then he had business cards made up and left at the local lumber yards and places.

Thus, he is often out of the house again by five o'clock on a handyman call, usually until 7:30 or 8:00 p.m. Currently, this is on Monday, Tuesday, and Thursday evenings only. On Saturdays, he often works overtime at his regular job and then puts in another two to three hours on a handyman job. Sometimes he works all day Sunday also.

> Beth: It really depends on how much work there is and how urgent the calls are. Also, what he feels like. If he doesn't feel like working, he won't. Normally, though, he really loves it. It's nearer a hobby than a job.

He is usually accompanied on his handyman calls by one or another of his three sons.

> Beth: He just says, "Okay, who wants to go with me tonight?" And usually someone will go. If they don't, well, he'll just go by himself.

Beth says that Bill does not put any pressure on the boys to accompany him. He pays them full wages when they do, and when he bids on jobs he always includes pay for a helper. However, he never hires "outsiders"; if one of his sons won't go, he'll go alone. Their oldest son, who lives five miles from them, still often accompanies his father on these calls.

Bill and Beth are members of the VFW (Veterans of Foreign War) and the American Legion. On Wednesday nights they either go bowling or to a bimonthly meeting of the VFW, "according to how we feel that night." This is why Bill doesn't do handyman jobs on Wednesdays. He keeps Friday evenings free also, and they often go to a movie. He sometimes works on Saturday nights, although often they go dancing instead.

> **Beth:** He used to be active in other things too, but now it's just the bowling and VFW. He found he was spreading himself too thin. He does quite a bit for the VFW. They have the Holy Ghost Parade here— him and some of the men from the post head the parade. They have four or five parades every year that they head. I bet they spend about half the day [on parade days] —on Sundays.

Beth herself is hardly any less active in her spare time. She chuckled as she related her activities of the past few months:

> This spring, I had practically every evening taken up. I was going to class Tuesday, Wednesday, and Thursday, but twice a month we had the VFW auxiliary meeting. Then on Friday nights, I bowled. Then Monday night, once a month there was the American Legion. My husband isn't active in that any more, but I'm still in the auxiliary.

She is taking commercial art, drawing, and painting in night classes and started these classes last spring for the first time.

> **Beth:** I hope to learn enough to get a job doing that. I told my teacher I wanted to learn every aspect of the commercial art, so now he's giving me special attention.

The classes had lasted from 7:00 until 10:00 p.m. She'd had to leave home at 6:30 to get there in time.

> **Beth:** At that time, I used to get home at 4:00. It didn't leave much time to fix a meal and get there. Lots of times, I'd fix a meal, put it on

the stove, and they all fed themselves. Like one boy would come home
at 6:15 from his job [part-time job at a service station]. I'd have to use
the car at 6:30, so he'd get back in time for that. Then if my husband
had a job to go to that evening, sometimes he'd eat early before he left,
and sometimes at nine o'clock or so after he got back.

Summer classes were stopped as a result of the passage of Proposition
13 in California, but Beth was hoping to resume in the fall.

Because Beth has worked at least part-time for most of her married life, I asked how she had managed child-care arrangements over
the years. This, she said, first became an issue when they lived in
Montana and she went to work in the hardware store with her husband when the youngest child was three.

Beth: At first, I used to take the two youngest with me to the store.
Then that got to be a problem, so I took them to a sitter's house. [I
asked how this became a "problem," but she either didn't hear or
ignored my question.] Even then we only lived half a block from the
hardware store. Of course, that was a quarter of the way across town!
[with humor] Sometimes I'd just leave them playing in the yard. They
knew where I was at and they could come and get me. If I knew I was
going to be gone quite a while, I'd leave them with a neighbor. It was
kind of hit and miss.

Q: You said that that job was part-time. What made you decide to go
to work full-time?

Beth: It was a necessity. Out here, the economy is so much higher than
it is in Montana. There you could get by on five or six thousand a year.
Here it takes three times that. I had decided that since there was an
opportunity for me to go to work, we would be better off if I did.
Now we've got to depend on that extra income so much, I don't know
how I'd do without it.

When she had first started full-time work in California, both she and
her husband worked swing shift, from 3:30 till midnight.

Beth: This created problems at home, so after a while—about a year—I
switched to days. The three boys were at home by themselves. [Their
daughter is five years older than the oldest boy and was married when
they moved to California. She did not accompany them.] The oldest
one babysat. He was either in the first year of high school or maybe still
junior high. Anyway, in the evenings, they were alone. They would cook

for themselves. They could all do that. But, like one time, the kids in the neighborhood was all playing and the middle one [son] ended up getting a bad slash in his hand. Then another time, they had a water balloon fight and one ended up with a broken ankle.

Beth's sister, who has children also, worked days, and the two women called on each other in times of emergency to take care of each other's children. However, Beth had not been happy with the situation and so decided to change to day shift when the opportunity arose.

> Beth: When I went to days, my husband was still on swing, so I'd be saying goodbye as my husband came in. This went on for a year, then he went on graveyard [midnight to 7:00 a.m.], and of course it was the same thing there. Then he was laid off.

Bill was unemployed for several months, but kept busy with his handyman business, and then was reemployed by a former company on the day shift. I asked how she had liked swing shift, apart from the problems it had caused with the boys.

> Beth: I think I preferred swing shift the best. It was quiet. No big shots looking over your shoulder all the time. We had a lot of privileges the day shift didn't. Like we was supposed to take 30 minutes for our supper break, but we always took an hour because the cafeteria wasn't open then, so a bunch of us would go out and eat. We had a lot of potlucks.

However, after she had switched to day shift, Beth said it dawned on her that she'd been missing a certain amount of social life by working in the evenings. So she had adjusted quite readily to day shift.

The younger of the two sons living at home has a job at a local service station. He works three nights a week from 4:00 until 9:00 p.m. and all day Saturday. (Because the interview took place in the summertime, neither of the younger boys was in school.) The older, whom Beth refers to as her "middle son," does not have a job at present.

> Beth: He's been putting in his applications everywhere. But he has been the one to help me around the house. He does the vacuuming while I'm at work. He cleans the bathroom. Then he made a batch of cookies. Things like that. He goes out with my husband on some of his handyman jobs. And he does woodworking at home as a hobby.

We moved on to a discussion of household work and who is responsible for various tasks. In the first part of our discussion, I received the impression from Beth that they all shared fairly equally. In particular, she seemed anxious to present her husband in the best possible light. When she explained his contributions to me, she spoke slowly and deliberately, looking me directly in the eye as if to ensure that I was fully grasping her comments. Nevertheless, as our conversation progressed, I became increasingly certain that Beth's objective situation in this household was not that different to the situation of some of the more dissatisfied women I interviewed.

Q: Who is chiefly responsible for the housework?

Beth looked surprised, and spoke in a slightly aggrieved tone as if hurt that I hadn't remembered.

> **Beth:** Well, remember, I said my middle son—since he's the one without a job now—he vacuums, cleans the bathroom, does the dishes. Generally, the deeper cleaning I have to do. He won't mop the kitchen floor. I have to do that. Then in here [indicating the living room where we sat] he'll just vacuum the middle of the room. Maybe he'll move this little table [the coffee table]. Once in a while, I have to move the heavy stuff and vacuum under them. I generally have to dust. The boys are responsible for their own bedrooms.
>
> **Q:** Who fixes breakfast?
>
> **Beth:** We get our own. The boys know how to cook well enough they can fix toast or cereal....

The younger son was in the kitchen eating pizza as far as I could make out, and he called out at this point, "scrambled eggs."

> **Beth:** Yes, scrambled eggs. One likes French toast. My husband and I don't eat breakfast. He has a cup of coffee. I have milk. Now on weekends when everyone's home, Sunday especially, I like to fix a big breakfast—hot cakes, waffles, things we wouldn't generally have.
>
> **Q:** Who cooks dinner?
>
> **Beth:** I do. Well, now, except sometimes when I'm going to be late. I have a standing hair appointment every Friday. Like in my last job, when I got off early, the appointment was at 4:00, so I didn't get

home till 5:30 or 6:00. Sometimes my husband would come and get me, bring me home, and he'd have the meal all fixed.

Q: How about the dishes?

Beth: Every month, it used to be the boys would take turns for the dishes. One month, it was one's turn, then the other one's turn. Now the younger one has a job, he pays the middle one to do his dishes.

[A loud chuckle from the kitchen from the younger son who was listening to us. He called out, "yeah, that's a good deal."]

Beth: The boys usually come home for lunch. Sometimes the way their schedules are they only have one class after lunch. So when I get home, the dishes are all cleaned up.

Q: Grocery shopping?

Beth: When my husband is home on a Saturday, we both do it. Otherwise, I do it myself. I take Saturdays to do stuff that doesn't get done during the week. Like the shopping and the clothes washing. I try to wash twice a week. On Saturdays, I strip the beds, do all that washing, put it away. My husband helps me with that if he's home. He folds the towels and sheets. I don't do any ironing. I hang it all up right out of the dryer. If my husband is working out in the garage, and the dryer quits, he'll just take the stuff out and put another load in.

She added with some satisfaction, "We all kind of work together."

Q: Yardwork?

Beth: The middle boy has a couple of ladies' lawns around here that he mows so he mows our yard at the same time. Of a morning before we go to work, we'll turn on the sprinklers for about 15 minutes.

I commented on the attractive flowers and shrubs in the front yard. Beth smiled proudly and said she does all the planting. She enjoys this.

In spite of Beth's explanation of the housework for which the middle son is responsible, her subsequent comments indicated that, in fact, much of what he does is a sort of occasional tidying up throughout the week.

> **Beth:** Most of the cleaning gets done on Saturdays, unless I feel it needs it during the week.

And she elaborated on her Saturday schedule.

> **Beth:** For a while, the three of us—me and the two boys—we'd get together and by noon we'd all be done. But doing it by myself, I'd start at 8:00. I'd do what I could while the boys were still sleeping. They'd get up at 11:00, then I'd work for about two or three more hours.

She cannot rely on the boys to help her on Saturday mornings, however. Sometimes they decide to go on a job with her husband instead, and, as she'd mentioned, they seldom rise before 11:00 anyway. She was tolerant of their sleepiness.

> **Beth:** I let them. They stay up very late and watch TV. They say they need their sleep. The middle one is like a bear if he doesn't get enough sleep.

The boys had first started helping her around the house some time after she had started working full-time.

> **Beth:** When I first started working full-time, they didn't help me. I'd come home so tired, I'd just pass out. I'd get in the reclining chair and just sleep for an hour. Boys being boys, they'd always come in and say, "What's for supper?" So I'd have to struggle up and see that they had a meal. After a while, I got used to it so I didn't have to pass out like that for an hour. Then four years ago, we moved into this house. We rented before. It's quite a bit bigger than what we had. The boys took more of an interest in helping me.
>
> **Q:** Have you ever sat down and systematically worked out some plan for sharing out all the jobs?
>
> **Beth:** Well, kind of, but it didn't really work out. We talked about the different jobs the boys could do to help me. [This was four years ago when they moved into the bigger house.] For a while there, everybody pitched in. Now they've gotten a little older, they're getting lax. For a while they were really good. I'd come home at night and everything got done. Until first one job wasn't done, and then another. They got an allowance, and they were supposed to do certain things. If they volun-

teered to do something extra, then they got paid extra. Of course, if they didn't do what they were supposed to, they didn't get the money.

Beth looked at me earnestly, as if trying to explain the absolute futility of expecting some kind of preplanned scheme to work.

Beth: It just didn't work out, because the only thing that lasted was the dishes and doing their own rooms.

She suddenly seemed to remember what she'd told me about the middle son and his helpfulness. As if to resolve the inconsistency, she added hastily:

The middle son helps me quite a bit. He vacuums... [she looked around the room as if searching for evidence] but only the middle of the room.

Thus, the picture was changing as we talked on. The boys do the dishes and take care of their own rooms. When the middle son has no job, he runs a vacuum cleaner around occasionally and maybe cleans the bathroom. *But* the major share of the work still gets left to Beth. She estimates she spends a couple of hours per working day on household work and cooking, and the bulk of Saturday is devoted to laundry, grocery shopping (which, as it turns out, her husband is very seldom available to help her with), and the bulk of the real household cleaning.

She was thoughtful for a moment after her latest comments about the housework, and her next remark caught me somewhat by surprise.

Beth: The boys think it's terrible they have the dishes to do and their rooms to clean up.

I made sympathetic clucks of amazement at this, and she continued:

That's because they're boys. Some of the boys in the neighborhood that are over here most of the time don't have any chores at home. I have to mind the boys that the dishes are still to be done, and then the other guys get mad because they want to go out somewhere.

We talked a little about these "other boys." Most had part-time jobs after school, but had free evenings, and spent a lot of time visiting her sons. She thinks that most of their mothers work, at least part-time. When her boys were little, their older sister had often helped the mother.

> **Beth**: Sometimes on Saturday she'd babysit. She helped me around the house—with the dishes. She was good at cooking. I had a bad accident once and was in the hospital for a month. She did all the cooking then.

However, only "once in a while" did the daughter do any cleaning or other household chores. Her mother's comments mirrored those I'd heard from other women in explaining why their teenagers don't help more.

> **Beth**: She was a teenager. In high school, she was a cheerleader, on the drill team, the 4-H, I don't know what else. She had all kinds of activities. She was gone all the time. If she happened to be home, she'd clean the house for me.
>
> **Q**: How about your husband?
>
> **Beth**: As a matter of fact, back then he never so much as dried a dish. He always used to say, "This work is woman's work." He would never do anything for the kids. He figured that was my job. As the boys got bigger, he'd do things—like tie their shoes, help them on with a shirt or sweater or overshoes. I think he thought they'd break when they were little.

She chuckled. And then went on to recall how things had changed.

> **Beth**: After I started driving a school bus [this was in Montana] I'd drive in the evening, taking the kids home. It would be late when I got back. After I came home one time, he had the meal fixed. He said, "It's only fair since you're helping earning the money, I'll help in the house." He'd wash or dry dishes or sweep. He's done it ever since.
>
> **Q**: Have you ever *asked* him to help?

After a short pause, she gave a slightly evasive response:

> I think most of it has been voluntary.

Bill, her husband, had returned to the house a short time before. He had glanced in at us from the kitchen and exchanged a friendly smile with me. Now, Beth turned and whispered to me:

> Right now, he's folding the towels for me. He's put another load in the washer.

She said this with conspiratorial pleasure, as if we were secretly observing a small child doing something cute. At this point, I suggested that we ask him to join us, and Beth indicated reluctance (probably because it was now approaching her bedtime of 9:30). As we went on talking, Bill (a rather short, slightly built man) started clearing off the kitchen table, where the boys had earlier eaten pizza, and it sounded as if he was loading the dishwasher. Almost as though he wanted to demonstrate his helpfulness in front of strangers!

As with many other women who start working outside the home, Beth feels her standards toward housework have relaxed considerably over time.

> **Beth:** I used to be a perfectionist, now I think "the heck with it." He [husband] folds the towels, and it's not the way I like them. And I think, "So what, they're done aren't they?" And who's going to look in the closet and criticize? And if they do, they have no business in there. My son vacuums in here—so he doesn't do the corners! [She shrugged as if to say, "So what!"]

I asked Beth if her husband put his "handyman" talents to work around their own house; I expected a prompt affirmative response. However, she hesitated for a few moments before reponding. Then she pointed to the wood paneling in the room we were sitting in.

> **Beth:** He did this. My sons did the mantel. He remodeled a bathroom one time.
>
> **Q:** He is responsible then for all the fixing and repairing that comes up?

She hesitated again and said "Yes" without much conviction. Then she added, "Or maybe the boys do sometimes." She thought about this and then said conclusively, "Yes, him or the boys will do it." I'm not sure whether her initial uncertainty was because such jobs very seldom come up in their household, or because they generally are left undone. In any case, this reaffirmed my impression that Beth was reluctant to say anything about her husband that might make me think he was not as helpful as he should be.

Q: Is there anything else you can think of that your husband or the boys are responsible for doing around the house?

Again, a rather long and anxious pause while she tried to think of something. Then her face brightened.

Beth: Him and my oldest son are in the process of building me a china cabinet. They've been working on it for a year. It's made of solid walnut. It's real hard to get the wood. Whenever they have any free time, they work on that.

Q: Beth, your daily schedule sounds quite hectic. What would a perfect schedule look like for you?

Beth laughed at this.

Beth: I wouldn't know what a perfect schedule would look like. If I had a schedule where everything got done, I'd be bored to death.

She recalled again her attempts after starting a full-time job to have her family help her in some systematic way to get all the household chores done.

Beth: I tried to make up a schedule but too many things come up and I couldn't stick to it. So I did what I thought was important and the rest waited.

Q: What changes in your life would you make if you were suddenly to become extremely rich?

Beth: I think I still would work. I really enjoy what I'm doing now. I might buy a few things. I might have someone come in two or three times a week [to do the housework]. I wouldn't want anyone in all the time. Just once in a while.

Beth says she enjoys housework if she has the time.

Beth: You see, I find myself enjoying some jobs of housework. If I've got the time, I don't mind doing it. Sometimes I'm not in the mood.

Q: Are there some household jobs you're not in the mood for more than others?

Beth: No, it applies to everything. Even cooking. Like once in a while, I'm in the mood for baking cookies. I'll make three batches, then put them in the deep freeze so they'll last a while. Then I might go for three months without making another cookie. Then I'll feel like washing walls sometimes.

She suddenly recalled something at this point and turned earnestly to me as she explained:

One thing—my windows seem to be neglected more than anything else. A lot of it is because some of them are kind of hard to get at. You have to take the screens off. Some are too high for me.

Q: You do the windows yourself then?

Beth: Sometimes my husband and I do them together. He'll do the outside and I'll do the inside. That's one thing I can't get around to doing too often. In the living room, one wall is mirror tile, which gets cleaned about as much as the windows. It's an all-day job.

But she was quite sure she wouldn't ever want a full-time maid.

Beth: I like to be master of my own kitchen. Do what I like in there, how I like, without other people around.

Q: Would you prefer to work only part-time if money were no object?

Beth: It's possible I might decide to work half a day, but I would go in five days a week as long as it was something I enjoy. Half a day wouldn't be bad if I didn't need the money. I'd go crazy not working at all.

Beth was the oldest of nine children, four girls and five boys. Her father had always worked and her mother had stayed home to take care of the house and children. The children were all expected to help around the house.

Beth: When I was in junior high, I'd sweep the floors. My sister and I shared a bedroom. We cleaned our room. Her and I did the dishes. Mom always left us with the dishes. She [mother] did a lot of sewing. She made her clothes and me and my sisters' clothes. My sister and I did the housework. Mom did most of the cooking. But when I got in high school, then I did.

As the children grew older, the various household chores were passed down. The brothers also helped with the dishes but never did vacuuming and sweeping.

> **Beth:** Father was one of those, he didn't do anything. He'd come home
> and read the paper till the meal was ready and he'd eat.

Beth's husband had grown up on a farm in Montana. He was the
youngest child, having one brother and two sisters. They lived in a
log cabin. At one time, one room of it was used as the local elementary school.

> **Beth:** He and his brother milked the cows, fed the cattle, did the haying,
> drove the tractors. The girls worked in the house, cooking and cleaning
> and washing. Their mother sometimes went in the tractors, too, to help.
> Their father did the outside work. They had hired men too.

We reflected on differences between her surroundings now and
the earlier days of her married life in Montana.

> **Beth:** Ninety percent of the women there [in Montana] didn't work.
> There was no jobs for them. I'd have neighbors over for coffee or go
> have coffee with someone else. Sometimes we'd meet in the one restau-
> rant in town and drink coffee and talk. I would do things with people
> all the time.
>
> **Q:** And it's different here in California?
>
> **Beth:** Oh yes. I broke my foot and was home for a month. I was so glad
> to get back to work. There was no one to talk to. Most of the women in
> this neighborhood work. There was no one to have coffee with even. I
> was bored stiff.

Clearly, the kind of life she'd led in Montana where few of the neighborhood women worked provided her with opportunities for mingling
with other women during the day, gossiping, and so forth. In a neighborhood where nearly all the women have jobs in the daytime, the
only way she can fully satisfy her sociable impulses is to go to work
also.

> **Beth:** I enjoy the people. I've always liked people. I like to be around
> people, talk, visit, compare notes. Gossip, I suppose you'd say. Staying
> at home, I'd miss that.

The job itself has not always been enjoyable for her, however. In
particular, her last job, which she left only a few weeks ago, caused
her much distress.

Beth: Sometimes, I used to come home from work feeling so upset I just didn't want to do anything. And then I dreaded going to work next day.

Beth stifled my attempts to inquire further into her unhappy work situation, saying "It's a long story." However, she did volunteer:

There was conflict with my supervisor. The jobs she was having me do. Being watched constantly. I didn't feel like doing anything.

Being happy at work, as she is now, enables her to approach her domestic workload in a positive way; whereas her former unhappiness had induced a lethargy that affected her home life too.

Beth says her husband enjoys his job. He enjoys his handyman business also.

Beth: He does it because he wants to, not because he has to. It's a hobby, like I would paint.

Moreover, although domestic chores are not something she generally enjoys facing when time is short, she stressed that she will not permit housework to interfere with things she really wants to do.

Beth: There are other things I just make time for. I paint in oils. It kind of relaxes me. Once in a while I sell a picture, or paint one for a wedding or birthday or anniversary.

She explained that on any night she feels like painting, or indulging in other crafts that she likes to do from time to time, she'll just do whatever has to be done with the dinner or laundry and then spend a couple of hours painting or working on her hobby.

Beth is well content with her lot and is indifferent to the women's movement.

Beth: I'm not a woman's libber. I guess you'd say I enjoy being a woman. I don't care to compete with men. It's important for widows and divorcees to be able to earn a living with a family. I'd like to see them do that. I don't have to. I'm working to help out but I'm not trying to compete with any man to get a better job or be equal.

She is very glad that she was able to stay close to her children when they were babies and feels sorry for mothers who have to go to work when they have babies at home.

> **Beth:** I think they miss a lot. They miss a lot of their kids' childhood when they have to loan their babies out to sitters. My daughter-in-law works, and her mother takes care of their granddaughter. She only sees the baby nights and weekends. Sometimes he [her son] will bring the baby over to me.
>
> **Q:** Do you enjoy sitting for your granddaughter?
>
> **Beth:** Yes, I enjoy it. I don't think she [daughter-in-law] realizes what she's missing, seeing it's her first child. I feel that way because of having four. I know they grow up so fast. It doesn't take long before they're out of babyhood and grown. The mother misses a lot of that.

However, Beth doesn't feel the children are particularly harmed by being sent to a sitter. She recalls a sitter they had for their own children and how she had felt that it was really good for the kids to get used to another adult.

> **Beth:** They got weaned away so they weren't hanging on my dresstails all the time. I thought it was good for them, so they don't have to be depending on me all the time.

She is not certain, however, about the effects on children who are left all day, every day, with a sitter but suggested, "It's good for them some of the time."

> **Q:** Beth, would you say it's your opinion that it's your husband's responsibility to earn the living and that you're just helping him with this when you work?
>
> **Beth:** Yes [firmly].
>
> **Q:** And that it's your job to take care of the household, and he's just helping *you* out by doing things in the house?
>
> **Beth:** Yes.

Some closing observations on Beth's case. There was an atmosphere of cheerfulness in the crowded little home, contributed mainly by the lighthearted conversation between the sons in the next room and their smiles and comments when they looked in on us from time to time. Beth was generally quite solemn, but there were times when her face lit up in genuine delight, such as when she pointed out that her husband was attending to the laundry as we talked and when she described the walnut cabinet the "boys" were making for her.

It seems that equity in the distribution of domestic work has never been an issue between Beth and Bill. She has not argued with him to help her and accepts gratefully whatever help he proffers. There have been struggles on her part to have her sons help out more. As it happens, the major competitor for the sons' time is the husband. Presumably, they would prefer to accompany him on a handyman call than help their mother with the cleaning. In fact, if the neighborhood boys seldom do the dishes, as Beth says, there are probably some peer pressures on her sons to avoid "woman's work."

The relationship between Beth and Bill, I would guess, is a warm one. For all the busyness in their lives, they set aside time to be with one another—to go bowling, dancing, to the movies. Although his handyman business is "more of a hobby," it does bring in money and therefore she cannot complain about it.

Beth, in contrast to women like Jean and Nancy, does not rely on rational organization to help her cope with the multiple demands on her time and energy. But she has made the dual burdens of work and family bearable by forcing herself to be more easygoing about her household standards, even sometimes neglecting the housework to find time for enjoyable hobbies.

Finally, as loving and close-knit a family as this appears to be, one is struck by the extent to which the world outside the home dominates their time and activities—both work and leisure. As with so many other urban families, it is difficult to reconcile the story of this family with the image of a modern family as a "haven" from a bureaucratic world.

The families interviewed were asked to estimate weekly time spent by husband, wife, and children on all domestic work such as cooking, cleaning, yardwork, maintenance of house and appliances, bill paying, and so on. The time estimates do not include time spent merely playing with children, but do include time spent feeding or bathing children, and helping them with homework.

Earlier, I noted that there was frequent disagreement between husband and wife concerning the amount of time each spent on household work. This issue was studied by Berk and Shih (1980), who point out that this kind of discrepancy should not merely be regarded as a methodological nuisance. It is, rather, likely to reflect differences in perceptions of reality among family members.[1]

In the sections that follow, I shall first discuss each interviewee's reports of the division of labor between wife and husband. This will be followed by a discussion of some of the factors that might reasonably be expected to affect the degree of egalitarianism or traditionalism in the family's division of labor. The final section in this chapter focuses on housework done by children.

DIVISION OF LABOR BETWEEN HUSBANDS AND WIVES

Table 7.1 shows mean weekly hours of housework for husbands and wives by employment status of the wife. In some families, the estimate from either husband or wife was missing, and such cases are omitted from the table. Part A of the table shows means of all usable responses (N = 23). Part B shows means of responses obtained from interviews where both husband and wife were present (N = 15). If there was a discrepancy, I accepted the wife's estimate for the time she spent on housework and the husband's estimate for the time he spent. When the husband was not present at the interview, I had, of course, to accept the wife's estimate for both of them.

This table (Part A) indicates that the housework time of full-time employed women in this sample is only half that of nonemployed women: 18.5 as compared with 34.6 hours per week. Husbands of employed women spend almost twice as much time on housework as husbands of nonemployed women (9.5 as compared to 5.5 hours per week), although their time spent still falls far short of the time spent by their working wives.

In looking at Part B of Table 7.1, it can be seen that when husbands' reports of their own time spent are used, the estimates are increased, with husbands of employed women reporting they spend 11.9 hours per week on household work.

---

[1] Berk and Shih found, incidentally, as I did, that differences tend to take the form of each partner attributing greater participation in household tasks to self than is attributed to himself or herself by the spouse.

Table 7.1.
**Mean Weekly Hours of Housework for Husbands and Wives
by Wife's Employment Status**

Wife's Employment Status	Husbands	Wives
A. All Usable Responses (N = 23)		
Full-time	9.5	18.5
Part-time/student	8.7	24.5
Nonworking	5.5	34.6
B. Responses from Interviews with Both Husband and Wife (N = 15)		
Full-time	11.9	17.8
Part-time/student	8.7	24.5
Nonworking	6.5	43.0

Note that when we use only those responses obtained when two spouses were present, the time estimate for the nonemployed wives is much greater than the average of all responses (43 hours per week as compared to 34.6 hours per week). There may be some tendency for a housewife to inflate her housework time in the presence of her spouse—with an employed wife perhaps not feeling such a need given her obvious great commitment of time to her job. This is pure speculation, of course.

There is a wide range in the number of hours reported for individual respondents (see Table 3.2). Among nonemployed wives, estimates range from 12 to 70 hours per week; for their husbands, the range is from zero to 12 hours per week. For employed wives, estimates range from seven and one-half to 30 hours per week; for their husbands, the range is from zero to 20 hours per week.

To reiterate an earlier warning, these 30 families do not comprise a scientifically selected random sample. Hence, the distribution in the table cannot be interpreted as evidence of a relationship between working hours and housework hours in the population at large. However, the table does demonstrate that findings for these families do not differ markedly from findings in the literature: working wives spend much less time on housework than housewives; husbands of working wives spend more time than husbands of housewives but still nowhere near as much time as the women do.

The time on household work is only one way of estimating husbands' and wives' contributions to the family. As already noted in Chapter 3 (Table 3.1), these husbands on the average spend far more time than do the wives in working away from home. In fact, when we identify those families where employed wives spend equal or greater amounts of time in employment than their husbands,[2] we find that in most of these cases the husband's contribution to housework is equal to or almost equal to that of the wife.

In spite of disagreements between spouses concerning the number of hours each spends on housework, there was, interestingly enough, overall consensus within each family as to whether husbands were "helpful" (that is, shared as equally in the housework as their work hours would permit), or "unhelpful" (that is, left most of the housework to the wife). Next, I discuss three factors that might reasonably be expected to influence husbands' helpfulness with housework. These are: availability of time, sex-role ideology, and childhood socialization.

AVAILABILITY OF TIME

All respondents at one point or another expressed the unequivocal belief that the single factor most likely to constrain time available for household work was time spent on the job, especially as far as wives were concerned. (This belief is, of course, borne out by the negative relationship generally found between these two variables.) Table 7.2 lists "helpful" and "unhelpful" husbands by employment status of the wife. "Helpful" husbands are defined as those who (1) are reported by both spouses (or by wife if only she is interviewed) to be willing to share as equally as their job permits in housework, *and* (2) spend an average of eight or more hours per week in household work. "Unhelpful" husbands are those who do not meet both these critieria.

On the whole, there are more unhelpful than helpful husbands (20 as compared with ten). Husbands of full-time employed wives

---

[2] Table 3.2 indicates that these were Interviews #8, #10, #13, #14, #17, #24, #26, and #27.

Table 7.2.
"Helpful" and "Unhelpful" Husbands by Wife's
Employment Status

Wife's Employment Status	Helpful Husbands	Unhelpful Husbands
Full–time	7	4
Part–time/student	1	5
Nonemployed	2	11

are more likely than other husbands to be reported as "helpful." Clearly, the wife's employment does not inevitably lead to a husband's helpfulness, and sometimes husbands of nonemployed women are reported to be helpful.

Part-time employed wives appear to more nearly resemble non-employed than they do full-time employed wives in that most of them have unhelpful husbands. This suggests that it is the real or perceived pressure of time—far more acute for a full-time than for a part-time working wife—and not simply the fact of the wife's employment that leads to the greater helpfulness of husbands. Probably for this reason the majority of nonemployed women report themselves to be satisfied with the division of labor. Some housewives say they do not like housework but feel it is only fair they do the bulk of it seeing that the husbands have to go out to work. Here are some quotations from housewives.

It seems to be the natural way things work [that she do the housework]. I have the time to do it. Also it affects me more than it does him if the house is dirty because I'm here all the time (Interview #7).

Don't think that John thinks of housework as woman's work. He doesn't feel that. It's just that things have evolved this way between us because it makes sense—I have more time (Interview #12).

I do everything. He does nothing [in the house]. Our division of labor is just how it evolved. I have more time, so I do it (Interview #15).

He doesn't do a thing. He doesn't lift a finger. I feel it's my responsibility if I'm not working at a job. I feel he should be free when he comes home (Interview #31).

Even when a wife does not have more available time than her husband, the fact that he earns the money is what counts. As one frantically busy full-time law student and mother of three says:

> I can't do anything about my husband's work. That's essential. He has to feed us (Interview #9).

In some cases, wives are reluctant to seek employment even though the husbands would help in the house; their reluctance stems from the fact that they feel the men will not do the work properly, as the women would wish it to be done. (Recall that Beth indicated she had forced herself to accept the way her husband folds the towels, which is not the way she likes towels to be folded.)

SEX-ROLE IDEOLOGY

It is reasonable to believe that a male with traditional beliefs about male and female roles might be less helpful with the housework than a male with more egalitarian beliefs. In the next chapter on sex roles, it will be shown that most helpful husbands profess to have egalitarian attitudes and most unhelpful husbands express traditional attitudes. However, the relationship between ideology and behavior is not as clear-cut as this statement would imply.

For one thing, both the unhelpful-egalitarian *and* the unhelpful-traditional husbands tend to explain their unhelpfulness in terms of *time.* For example, in one dual-worker family (Interview #20), husband and wife claim to have very egalitarian attitudes about sex roles. However, because she is a schoolteacher with "free" summers, both she and her husband consider it only equitable that she bear a heavier share of the housework throughout the year. Similar views were expressed in the other families where the wives have only part-time employment or are students.

For the men whose expressed ideology conflicts with their behavior—that is, the unhelpful but supposedly egalitarian husbands—a rational explanation that pleads lack of time is one way to resolve the inconsistency. The fact that even those whose ideology and behavior are consistent—the unhelpful-traditional men—use the same kind of explanation, rather than invoking their normative beliefs to justify their behavior, suggests that the rational explanation is considered the more acceptable.

Incidentally, the two helpful husbands of nonemployed women (see Table 7.2) justify their helpfulness in terms of their upbringing and their ideological beliefs. The wife of one of these men (Interview #19) says:

> He isn't one of your male chauvinists. He just never had the impression that there's men's work and woman's work. We don't even need to say anything to each other; we just work real good together and everything falls into place.

The husband added:

> I've just never thought of anything different. I just can't be anywhere sitting on my can waiting for someone else to do something and be comfortable.

The relationship between the husband's helpfulness and sex-role ideology is discussed further in Chapter 8.

CHILDHOOD SOCIALIZATION

There seems to be some tendency for husbands to be helpful to their wives if, as children, they were required to do housework for their parents. Similarly, a lack of current helpfulness was often explained in terms of the husband's lack of appropriate experience. One working wife in a blue collar family bewailed her husband's unhelpfulness, but said:

> That's one thing with my husband. He never did it as a boy. If you've never really done it, then you don't know how (Interview #17).

Questions concerning husband's and wife's housework experiences as children were systematically asked from the tenth interview on. Responses were obtained from a total of eight helpful husbands and 13 unhelpful husbands. Six of the eight helpful men listed such chores as housework, cooking, cleaning, dishes, grocery shopping—or what might be considered traditionally "female" chores—in addition to traditionally "male" chores such as taking out garbage and yardwork. Of the 13 unhelpful men, only four listed "female" tasks, five others said they had done yardwork, and the remaining four said they had done "nothing."

There, thus, seems to be some relationship between perceived or actual competence and the willingness to perform the work. Of course, this needs further empirical investigation, but the relationship does seem to be a reasonable one. As another respondent suggested:

> He feels that doing woman's work is bad enough. But to show he can't even do it properly, that would be terrible!

There was, incidentally, no relationship between the amount and nature of housework done as a child by the *wife* and the family's present division of labor. A few wives reported having never done much to help their parents. Some felt their parents had erred in being so undemanding because the adult role of housewife proved to be difficult to fill without some prior training. One wife (Interview #9), a full-time law student married to an "unhelpful" attorney, stated flatly that she had been raised to believe that she had a brighter future in store than spending her time on menial chores. Her tone was bitter as she explained that as a girl her parents had always had household help. All she and her sister had ever done was to make their own beds and occasionally help with dishes. And now those are the only two chores, she says, that she doesn't feel intensely resentful doing.

Rather surprisingly, there seemed to be no relationship between the division of labor reported for *parents* of the interviewees and their present division of labor. Most respondents said that their parents were traditional in the way they divided household work, with a very few reporting their fathers had done dishes or cooked occasionally. In only three cases did husbands report their parents to have had an egalitarian division of labor: one of these is a helpful husband himself, but the other two are among the unhelpful husbands.

CHILDREN'S HOUSEWORK

Earlier studies have found that teenage children are an important source of domestic help in modern families. Refer, for example, to the findings from Walker's time budget studies (Walker, 1973; Walker and Gauger, 1972, 1973). Walker found that for mothers working 15 hours a week or more, almost 30 percent of the total housework was performed by teenagers; for women working less than this or not at all, 20 percent was done by teenagers. Similarly, Bahr (1974) reported that when adolescent children are present in a family, they, rather than the husband, tend to relieve the working wife of household chores. In the case study at the beginning of this chapter, we saw that when Beth went to work full-time, she turned to her sons, not her husband, as the primary untapped source of household help.

All the families interviewed were asked to describe what their children did in the house and what their attitudes were toward children's participation. There were 21 families with at least one child aged seven or older. In 16 of these, parents reported having strong feelings—amounting to what might be described as a "family policy"—concerning the desirability of children contributing to household work. Typical reasons given for this attitude were along the lines of, "They are members of the family and ought to share in all the work," and "They need to learn how to do these things so they will know how when they grow up." This last statement was sometimes followed by an anecdote relating the sad experiences of a friend who had *not* had this childhood training and had experienced difficulties in adult life as a result.

As mentioned earlier, some women complained that their own parents had erred by not being demanding enough of their children. One wife (Interview #30) said she feels that her childhood would have been more satisfying and not so "boring" had she been made to share in the chores—although, as she says, "at the time, I thought I had it made."

The remaining five families, who report neutral or even somewhat negative attitudes toward children's participation, fall into two groups. One group consists of full-time housewives whose children do little or nothing to help in the house (Interviews #12, #15, #18). The other group consists of employed women whose children do, in fact, contribute fairly heavily (Interviews #17, #23). Two of the nonemployed women do not spend much time themselves on housework and imply there is no need for the children to do anything. One said, "They might as well enjoy themselves while they're young." The third housewife (Interview #15) said, but without conviction, that her children really ought to do more but they have no time because they are so busy with after-school activities.

The two employed mothers whose children do help out appear to regard the necessity for the children's contribution as a negative consequence of their employment. Neither had a well-articulated set of ideas concerning the issue of children's help. They both reported difficulty in getting all the help they needed from their children and saw this as just one extra "hassle" that accompanies having to go to work.

Except for these two families, parental philosophy appears to be consistent with children's behavior. However, the actual amount of time spent by each child varies considerably—from two to 15 hours per week. (See Table 3.2 for the average time spent by children in each family interviewed.) Typically, the first duty likely to be assigned to a child is the cleaning of his or her own room, followed by table setting, dishwashing and kitchen cleanup, taking out trash or garbage, weeding, and sorting laundry. As children grow older, they are likely to have such chores as vacuuming, dusting, and floor washing added to their duties. In no family was cooking the prime responsibility of a child, although some families spoke with pride of their child's ability to cook at all—even if this was only making ready-mix desserts and cookies.

The distribution of families in this sample tends to preclude the making of generalizations concerning the effects of the wife's employment on children's housework. This is because most of the women with younger children were not employed; thus, the effects of the child's age might well be confounded with employment effects. However, *all* families where mothers had moved from nonemployed to employed status reported that the children contributed considerably more as a result of the mother's starting work.

There was very little evidence that children's tasks in these families are sex-typed, contrary to the findings reported by Lynch (1975).[3] In only one family (Interview #32) was it stated that the daughter primarily helps the mother inside the house whereas the sons primarily help the father outdoors. In the remaining families, both sons and daughters were expected to help with housework in varying degrees, with the number of hours of such housework and the distribution of tasks being unrelated to the sex of the child.

Another factor, reported by six families, was that children tend to be excused from household chores to the extent that organized activities outside the home are occupying their time. This issue is explored more fully in Chapter 9.

---

[3] In her study of 806 children, Lynch reports that sex differences in the allocation of tasks appear in the 10–12 age bracket, although they are not present for younger children.

CHANGING PATTERNS IN A MARRIAGE

The following is a detailed account of one family (Interview #32) that illustrates differing patterns of housework distribution in different stages of the family life cycle.

Ben and Irene were married while both were college students. Their first child arrived very soon after they were married. They now have five children, who range in age from four to 16 years. In the early years of marriage, both struggled to keep up their college classes while working part-time to earn money. They shared in all the housework and child care equally. He would babysit while she went to work or to class, and vice versa.

Ben reports that the first real shift in their sharing pattern occurred several years ago when they moved to a fairly large house. This necessitated much outdoor work—fixing the yard, painting the house, and so on. He found himself increasingly spending time outside while Irene worked inside. However, he continued to help out with much of the grocery shopping and housecleaning until the children grew old enough to help too. Ben says, "As they grew older, we put more on the kids. *I got out of it*" (Emphasis mine). Soon, husband and wife were sharing only the grocery shopping.

About two years ago, Ben decided to start a new job at his present company, which he realized would require really long working hours if he were to make a success of it. At that point, Irene decided to leave her full-time job because she found that she could not handle both a job and the greater burden of household responsibility that fell on her with his being increasingly tied up with his job. Today, she works sporadically as a substitute schoolteacher. The present situation is not satisfactory to her, however. Of the substitute work she says, "It never rains but it pours." That is, there is either no work at all for long periods, or else she is called in full-time for several months at a moment's notice. She genuinely loves teaching and misses her work when none is available. As a housewife, she feels isolated and bored. She is also distressed at the growing separation between her activities and those of her husband. (She said, rather accusingly, that *he* did not seem to mind this, and he didn't contradict her.)

Doing housework was something that Ben had done from an early age. As well as helping his mother (his father had died when he was very young and his mother worked), for five years during his teenage years he had cooked and cleaned for a neighborhood woman for pay —"sort of like a housemaid," he said.

Thus two factors combined to produce a sharing pattern for Ben and Irene early in their marriage: the heavy time pressures they both faced from school, work, and their growing family and his childhood experience at doing household work.

The factors they mention that led them away from this sharing pattern were also mentioned by many other respondents. First, there was the move to a larger home, which required outside work. Outdoor work has generally been considered "man's work," and it seems husbands tend to accept it as their responsibility—possibly because much of it involves physical strength. Second, as children grow older, they appear to relieve their father of duties inside the house at a more accelerated rate than they relieve their mother—although they relieve both in many cases. Ben's indoor chores—such as the dishes and vacuuming—were probably seen as more easily handled by the children than his outdoor tasks. With his wife then perceived as getting help for "her" inside work, Ben undoubtedly felt more free to limit his efforts to the outside work.

Irene reports that with her husband now working very long hours away from home, their sons are increasingly required to help him in the yard, and she has difficulty finding "indoor" helpers for *her* except for her one daughter.

This particular family's history affords the opportunity to examine the relationship between sex-role ideology and domestic behavior. Both husband and wife come from homes with very traditional ideology. Their behavior in the early years of their marriage clearly conflicted with this ideology: she went out to work and he shared equally in the housework. Yet, over time, the various factors mentioned—the move to a larger house, the growing availability of children to do the housework, the offer of a better job for him requiring longer hours—have all had the effect of shifting his behavior back into more traditional patterns. With the extra pressure on her, due to the withdrawal of his participation in the house, she has left her full-time job to become a housewife. This is in spite of the fact that she has *very* egalitarian ideals as regards family roles and is quite distressed at what she sees as her family's steady movement toward traditional patterns of behavior.

For Ben, it seems that the traditional beliefs acquired during his formative years have exerted a continuous pull—overruled only by such exigencies as the necessity for his wife to earn money when they were first married—leading him to seize opportunities to modify his behavior in a traditional direction whenever shifts in their practical circumstances present such opportunities.

The influence of ideology was underscored further during an interesting discussion that developed during this interview. Husband and wife were explaining some of the sources of their present discontent with their lives—and it was fairly evident throughout the interview that there are many conflicts in this household. He feels that she does a rather poor job of organizing the household. (As mentioned in Chapter 5, he is an "organizer" and Irene is not.) She resents the long hours he is absent from home every day and very much misses having a regular teaching job. The family moved to California two years ago in order for him to take his new job, and they all deeply miss the friends and relatives they left behind.

They apparently spend a fair amount of time discussing ways to improve their lives. One possibility, which Irene is espousing, is for them to return to their home state. As such a move would mean that he would be unable to advance further in his present career, she has suggested that he then return to college to train for a new career, and —while he plays the roles of student and "househusband"—she will go to work full-time to support them all financially. They both feel this arrangement would work extremely well because he is not only a good housekeeper, but he quite enjoys household work, and, as already mentioned, she greatly enjoys being a teacher. However, Ben says that—as much as this idea appeals to him—he cannot possibly consider it seriously, because his pride would not allow it.

> **Ben:** It would damage my self-respect [to have his wife support him] . . . .
> Males in my family were always breadearners; they never did housework.

SUMMARY

We have seen that for these 30 families a husband's helpfulness in the house seems to be as much if not more a function of time constraints imposed on his wife by her employment than of ideological beliefs about male and female roles. However, the influence of ideology cannot be dismissed lightly. Note, for example, how Ben used traditional ideology to *justify* his pursuing his career to the extent that Irene was forced to abandon hers. It is not clear whether he personally endorsed traditional beliefs about sex roles or was simply using them to legitimate his desire to "get out of" housework and devote his time to activities he enjoyed more.

As we will see in the next chapter, even couples whose domestic division of labor is quite egalitarian often reveal a yearning for more traditional family roles.

CHAPTER *VIII*

Sex-Role Ideology

In this chapter, I am concerned with the ways that the organizational environment, through its impact on domestic behavior, affects the sex-role ideology of individuals.

Sex-role ideology refers to people's beliefs about appropriate roles for men and women. As used here, the term "ideology" is equivalent to what in the literature is often referred to as "preferences" (or, for economists, "tastes"). However, I deliberately avoid talking about preferences when referring to normative beliefs, because "preference" is too easily confused with the idea of a *personal* choice or ideal for behavior. And it seems that neither one's current behavior nor one's normative beliefs are necessarily related to one's personal choices or aspirations.

The next case study describes a working couple, Mike and Chris, who try hard to maintain an equitable division of household labor. Their ideology is as egalitarian as their behavior in that they believe that sex roles should be a matter of individual choice rather than societal prescription. Yet they plan to make the change to the more traditional roles of husband-provider and wife-homemaker as soon as their economic circumstances permit.

Mike and Chris (Interview #24)

The interview with Mike and Chris took place at eight o'clock on a summer evening. Chris had warned me that Mike would be tied up

with a business engagement early in the evening, but she said he might
join us later. Their house was on a pleasant suburban street in a housing tract now about 20 years old: mature shrubs and trees, a quiet
settled look. It was not an opulent suburb, but it was pleasant and
respectable.

Their house was pleasant and respectable too. Chris greeted me
in a friendly but slightly reserved way and showed me to a seat at a
small round table in the window of what seemed to be a sort of family room. An archway led through into a kitchen beyond, and the
living room was at the back of the house on the other side of the
wall facing me where I sat. Their ten-year old daughter, Jenny, came
to steal a shy glimpse at me and then retired to the television in the
living room. They had a dog and a cat, both of which made themselves
evident throughout my visit. I was immediately offered a cup of coffee and chatted to Chris as she fixed the two mugs of coffee for us.

Chris and Mike both work for the same large electronics firm but
in very different capacities. He has a middle management position;
she is a secretary. They met at work and have been married only a
few months. She quickly set me straight when I asked if she had been
his secretary.

> Chris: No. I don't think those secretary-boss things usually work out.
> It's because of your position. You know [searching for the right words]
> ...like if you're subservient....Oh, I guess that's not the right word.
> But, anyway, in that kind of position...the boss-employee relationship
> ...I just couldn't imagine a marriage resulting.

I didn't debate the point. Chris went on to describe their typical
workday. She leaves home in the morning about 7:45 and gets back
about 6:00. Work is a half-hour commute from home. She and Mike
commute together about half the time. However, he often has to stay
late to catch up on extra work or meet with clients. On the night of
our interview, for instance, he is attending a cocktail party for some
clients. He tries to keep such commitments to a minimum.

> Chris: Like tonight, his boss asked him to stay till 9:00 or 9:30, but
> he's going to try to leave by 8:00.

Official work hours are 8:00 until 4:30, but Chris enjoys flexibility
in her hours.

> **Chris:** I have the best boss in the whole company. He lets me go into work later and stay later than most employees. That way I can share a ride with Mike both ways. I could be home by 5:30 most days, but most days I have to shop or do errands or something.

This is the second marriage for both of them. Chris was divorced about four years ago. She has no children of her own. She has worked since she left school at the age of 16, and always as a secretary. In her former marriage, she and her husband lived in an apartment. Housework wasn't much of a problem, as she recalled.

> **Chris:** We split 50-50. It was four years ago, so it's hard to remember. He did most of the cleaning. I did the cooking and laundry; he did everything else. I didn't like the housework. Well, he didn't like it either, but I was less flexible back then. So he did it.

After the divorce, she lived alone. Again housework wasn't much of a problem.

> **Chris:** I was living alone. I just had an apartment. I did everything, but I only had to clean up after myself.

Then she and Mike married, and she found herself with not only a new husband but also a child *and* a house. This combination was quite overwhelming to her. What is more, they had given themselves no opportunity to think through ahead of time the details of how they would manage the practical side of their lives.

> **Chris:** It was such a whirlwind thing. [Some hesitation here.] My husband and I had some marriage problems. [Another pause.] It was a combination of lots of little frustrating things. One of them was the housework. There was so much more cooking to do . . . so many people. I never had any time to myself. There was always something to be done.
>
> **Q:** How did Mike manage before he married you?
>
> **Chris:** Mike was a single parent for three years. He used to have a cleaning woman. I inherited her when we got married. She came in twice a month for about four hours. But she didn't do that hot of a job. She was a really strange woman. She wouldn't clean if someone was in the house, so we always had to ask Jenny to leave when she came. Then she wanted her own key and everything.

Q: So you don't have her come anymore?

Chris: No. Also we're trying to save money so we can buy a house.

I hadn't realized until this point that they did not own the house they were in. We talked a little about the neighborhood. Chris and Mike both like its quiet settled quality but think that prices of houses in the whole Bay Area are "out of sight." Chris said they were hoping Mike would soon be transferred to a cheaper area of the country where they would be able to afford a house more readily. Mike enlarged on this later in the interview.

Q: How do you and Mike handle the housework now?

Chris made a face, and gave a little wave with her hand. When I first arrived, she had murmured something to the effect of, "Please excuse the mess," a remark I ignored as the room looked clean and neat to me. Now she said:

> Not well as you can see. [I made mumblings of, "it looks just fine to me," and she shrugged.] We split it three ways. Jenny does a fair share of housework. We sat down when we first got married and decided who likes what the least. So now I pay the bills, do the laundry and ironing, the cooking and shopping. My husband does the yardwork, mending and fixing... the cars... the windows and floors. Jenny takes care of the animals; she loads and unloads the dishwasher and does the vacuuming. We just let the rest go.
>
> **Q:** Has Jenny always helped around the house?
>
> **Chris:** Probably less than a year. She was in child care before that. She used to go straight to the sitter's house after school.
>
> **Q:** And does she help willingly?
>
> **Chris:** We have to prod her. I try not to lay it on too heavy. As long as she gets her stuff out of the living room by the time we get home. She takes the garbage out too. Then we ask her to vacuum the place once in a while. She doesn't like to vacuum, so I try not to ask her too much.

Earlier, Chris had mentioned vacuuming as being Jenny's responsibility; this exchange made it seem that Jenny didn't do too much of it, in fact. Still later, Chris admitted:

I do some of it [vacuuming]. Jenny does more than I do. We pay her
an allowance for it. If she blows it, she doesn't get her allowance.

Chris estimated that Jenny probably spends a total of half an hour a
day on all her household chores.

Q: What kinds of things did Mike do around the house before you were
married—while he was a single parent?

Chris: He did the laundry and personal stuff. The cleaning woman cleaned
the frig. She did all the cleaning.

Q: Did Mike do the cooking?

Chris: They didn't eat home too much. I think they ate out all the time.
At least, I haven't seen much evidence he knows how to cook!

It is important here to interject a note about the *tone* of voice
used to make these remarks. There could have been, for instance,
considerable bitterness underlying the last remark, in view of the
fact that having to cook "for so many people" was one of the things
Chris had found so burdensome when she married Mike. We might
imagine, for example, that Chris would be angered at a husband who
had seldom bothered to cook for himself but was willing to burden
his new wife with the cooking for the whole family. However, Chris'
tone was not bitter. It was matter-of-fact, and as this interview developed and Chris', and later Mike's, ideological beliefs about family life
and male and female roles emerged, it became obvious that she felt a
vague sense of guilt that Mike had to worry about housework at all
and frustration at her inability to run the household as the "perfect
wife and mother" would.

Q: How much time do you and Mike spend on household work?

Chris: Let's see. I don't cook breakfast. Dinner is about one hour a
night. I try to get something done every night. One day, I'll do the
laundry. The next night, I'll iron. It's probably two hours a day alto-
gether, and then perhaps a total of about five hours at the weekend.

This amounts to about 15 hours a week. Chris thought that sounded
about right and thought Mike probably spent the same amount of
time as she did.

Q: Do you try to organize your housework at all, Chris?

As with nearly all the interviews, I felt slightly surprised at not being asked to interpret my question more fully. ("What do you mean, *organize?*") Most people, it seems, know or think they know what this implies.

> **Chris:** I try. The only thing I really have control over now is the grocery shopping. For the first time in my life, I can plan out a week's worth of food without having to run to the store all the time. The laundry is pretty under control too. The rest of it is out of control, I would say. [I looked up and smiled and she smiled back. But she was serious.] I don't have a schedule that I vacuum and dust at certain times. I never have.

So "organizing" to Chris means having schedules and being in control.

> **Q:** What changes in your life might you make if you were to become very wealthy?

Chris didn't hestiate for a moment. I am sure if I hadn't asked such a question, she would have found some way to bring up their plans for the future.

> **Chris:** [Eagerly] We *are* planning to make some changes. We're planning to move, hopefully quite soon. We'll find out in a couple of weeks if we're going to move to New England. If we move, I'll quit work. We'll live on Mike's salary. I'd *love* to have just one job. Right now, I have two jobs. [That is, as a secretary and as a housewife.]
>
> **Q:** What sorts of changes in your life do you anticipate if this move occurs and you end up staying home instead of working?
>
> **Chris:** I want to have a baby. I'd do more sewing and things like that. Then also with Jenny. I think how she's growing up so fast. I want to spend time with her. She really feels deprived—most of the mothers in this neighborhood don't go out to work. I'm about the only working mother. So I'm not available to drive her anyplace.

Incidentally, Jenny's parents had been divorced for five years at this time. (Jenny's mother lived not too far away and so was able to visit occasionally; however, Mike said later in the interview, with great bitterness and disapproval, "Her mother doesn't bother to exercise her visitation rights much.") Chris continued:

My mother thinks I'm crazy. All my family are very ardent feminists. They think I should be doing something meaningful like going back to school and getting a degree. [But] This is what I want to do. I think—I know—I'm going to love it [being a full-time housewife].

Chris is the oldest of four daughters.

Chris: One sister graduated from college. She's working as an accounting clerk. She's thinking about going to law school. Another sister has also graduated from college; she's a lab technician. She's thinking of going to med school. The youngest didn't go to college; she works in a bank. She's the only one of my sisters who's also married.

When Chris and her sisters were young, their mother stayed home. The girls were never asked to help out in the house.

Chris: Mother did everything. We never had to do anything. We cleaned our own rooms and did our own ironing, but that was all. We didn't have to help with the dishes—nothing like that. Occasionally, we were asked to help out if company was coming, but it was never one of our jobs.

Their father never did any work around the house either. When the girls grew older, the mother found a job. She is now an office manager, sometimes works really long hours ("12 hours a day," Chris said) and really loves her job.

Chris: Now she doesn't do anything in the house, and my father doesn't, so the place is a terrible mess. Mother never has been a very good housekeeper. In the last couple of years, things have really slipped. She cooks and does the laundry—things they have to keep up with. Every now and then, when things get too bad, they have a blitz and grab whoever is over—like one of my sisters or myself—and get things cleaned up. It's really bad though. I don't know how they can stand to live like that. About all my father does these days is pick an hour before company's due to arrive to sort out three years' worth of magazines. They have a very nice house though—you know, it's quite an expensive house.

Q: Would you expect your own children to help in the house even if you stayed home?

Chris: Yes, I would. I'd raise them to be like Jenny. Children are happier if they have a certain set of small things they have to do to help.

This echoed the comments of some of the other women interviewed. Like one of those women, quoted in the last chapter, it is only in retrospect that Chris feels her upbringing should have been different.

> **Chris:** That's how I feel about it now. At the time, when I was growing up, I thought I had a pretty good deal.

We returned to Chris's plans for becoming a full-time housewife. I asked what changes in housework arrangements she thought would occur.

> **Chris:** I think I'll do most of the vacuuming and dusting. Jenny will still have some responsibilities like taking care of the cat and dog. They're her cat and dog. I don't want to do it all. I expect to take most of the burden off Mike. I would expect him to take care of the yard and the cars still. He's really looking forward to it too. Back there [i.e., New England], we can afford to buy a house. Around here, we can't. I know I'm going to love it. [This was a phrase she repeated numerous times in connection with her plans to leave work and become a full-time house-wife.] It's so frustrating now. I'm at work—well, usually it's busy—but sometimes I think, "There are so many things at home I want to do—I really should go home." I think I'll be more fussy about the house. Right now, I'm pretty relaxed. Mike likes it cleaner than I do. I wouldn't mind doing it if I had the time.

Our interview was interrupted briefly when Mike came home from his business cocktail party. Chris introduced us. Mike was polite but seemingly a little distant. His daughter greeted him joyfully, running out of the living room to hug him and embarking immediately on a long and excited recitation of the day's happenings. Chris went to fix some coffee; she and Mike didn't say much to each other apart from a quick "Hello." I caught a glimpse of Mike and his daughter as we continued our interview. Jenny was sitting on his lap, and he was cuddling her. I asked Chris if she would like us to stop our conversation for a while, so she could get his dinner, but she said, "No, that's okay. It's ready. He can heat it up." A little later, he went into the kitchen and fried some chicken in a pan. He smiled through the door at us and apologized for the noise of the hissing pan.

> **Q:** What do you think about the women's movement, Chris?

Chris: It depends. I think it's generally a good thing. The cost of living forces most people to have two careers. It's good that women should earn as much as men for a comparable job. I just hope it doesn't go too far though. Like my family is so opposed to what I want to do [i.e., leave work]. They don't think it's a fulfilling type of thing for me to do. But I want to do it. And if I don't like it, then I can always go back to work.

I asked Chris how she felt about mothers of young children going out to work. Her response revealed the ambivalence common among many of the people I talked with.

Chris: I personally think that children are very impressionable. The more you can be around them, the more you can influence their values, teach them your ideas of right and wrong. I think it's very important to be around. [*But*] I have mixed feelings though. I know several working mothers whose children are in child care. The mothers are happy going to work and the kids are sweet kids. It doesn't seem to harm them. I personally want to be around. It's probably okay if you have reasonable child care—that's proficient and caring and not too impersonal.

We discussed male and female family roles.

Chris: I've always worked. The traditional thing has never been true for me and never for my generation.

But clearly Chris' personal preferences are in favor of the "traditional thing."

Chris: I guess I'm kind of old-fashioned. That's probably why it would be best for me [i.e., to leave her job]. I know it would be best for Mike.

Q: Why do you say it would be best for him?

Chris: He's very involved in his career. You see, he *has* a career. I have a *job,* and I'm just not interested in a career. I think it's a big burden on him to work all day and come home and do housework with me. I don't like to see him pushing a vacuum. It makes me feel like I'm not doing my job.

Q: How about if you had enough money to be able to pay for really good household help? Or how about a part-time job?

Chris: Well, it might be a good solution if you had good household help. A part-time job might be all right too. But they're usually not very exciting. I can't think of anything I'm capable of doing well that I could do part-time. I've thought about doing something at home, like typing term papers, that I can earn a little money at and just do at my own pace.

Q: How will you feel about not earning a paycheck, not bringing home money of your own?

Chris: That will seem strange. I've thought about it a lot. I'm not a big spender though. I don't spend a lot on clothes and things. Mike and I have a joint checking account. We just put all the money in and spend it. We don't think about separating it. We make joint budget decisions. When we were first married, Mike had a lot of bills. They're almost all paid off now. We're saving a lot more money.

I asked Chris if she thought Mike would be willing to join in our conversation. She called out to him, and unfortunately he was about to start eating his warmed-up chicken. I hastily explained I'd be willing to wait, but he said "It's okay. I can heat it up again." Judging by the eagerness with which he joined us, it seems that he was eavesdropping on our discussion and was anxious to join in.

Q: Mike, how do you feel about Chris leaving work and staying home?

Mike: It will really free me up from Jenny's problems and things. Like her camera was stolen the other day and she called me at work. Did Chris tell you [that] I was a single parent for three years and it's been getting to me? To some extent, it's interfered with my job. I've let my managers know I have this responsibility, and they've been very understanding. But I've always wanted to go into field sales, and that's something I haven't always been able to do because I couldn't travel. So this has really hindered me. If Chris is able to stay home, I'll be able to travel without worrying. Not that I want to leave them, but I feel I'll be advancing in my career.

He paused to think for a moment.

I think I would have a closer relationship with Chris. Like she said before, she has two jobs now. She'll be able to prepare meals in a more leisurely way, do her household duties. I'd still clear the table and do the dishes.

I said, "You would?" or something to this effect, because his last sentence rather surprised me.

> Mike: Yes. I always did such things before. I still will. Chris will be more relaxed. I can relate to her more. That will benefit Jenny's life too.
>
> Q: Mike, how do you feel about sex roles in the family? Do you think it's all right for a woman to have a career and a family?
>
> Mike: I have some old stereotypes I fall back to. The ideal situation is for two people to be compatible. If a man marries a woman who is a career woman, he should know that and accept it. If she doesn't want to work, that's fine; there are other benefits. The part of feminism I really resent is when they say that a woman who *likes* the role of housewife is really missing something. As I see it, the whole point of feminism is for a woman to have a choice. That's what feminism means. I told Chris she could choose what she wanted to do. I've had feminists working for me, and it's hard to be sympathetic with their point of view because they're always so defensive.

Mike went on to discuss his parents and his early youth. His father is now 70 and his mother 62. Theirs was a most traditional relationship.

> Mike: My mother never worked. Six months before I was born, she quit. She can't drive a car. She does what my father says. [Chuckling] Recently though she's been asserting herself.

I started to say, "Because of the women's movement?", but he interrupted before I finished the question.

> Mike: No, no, not because of that. She's just bored following him around. She went off to try to get a job and was real upset because she couldn't find one. He was kind of afraid that she would.

Mike and Chris exchanged glances here and laughed. Chris said, "She's a terrific person," and he agreed, still chuckling. He has one sister, four years younger than he.

> Mike: We lived in snow country. I used to take care of the yard and had a lot of snow shoveling to do. I also cleaned the cars. I was supposed to straighten my room, but . . . I was a real slob till I got older.

He listed the other duties he had when he was a youth: helped with the grocery shopping on occasion, cleared the table, helped prepare the food, painted the house, which had to be done every three years.

> **Mike:** My sister didn't have any duties at all. I was very resentful of that. She was the apple of my father's eye. I had a lot of responsibilities. Her life is still quite a turmoil. She never has enough time to do anything. This is her second marriage. She was a single parent for a while with two children, and her life was a disaster. But we won't talk about that.

Again, he and Chris exchanged glances and laughed as though the two of them often discussed his sister's situation. He didn't directly draw any parallels between his sister's adult life and his own: they both are in their second marriage and both have contended with the responsibilities of being a single parent. The implication was that his own situation is not as bad as his sister's or that he is handling it better in some way. He went on with a more tolerant note in his voice, as though explaining to me why the sister's life is not turning out as well as his own.

> **Mike:** She had no responsibilities. I did. It's made me more serious. I was buying my own clothes from the age of 16 on. I put myself through college. I worked full-time since the age of 19.

He went on to describe his work history. At the age of 19, he took a full-time job while he was still at college. He got a Bachelor of Science degree in marketing. He is now 30. For the past five and one-half years, he has been in an electronics-related industry. Whenever either Mike or Chris talked about his career, their almost reverent tone made it plain that this was a serious subject in their home. He is anxious to get into field sales, thus escaping from "a job with structured hours that ties you to a desk." Being a single parent has, of course, forced him to turn down any such offers that have come his way in recent years. Up until last spring, he was attending night school and working on an M.B.A. But eventually he had to give this up.

> **Mike:** I just couldn't juggle all that. I used to take Jenny with me, and she'd stay in the cafeteria while I went to class. She was quite happy, but it just wasn't right. It's just no way to bring up a child—in a cafeteria.

Q: What differences have there been in your household life since you
and Chris were married?

This question caused momentary discomfort. He looked at Chris, as
though wondering what she had told me earlier. I prompted him.

Q: Of course, you had a cleaning woman before, didn't you?

Mike: She didn't do that great of a job. [Briskly, getting down to the
business of answering my original question.] We have more work to do.
I guess I'm more hangloose about the house [now]. I'm getting a little
more lax about it. I accept more. I'm a picker-upper—a role I got into
when I was a single parent. Chris thinks I'm obsessed.

Chris kept quiet throughout this discussion and seemed a little tense,
as though not quite sure what he was going to say. She relaxed after
a few moments. He seemed to be taking care not to cast any asper-
sions on her household abilities and instead to blame himself for his
pickiness. He repeated that he is trying to train himself not to be quite
so fussy.

Q: What kinds of changes do you anticipate if Chris leaves work? Any
changes in decision making for instance?

Mike: We'll try to keep it equal. Some of our roles and responsibilities
will shift. We'll try to have a 50-50 vote on everything. My first wife
was the type of person who let me decide *all* the time. I didn't want
that the second time around. It's important for my wife to be the kind
of person who can make decisions—give her opinion.

Mike turned to Chris at this point, addressing her directly:

I think I've been pretty reasonable. Anytime I get a job offer, talking
it over with you.

Although there was a half-question in his comments, she did not
reply; however, her expression implied agreement.

Q: Do you involve Jenny in making any of your decisions?

They both shook their heads at this. Mike said:

We've been a little dictatorial about the things we've asked her to do. She doesn't enjoy doing them. She's home all day though, and she has the time.

Chris added, "And she really doesn't do much—about half an hour a day."

Mike: It's important for a child to have these responsibilities. My sister had none, and she has trouble making toast without burning it.

Up to this point, Mike and Chris' story can be summarized as follows. Mike had grown up with two quite traditional parents. His mother hadn't gone to work, and his father was quite clearly boss in the house. His first wife, it seems, was ready to assume a similar role. However, Mike disapproved. He didn't think women ought to be *that* compliant and unassertive; he felt they ought to exercise choices. As a child, he had done a lot of household chores and, in common with other men who had similar childhood experiences, did not shy away from helping his wife.

Chris' background was rather different. She had not been obliged to do housework as a child. Moreover, her family apparently downgraded the importance of a woman's competency in the home in comparison with success in a job or career. These factors—his having become proficient at housework as a child and her having grown up in a family supportive of nontraditional roles for women—make their present role-sharing behavior rather predictable. But note that what they both really want is a more traditional situation. She wants to be a full-time housewife; he wants to build his career, and they both feel this is possible only as long as he is relieved of household burdens.

Further discussion revealed, however, that Mike has some uncertainties about his career, or at least his present choice of career.

Q: How do you feel about husbands and wives reversing roles?

Chris immediately shook her head at my question and said, "Oh, no." But, surprisingly, Mike showed some interest in the idea.

Mike: I'd feel worried telling people about it, but I'd enjoy a year off. I'd work on various projects. I like photography. I'd do that, some research. I really don't have much of a chance to do things like that.

He confirmed that he would be quite happy to run the household during his year off. But Chris said, "I couldn't stand that, seeing him cook dinner." When I asked her why, she said:

> It's because I have a hard enough time accepting the fact that I can't do everything. It makes me feel guilty. I feel I'm not doing what I'm supposed to do when I see other members of the family doing the wife's job.

We went on to discuss the hypothetical situation of their becoming extremely rich. This led to a cheerful and laughing discussion of their fantasies. Mike said:

> I'd buy a nice house in a place where I'd like to live—probably not around here. Somewhere in the country but within California. Upper Marin County would be nice. I would hire someone to do all the errands and cleaning. There's no point in you [i.e., Chris] cooking unless you wanted it. I wouldn't want a live-in maid.

But Chris said, "Oh, I wouldn't mind." He suggested he might resent the lack of privacy, and she laughingly suggested private quarters for the maid. Mike continued:

> Oh, the fantasies we have. I'd like a Ferrari. I'd like to have a lot of animals. We could travel all over, to Europe....

Chris was saying, "Oh, *yeah*," with her eyes shining. Unlike some people—who found the question not worth the energy to answer because of its total irrelevance to their lives—Chris and Mike enjoyed considering the prospect of unlimited money and what they would do with it. They seemed equally enthusiastic about their very real plans for the near future—the proposed move for Mike to a new job and Chris giving up work. I was sure when I asked Mike if his fantasies included giving up *his* job that his answer would be in the negative, given the weight both of them placed on Mike's career and his desire to pursue it fully. But my guess was incorrect.

> **Mike:** I probably would give up my job [in the event of becoming extremely wealthy]. Maybe go back to school. Probably spend a lot of time doing something like photography. I enjoy aspects of my job; aspects of it are frustrating.

He was thoughtful for a few moments before expanding.

> **Mike:** I don't have any engineering background. I worry about that. I always feel sort of inferior to others at work because of my lack of knowledge. This is foolish. My superiors are always telling me it doesn't really matter.

Earlier, I had asked Mike if he would consider taking up his studies again now that he had Chris to take care of Jenny. He had responded, "Yes, possibly," but with distinct lack of enthusiasm. I wondered now if his decision to give up night school had been influenced not only by the difficulty of being a single parent but also because he found the course work itself difficult.

Mike spoke again about his desire to have a job with flexibility in the hours:

> I don't like too regimented a schedule. I'd like to be in field sales where I can manage my own time. I wouldn't really mind a structured job as long as the work is challenging. But I would prefer the flexibility to take a day off anytime I wanted. [With a smile, getting back into the fantasy mode.] It would be ideal to have my own company and have a manager who's sufficiently trained to take over and run the place while I have a month off anytime I feel like it.

Mike's dinner was by now too cold to eat. I had mentioned it a couple of times while we talked, but he brushed off my concern with remarks like "No, no, that's all right. I'm enjoying this. Do you have any more questions?"

It seems their social life is fairly quiet at the moment, perhaps because of difficulties of finding time for entertaining and also perhaps because they have not yet found a mutual circle of friends. Mike doesn't bring business acquaintances or clients home for meals. Before he joined us, Chris said, "I wish he would though. I love cooking for company." However, later, Mike said, "I like to have people around. Chris enjoys time to herself. [to Chris] Isn't that fair to say?" Chris didn't repeat her earlier comment to me; instead, she just murmured agreement.

At the close of the interview, I couldn't help wondering aloud whether Chris would enjoy her prospective role of housewife as much in fact as in anticipation. Chris smiled and admitted there was a possibility she might not; however, she was most anxious to give it a try. Chris admits freely that she works primarily (if not solely) "for the money." Her job seemingly does not provide her with much intrinsic satisfaction, nor does it have the same potential for external rewards of pay and prestige as does Mike's job. It is, thus, worthwhile for Chris to tackle a new and relatively untried route to a fulfilling and challenging life in the roles of full-time housewife and mother. At the same time, Mike feels that *he* cannot realize the full potential of his career while he is burdened with household duties. The traditional male-female family roles, thus, seem to be ideal for them. Nevertheless, Mike firmly espouses the cause of equity. If a wife goes to work, he feels the household chores should be evenly divided. Moreover, sex roles should not be a matter for societal prescription. They are a matter for individual preference, which a couple should reconcile before marriage.

A review by Scanzoni and Fox (1980) of research performed in the 1970s on family roles reports the following. First, over the past decade, there has been a gradual shift toward less traditional, or more egalitarian, attitudes on sex roles. Second, based on findings from studies of the division of labor (such as those reported in Chapter 2), gender-related domestic behavior has been much slower than ideology to move away from traditional patterns. The authors conclude that these findings indicate that changes in norms occur faster than changes in behavior. These conclusions are, of course, consistent with a "consciousness-raising" approach to social change. That is, first people's attitudes change, and eventually the changed attitudes lead to changes in behavior.

Not everyone would agree with this proposed direction of causality. For example, Chafe (1972) suggests that behavior must be changed *before* any new ideology can take hold. He presents evidence to show that ideological movements, including those promoting equality between the sexes, have had relatively little success over the years in changing people's behavior. Certainly, the prevalent ideology during the 1950s (as described in Friedan's *Feminine Mystique*), which stressed that women belonged in the home, did not prevent steadily increasing numbers of married women from entering the labor market. According to Chafe's argument, now that the cycle of behavior

that perpetuates the status quo has been interrupted, different definitions of sex roles will likely replace the traditional ones.[1]

In this chapter, I have pulled together findings from the 30 interviews that might shed light on the relationship between behavioral
and ideological change. In order to gauge existing normative beliefs
among the families in my study, respondents were asked how they
felt about such issues as traditional sex-role definitions, the women's
movement, and working mothers and if they approve of role sharing
or of men and women exchanging family roles.

The attitudes of people toward an issue as pervasive and deep-
rooted in socialization, culture, and habit as sex roles are both complex and varied. However, these respondents could be categorized
fairly readily into one of three groups: traditional, egalitarian, and a
third group comprising people who claim to have an egalitarian ideology but traditional personal preferences. I shall call this third group
"mixed."

The traditional category includes those who believe in the custo-
mary sex-based division of responsibility within the family—that is, it
is the husband's duty to earn a living and the wife's to take care of
the home and children. However, all people in this traditional group
say they feel it is fine for a married woman to work outside the home,
provided she does not have young children (and what constitutes
"young" varies among individuals), and provided her working does
not interfere in any way with her family duties. Most of these same
respondents also feel it is all right for a husband to help his wife with
housework if she is especially busy (as when she has a full-time job);
however, this "helping" is seen as a personal favor that can be with-
drawn at will and *not* as a transfer or sharing of responsibility for the
home.

Respondents in the egalitarian category have quite different views.
They feel that family roles should be completely flexible and reflect
individual preferences. If the husband and wife want to exchange
roles, with the wife earning money and the husband taking care of
the house, this is perfectly acceptable. If they wish to share both sets
of responsibility equally, this is fine too. No one in this category,

---

[1] For a good review of the literature dealing with normative definitions of
sex roles, see Holter (1972). For a review of studies dealing with changes in sex-
role definitions, see Pleck (1976).

however, suggested that traditional roles are *wrong;* rather, they felt that it is good for people to have a choice.

The third ("mixed") category consists of people who express egalitarian beliefs but who claim to have quite traditional personal preferences. A typical respondent here might, for example, state that husband and wife should share equally in the housework if both have full-time jobs, but that the preferred situation for the respondent personally is one where the husband earns sufficient money so that his wife does not have to work. This attitude differs from that of the traditional person who believes in spouses helping each other out when necessary in that those in the mixed category believe (along with the egalitarians) in the sharing of breadwinning or housekeeping responsibilities if circumstances warrant. They differ from the egalitarian respondents only in that they feel a traditional division of labor works best for them personally or—if their present behavior is egalitarian— that it is an ideal to which they aspire in the future. Thus, Mike and Chris fit into the mixed category as do Bob and Nancy (Chapter 5). Beth (Chapter 7), on the other hand, is in the traditional group: she believes that housework is *her* job and that earning a living is his.

Note that none of the people interviewed is so traditional as to believe that married women—even if mothers—should not work under any circumstances; nor is anyone so egalitarian as to believe that equal sharing in all responsibilities is the *only* course of action any couple should ever consider.

Assuming that working wives and helpful husbands represent egalitarian rather than traditional behavior, we can examine the relationship between ideology and behavior in these 30 families. First, Table 8.1 shows sex-role ideology expressed by husbands and wives by employment status of the wife. As this table indicates, almost all the employed women have either egalitarian or mixed views. Only three employed wives (two work full-time and one part-time) have traditional views. These three women all said that they work for the money and for personal enjoyment but stressed that they would not hesitate to give up their jobs if these were to interfere in any way with their domestic duties. The ten nonemployed women had either traditional or mixed views. Among the husbands, those with employed wives are most likely to have egalitarian views; there are equal numbers in the mixed and traditional groups. Curiously, husbands of nonemployed women are not as likely as their wives to be traditional; most fall in the mixed category.

Table 8.1.
Sex-Role Ideology of Husbands and Wives by Wife's Employment Status*

	Wife Employed	Wife not Employed
Wife's Ideology		
Traditional	3	5
Mixed	5	5
Egalitarian	8	0
Not known	1	3
Husband's Ideology		
Traditional	4	2
Mixed	4	6
Egalitarian	6	1
Not known	3	4

*Part-time employed wives and full-time students are included with the employed wives.

Table 8.2 indicates sex-role ideology of husbands and wives by helpfulness of the husband with housework. The relationship between the wife's ideology and her husband's helpfulness and between the husband's ideology and his helpfulness are roughly parallel. Where ideology is traditional, husbands are more likely to be unhelpful than helpful, as we would expect. Also, for the men, those with egalitarian ideology are more likely to be helpful than unhelpful. We will discuss each of the three categories in turn and describe in more detail some of the seeming anomalies.

Note that there is one helpful husband with traditional ideology. This is Joe (Interview #26), whose wife is employed full-time. Both Joe and his wife, Paula, have always had, and still do have, very traditional ideas about sex roles. For example, Joe stated vehemently that any man who would consider switching roles with his wife by becoming a househusband was "weird"; his wife nodded her agreement. She works, she says, "to give me something to do—and for security in case something happens to Joe." He enjoys the extra income her job provides but has somewhat mixed feelings about her going to work.

When they were first married, Paula was a full-time housewife. When her youngest child started kindergarten, she went to college for

Table 8.2.
Sex-Role Ideology of Husbands and Wives by Husband's
Helpfulness with Housework

	Helpful Husband	Unhelpful Husband
Wife's Ideology		
Traditional	2	6
Mixed	3	7
Egalitarian	4	4
Not known	2	2
Husband's Ideology		
Traditional	1	5
Mixed	3	7
Egalitarian	5	2
Not known	1	6

a few years (full-time) and then started working in her present occupation as a public health nurse. Apparently, the other family members did not help in the house when she first started going to college. "It was due to my complaining more than anything else," she reports, that led eventually to the whole family deciding on an equitable division of labor that would relieve the burden on her. Now she feels she has a very comfortable schedule. It seems it was probably not only her complaining, but also her husband's appreciation of the extra income, that led to the reallocation of housework. When asked if he'd prefer that she leave her job, he hesitated and avoided the question.

Joe: I told her, you don't have to work at all.

She responded very sharply.

Paula: You didn't say that.

To which he hastily and placatingly replied:

As far as our standard of living, moneywise, it's a lot easier. That's made a lot of difference.

Further discussion with this couple revealed that threatening to quit her job is one device this wife uses to insure getting cooperation from her husband in the house!

Of the seven husbands with egalitarian views, most are helpful, as we would expect. The two anomalous egalitarian-but-unhelpful husbands have both been discussed earlier. One is Larry (see case study in Chapter 4) who claims to spend eight hours a week on housework but agrees with his wife that he does as little as he possibly can. The second is the husband of a schoolteacher (Interview #20, mentioned in the last chapter), who spends only six hours a week on household work and justifies his relatively low involvement on the grounds that his wife has all summer in which to relax.

The seven unhelpful husbands in the "mixed" category all have wives who either do not work (six cases), or work part-time (one case). Thus, their egalitarian ideology is paired with an attitude of "this situation works best for us" to justify their unhelpfulness. Others have noted in commenting on the supposedly more egalitarian beliefs of better educated men that, in fact, many men find it relatively cost-free to espouse an ideology of equality between the sexes (Scanzoni and Fox, 1980). To the extent that a couple's actual behavior is a result in large part of a process of negotiation between two individuals, it is only those men whose wives insist on complete role sharing who have to put their ideology to the test. These seven men have not been faced with such a situation.

In all, there are six couples (Interviews #8, #10, #13, #24, #26, #27) whose behavior indicates a sharing of both market and domestic roles: that is, both husband and wife work outside the home for approximately the same number of hours per week *and* both contribute roughly equal amounts of time to housework. In order to demonstrate the range of normative beliefs that accompany this egalitarian behavior, I shall briefly describe each of these families.

In one young family, he is an electrician and she is an assembly worker (Interview #27). They have two preschool children. She works because they badly need the money. They work different shifts. He actually works shorter hours than she and spends as much or more time with the children than she does. Both say that "reverse roles" are fine. They feel that children need a parent at home, but this can be either father or mother. Neither of them would object to being either breadwinner or homemaker. Whether either or both of them go out to work depends on the job market and their financial needs.

This, then, is a couple with egalitarian beliefs to match their sharing behavior, beliefs that they claim they have always held.

A second case is that of Bob and Nancy (Interview #8), whose interview was described in detail at the beginning of Chapter 5. Recall that he is completing his doctorate and works part-time as a research assistant; she is a schoolteacher. They have one young baby. Both say they enjoy working. However, she says she would rather have stayed at home with their new baby but continued to work because they needed the money. Both claim to have very egalitarian views concerning male and female roles. They are slightly ambivalent about the issue of mothers of young children working and are inclined to feel that the *mother,* not the father, should stay at home with the baby if possible (although in their case, the father—being a student—sometimes spends more time with the baby than does the mother). They feel they will shortly move to wherever the *husband* can find a good job, and she will then either give up work or work part-time until her child is older. Thus, this is a couple with egalitarian beliefs that match their current behavior, but with quite traditional preferences concerning their future behavior.

In a third family, Mike and Chris (Interview #24), discussed at the beginning of this chapter, he holds a management position and she is a secretary. This is the second marriage for both of them, and his child lives with them. In her first, albeit brief, marriage, both she and her husband worked and both shared equally in the housework. In his first marriage, his wife did not work; they had one child. After his divorce, he took custody of the child and was a "single parent" for three years before remarrying. He says it severely hampered his career to have to take responsibility for the house and child. Both say they have egalitarian views concerning male and female roles: dual-career families are fine, and so is "role switching." However, *they* are greatly looking forward to the time when he receives a promotion, when she plans to leave her job and become a full-time housewife. She finds secretarial work boring and the dual responsibilities of work and home rather overwhelming; he would like to have full time to concentrate on his career. This, then, is a "tolerant" couple: an egalitarian lifestyle is fine for those who want it; equal sharing in the home is essential if both husband and wife must work; but, for them, traditional roles are ideals to which they aspire.

In a fourth family (Interview #10), both husband and wife hold management positions. This is the second marriage for him. After their marriage, a few years ago, she left her job to stay home for a year or so but has now returned to a full-time job. She has mixed feelings about working. On the one hand, she enjoys the stimulation and prestige of her job. Also, as a full-time housewife, she had found that mundane domestic problems assumed an unwarranted importance to the point of causing constant quarreling in the family. However, she feels the children (her husband's two daughters from his previous marriage) need more "parenting" than they get with her working, and she thinks that probably a part-time job for her might be the solution. Both profess egalitarian views concerning sex roles. However, he says he doesn't personally *like* housework or childrearing. This, then, appears to be another "tolerant" couple, who have egalitarian views but who feel that somewhat more traditional roles might work out better for them.

The fifth family is that of Joe and Paula (Interview #26), discussed earlier in this chapter. He is a line manager in an electronics plant; she is a public health nurse. She works both for money and for enjoyment. He helps with the housework because he values the money she earns and because she has apparently made the receiving of such help a condition of her working. Both have very traditional views about sex roles. They feel it would be quite wrong for husband and wife to trade roles; it is definitely the man's responsibility to earn a living, and the woman's to take care of the home and children. This, then, is a clearly traditional couple as far as ideology goes. They both perceive practical advantages in the wife's working, and their sharing behavior in the house is a practical response to time pressures.

Finally, there is the case of Ted and Marsha (Interview #13), who were discussed briefly in Chapter 5. He is a real estate salesman, and she is a personnel clerk. Ted says he always used to believe that "a wife should never work." Unfortunately, a few years ago, he had a severe heart attack and has been able to resume full-time work only in the last couple of years. The family has, thus, depended on the wife's income for some time. Ted admits that his attitude has completely changed toward the issue of a wife's employment.

Q: Did the fact that your wife had to go to work lead to the change in your attitude?

Ted: It's been a gradual transition. I'd really have to think for a long time to be able to say what was the crossover point. My feelings are just different today. Now, just for an example, when I was working at [his former employer] one of the secretaries there—now she'd be a real woman's libber today—she was always screaming about equal pay for equal work. I used to say to her, "Gee whiz, that's just the way things are. A man is expected to be head of the household." Today, I see the inequality of that. But just when the pendulum started to swing, I really couldn't say.

Ted's answer evades my question somewhat; however, I cannot help but feel his family situation *must* have had an impact on his philosophy. While he was recuperating from his heart attack, he helped his wife in the house because, he says, "I was just doing what I could to make the situation equitable." That is, she had far less time than he to handle the housework. Now, however, he continues to help out. In fact, both he and his wife report their present division of labor to be·completely egalitarian.

Even in this family, shades of her traditional upbringing still haunt Marsha, the wife, occasionally. She says it took a particularly long time for her to accept having Ted do the ironing.

Marsha: This really bothered me. I just don't want my husband ironing. I really felt bothered by it. I bet you didn't know, did you [to Ted]. There was many a time I had to leave the room because I couldn't stand to watch you doing the ironing. That just seemed to be my responsibility.

When asked why this particular activity seemed particularly inappropriate for her husband (she had not expressed such qualms about other household chores), she said, "My mother always did the ironing," adding thoughtfully, "I don't know—he can iron quite good." He nodded enthusiastically and with amusement as she spoke. He obviously does not object to ironing.

In brief, the first case illustrates a positive association between behavior and ideology. The next four cases illustrate rather loose connections between behavior and ideology. Although, in three of these four instances, the couples profess to hold egalitarian beliefs consistent with their present behavior, they all claim to personally aspire to more traditional patterns of behavior—patterns that they plan to adopt as soon as they are able. The final case illustrates a situation where ideology changed after a change in behavior.

SUMMARY

Many of those who adopt a fairly clear-cut traditional *or* egalitarian stance behave in ways consistent with their beliefs. However, for a number of respondents, there appears to be a rather loose connection between ideology and behavior. For example, as we have seen, many couples who have both egalitarian beliefs *and* egalitarian behavior claim to aspire to traditional roles. Such aspirations do not necessarily imply conflicts in values, remembering that the egalitarian respondents I interviewed in all cases placed heavy emphasis on the desirability of individual *choice* of roles and that in no case was there an outright denunciation of traditional roles. When there are differences between current behavior and normative beliefs or personal preferences, there is a tendency to explain these as functional adaptations to immediate practical contingencies.

The question we set out to answer in this chapter was: Does the organizational environment, through its impact on family roles and behavior, ultimately change sex-role ideology? I mentioned earlier some findings reported by Scanzoni and Fox indicating that changes in ideology have occurred at a faster rate in the last decade than changes in family roles. On the basis of my 30 interviews. I would suggest that probably there is little connection between these two trends. That is, we cannot assume that changing ideology is *causing* the small changes in family roles that have been observed.

The normative attitudes that people espouse undoubtedly follow fashion to some extent; thus, the better educated today are likely to engage in a rhetoric of equality between the sexes, and this is not necessarily related in any way to their behavior. They can always take the option, as several of my respondents do, of claiming "but the traditional way works best for us." Actual changes in family behavior seem likely to result not so much from ideological shifts but from practical concerns like time pressures.

As Harriet Holter (1972) noted, most sociological, anthropological, and social-pyschological theories of sex roles point to changes in society's economic system as the primary determinants of change in sex roles. It does seem likely that the growing acceptability of a rhetoric of sexual equality has followed from the dramatic increase in recent decades of the numbers of married women entering the labor force. However, as we have seen, just because husbands and wives are increasingly sharing the breadwinner role, this does not inevitably mean they will share the domestic role too.

Recall that among the couples interviewed here, whether they do or do not share domestic roles, they tend to use the rational explanation of time or lack of it to explain their behavior. Even unhelpful husbands of working wives are generally *more* helpful now than they used to be before the wives started working, and this is because family members generally *must* contribute somewhat more if they want to be fed, have their clothes laundered, and so on.

I would suggest that changes in family linkages to the occupational world bring about both ideological shifts and, independently, some changes in domestic roles. The rhetoric of either sexual equality or traditionalism can be used to justify one's current behavior if necessary. Quite traditional behavior can coexist with nontraditional ideology by emphasizing "free choice of roles" rather than "role sharing" in defining the latter. Finally, given that a husband's helpfulness is more likely to be a reflection of time pressures on the wife than of ideology, it is quite reasonable to find men with traditional ideology doing the housework.

CHAPTER ***IX***

Children's Activities

Children in modern families have links to organizations outside the family just as their parents do. Most attend school regularly, and many work part-time. (Although, as it happened, children were employed in only two of the families I interviewed.) Obviously, school requirements place constraints on domestic life. A nonemployed parent takes school hours into account in planning her or his day, employed parents must arrange for supervision for children when working and school hours do not coincide, family vacations must be planned to overlap with school vacations, and so on.

In addition, there is yet another external child-related source of time constraints for the family. This comprises a whole host of structured extracurricular activities, which include being on a sports team, being in the school band, belonging to scouts or some other young people's organization. In my naiveté, I had assumed that these extracurricular activities would have a relatively trivial impact on family life, given that they are completely voluntary. It seems this assumption is incorrect. In many families, child-related activities like this occupy a large amount of time for both parents and children. Moreover, as the next case study illustrates, many families regard them as far from trivial.

The final case study is of Max and Susan, who have two young sons. Max is an engineer; Susan is a full-time housewife.

Max and Susan (Interview #29)

It seemed to take hours to reach Max and Susan's house. They live in one of the newer suburbs of San Jose. Mile upon mile of housing developments, neighborhood shopping centers, expressways, stop-lights—where only a few years ago, there had been prune orchards. When, finally, I arrived outside their neat, almost new, two-story home, I had the sudden wild fantasy of being deprived of directions to take me back to familiar territory and being lost forever in this suburban wilderness of endless, seemingly identical, tracts.

As soon as I arrived, I was shown to a comfortable couch in the living room, which faced onto the street in front. It was twilight on a weekday evening, and some of the neighborhood children were play-ing ball outside. Max and Susan's two boys were in the family room watching television. The living room was neat, and on the table beside the couch where I sat there was a bound copy of Max's dissertation (which I didn't notice till it was pointed out to me some time later).

They were polite and seemingly eager to be cooperative but a little tense at first. At the beginning, I asked questions and they gave brief formal responses. However, this situation changed very quickly as they relaxed and we focused on topics they clearly enjoy talking about.

Max and Susan are in their early 30s. They have been married for 12 years and have two sons, aged 11 and nine. They were married as soon as Max got his bachelor's degree. He then immediately started to work on his doctorate. Susan worked as a clerk for several years before marriage and continued working for a few months in the col-lege bookstore after they were married. She quit shortly after becom-ing pregnant with their first child—about nine months after they were married—and has not worked since.

Max left school before completing his dissertation and accepted a job in the Midwest. They were there for two years while he worked and wrote his dissertation in his spare time. When he finally got his Ph.D. he accepted a job in California. Max is an electrical engineer. He has been with his current employer about 18 months, and only four months ago was promoted into a management position.

This couple's situation illustrates a dilemma reported by several of my respondents. On the one hand, Max is anxious to achieve suc-cess in his job, but he also feels it is important for him to spend time with his children and finds it extremely difficult to handle both his job and parental duties as well as he would like. Susan's concerns are similar. She also wants Max to succeed in his career, but she is frustrated at the way his long working hours interfere with their family life.

Whenever the subject of his job was broached, it was obvious from Max's expression and the note of anxious concern in his voice that it is both very important to him and that he is somewhat fearful of failing.

Q: Why did you decide to work for this company?

Max: They have a good reputation as an employer, so I was interested in getting in there. When the opportunity came, I took it. They're employee-oriented—they're interested in the employee's career goals and development. *And* they have a reputation for no layoffs.

He announced this last sentence as if this represented the absolutely crowning appeal of this particular employer. His wife nodded approvingly and said, *"Security."* He said, "Yes, that's right." He was to mention this several times during the course of the interview as one of the most important attributes an employer can have.

Max: Comparing this job to my last job, I have more sense of security. That affects us as to how we can spend money, make a purchase. In my previous job, I would always worry if I'd be stuck with all these bills. That doesn't become nearly so much of a concern with [present employer].

Q: Do you have to work much overtime?

Max: It varies. I average a nine-hour day. I do occasionally go in at the weekends—Saturday or Sunday—to try and catch up. Three or four hours.

Q: Does the company pressure you to put in overtime?

Max: It's only since I got into management three or four months ago.

He paused for a while here, and I waited as there was obviously something on his mind.

Max: They had this training class for new managers. Everyone there said you have to put in extra time to get ahead.

Q: You mean the instructors told you that?

Max: No, not the instructors. It was the consensus of the class that we had to work overtime if we wanted to get ahead. [He looked up at me and gave a humorless laugh.] I have noted though that many top managers only work an eight-hour day.

Q: You know, one of the people I interviewed mentioned that a manager's work is never finished anyway, that it's just a question of making a decision to cut off your work at a certain time. This person decided that five o'clock was it for him. He never worked overtime. Do you feel that philosophy wouldn't work for you?

Again, Max thought for a while before responding.

Max: I feel probably with more experience in the job that would be the case. Right now, I'd feel more comfortable getting more done. I'm never really caught up. [His anxiety was apparent in his tone.] If I was in the same job for a couple of years, I'd feel more caught up.

His wife, who quite frequently interrupted by volunteering what she thought his feelings were on the questions raised, reminded him:

Well, just recently, you've been doing all this interviewing.

Max explained that he'd been attempting to hire a new employee and had had to spend a lot of time interviewing candidates for the job. This whole process had caused him to fall really far behind in his regular work, and he now had a big backlog. He continued:

My last job was even worse. [He confirmed that he was referring to his former company.] I had engineering responsibility for a manufacturing line, which was three shifts, five days. I might get home at 7:30 and get a call at 10:00, and I was expected to go back. I was averaging a ten-hour day routinely, plus a couple of weekends now and then.

Q: Did those long hours have a bearing on your decision to leave that job?

Max: Yes, yes. It really got to me. Often, I'd come home too late for dinner. I'd miss the kids' game practice. All those things. In this job, I'd feel no qualms if I go in early and come home early. In the other job, people would look at you funny if you walked out at 5:00 and everyone was still working.

These remarks made it seem that his present working hours are quite satisfactory. However, the very next question I posed to Susan raised doubts that she thought so.

Q: How do you feel his work affects your life, Susan?

Susan: Well, he *still* never gets here for dinner. I'm adjusted to it. We just don't have dinner together.

Max seemed a little embarrassed at her comments. Throughout the interview, however, he appeared to be unwilling to contradict her and would tend to restate his remarks to try to reconcile any inconsistency in their responses.

Max: [earnestly] It really doesn't pay me to leave before 5:30 because I just hit all the rush hour traffic.

Susan: Oh now I don't mind as long as we eat [i.e., early]. The kids and I eat together and I save his dinner for him. This works very well. He's no problem with warmed-up food. He's no problem; even if it's dried out, he doesn't complain.

Max: This may all change in the future. They're going to move our plant to San Jose. That will cut 100 miles a week off my commute. It will probably take 20 minutes to half an hour for me to drive each way. [At the moment, it takes 40 to 50 minutes each way.]

Max was thoughtful again.

Max: I don't know if that will change things drastically. I'd be getting home more at 6:00, I suppose.

Max was sitting alongside me most of the time, and when he responded he most often looked down at his hands or the coffee table, occasionally at his wife, and sometimes he looked directly at me. He looked at me now and said, as though it were a dramatic statement, "In my working week, I spend less than 25 percent of my waking time here."

Q: When you come home, do you tend to leave your work at work? Or do you sometimes bring it home with you?

Susan answered:

He doesn't bring his work home that much. There are times when he's really bogged down a lot he'll be tireder than usual. He'll get home and doesn't want to be bothered. We don't talk about this job. [She paused and restated this.] *I* [with emphasis] don't talk about his job.

Q: Why is that? Don't you like to discuss your work at home, Max?

Susan looked astonished and then turned to Max, asking: "I don't know. Would you *like* us to talk more about your job?" She said it as though such an idea had never occurred to her before. Max was silent for a while, looking down at his hands and thinking.

Q: Is it technical?

Susan nodded, and then Max said slowly. "I don't bring problems home.... I have enough of it there." I could not help noticing his awkwardness and seeming ambivalence. It had taken him quite a while to formulate that response and even then he seemed not quite sure that he really meant it.

Susan: He does tell me about people-oriented things that happen. Like when he's interviewing. [Max silently nodded agreement.]

At this point, Susan drew my attention to Max's dissertation on the table beside me. She said, "Just look at the title." I read it out loud; it did indeed sound very technical. And she said rather triumphantly, "See why I don't talk about his work!" We all laughed, and this seemed to relieve a certain tension that had been building over what seemed to be Max's implicit condemnation of his wife for not taking more interest in his work.

Q: What kinds of things *do* you generally talk about?

They alternated at suggesting various things: their friends, something in the news, the kids, household projects, "what we're going to do for the day," planning a camping trip. Then Max, who had evidently continued to mull over our earlier discussion about his schedule said:

All the time I was in school, it was 24 hours a day. I couldn't spend much time with the kids when they were younger. I'm trying to see more of them now.

Max obviously felt it was important to be involved in his sons' lives
and wanted to express this thought to me—possibly because he felt
Susan's comments about his never being home for dinner might give
me the opposite impression.

I asked Max to describe his daily schedule and how it was affected
by the flexible scheduling policy his present company has.

> **Max:** I leave home about 7:30 and get home about 6:30. The flexible
> scheduling allows me to leave at the time I do. I sometimes get to work
> at 8:30. I'm trying to schedule my time to hit the end of the rush hour
> instead of the middle. When I was coaching the soccer team, I was able
> to start at 6:30 [a.m.] and get home at 4:30.

In spite of the flexibility allowed, he does tend to stick to the same
schedule within a half hour or so.

He had mentioned coaching the soccer team, so I asked him what
sorts of extracurricular activities he was involved in with the children.

> **Max:** I don't do anything outside the house in the summertime, but in
> the school year I'm quite heavily involved in their after-school activities.
> Last year, I was chief of the Indian Guides and coach of Don's soccer
> team. Then in baseball season, I was involved with Peter's baseball games.

He estimates he spends about seven hours a week in such activities
during the school season. I asked Susan what kinds of voluntary activities she is involved with and the amount of time she spends on
each.

> **Susan:** I volunteer at school . . . the PTA. I do different things. Once a
> week I go there with the perceptual motor class—it's like a gym class.
> That takes an hour a week. Then I'm hospitality chairman at the school.
>
> **Q:** What does that involve?
>
> **Susan:** We have different functions. Once a month, we have nightly
> meetings, about one and a half hours. About five functions through
> the school year. A lot of the time I'm tied up on the phone—who can
> bring what, things like that. The function itself is about two hours, and
> there's the preparation for it.
>
> **Q:** Do you spend much time driving the kids to various activities?
>
> **Susan:** I'm always driving them. This isn't in the summer time. They
> have music lessons. Once a week there's their organ lessons. That ties

me up about one and a quarter hours. See, it's too far for me to leave
them there and go back, so I have to stay. Then their religion classes.
That's about a half an hour's driving each week. Baseball or soccer....

Q: You and Max take them together?

Susan: No, that's for the *other* son. They're on different teams, so Max
can't take them both at the same time. That's about an hour a week of
driving. Plus a game on Saturday, which I attend.

She estimated probably six and one-half hours a week were spent on
child-related activities of this sort.

The theme of the desirability for children to have supervision and
to have a parent to take them to after-school activities was carried
through the next part of our conversation.

Q: Have you ever considered going back to work?

Susan: No, I don't want to.

This was firmly stated. I asked what she felt were the advantages of
her not working.

Susan: I can do what I want with my time. Volunteer work I can say
no to. I enjoy the freedom. I worked four years before we got married.
I know what it's like. I like being able to take the kids to lessons. The
working mothers around here have to depend on other people. I can do
what I want to get the housework done in the week. Then we can have
the weekends free.

In spite of her comments about the flexibility of volunteer work,
when I asked what most upset her daily life she replied:

During the summer, it's not bad. [But] During the school year, it's
mostly interruptions. [And then seemingly remembering her earlier
remark about volunteer work] I *can* say no to volunteering, but I
really don't. I have less time to do things once the school year starts.

There was some kind of squabble occurring in the family room
between the two boys. Max went to attend to them while I continued talking to Susan. I could hear Max's raised voice, the sound of
some spanks and crying, and then Max came into the hallway and
ordered both boys upstairs to bed. They went, with a lot of wailing

from one of them. (It was only about 8:30 in the evening.) He seemed embarrassed and upset but was not responsive to my inquiring smile. About 15 minutes later, Susan went up to the wailing child and succeeded in quieting him.

Q: Max, what kinds of things most upset your daily life?

The problems he described could perhaps only arise in an organizational environment, such as the one we live in.

Max: I would say sometimes the kids' schedules will start to bog us down. We'll go six months in a row without ever being able to sleep in on Saturday if we have a nine o'clock game. By November, you get pretty worn out.

Q: Seeing these are voluntary activities couldn't you just cut out some of it?

Max: We *want* the kids to be in some kind of organized activity. We've paid money for them to do it. We want them to do it. And *we* want to do it. It's just sometimes it gets so hectic. Practising two or three nights a week, and then the game. We have to drop them off, pick them up. Some day, maybe you're not feeling that great; you have to get up at five o'clock to be at work at 6:30, so you can come home early for the game.

Q: What do you feel is important about this kind of organized activity?

Max: I see too many kids who don't have their time occupied—getting into trouble. Or the kids are bugging *us* all the time. It teaches them discipline.

Susan: It's good for them. One son doesn't feel too good about himself, but then he got the pitcher position. [In a tone indicating that this clearly improved the son's self image.] It brings out something in them.

Till now, I had the impression that the boys themselves were eager to participate in these activities and wondered if they could be persuaded to give up at least some of them to ease their parents' burden somewhat.

Q: Do you think your sons would be disappointed if you did cut back on some of these activities?

There was vehement headshaking from both of them.

> **Susan:** Our sons probably wouldn't want to be in baseball or soccer or organ classes or anything, but we want them to do it. I tell them they don't have a choice.
>
> **Q:** You mean, even if they asked to be allowed to drop something you wouldn't agree? (Vehement shaking of the head from Max and Susan] Well, is there some age at which you think they should be allowed to choose for themselves?
>
> **Max:** They often grumble initially, when we start something new, but then after a while they get to enjoy it.
>
> **Susan:** At some time in the future, we'll let them have a choice.
>
> **Max:** I think some time soon we're getting to that point.

He reiterated, "But usually they're happy about it after they've started."

Max and Susan's philosophy toward organized activities for their children was far from unusual among the families I interviewed, although theirs was perhaps the only case where the parents admitted going against their children's desires in promoting such activity. We discussed this issue at some length. They did not take a defensive or apologetic stance. They were in full agreement with each other, and their opinions were strong and unequivocal. Two main themes ran through their argument. One was that one must expose children to a variety of activities. Left to their own devices, the children will tend to avoid anything new. Once they have been exposed to an activity—a new sport, music lessons, and so on—then the children are in a better position to decide whether or not they want to participate.

> **Susan:** Until then, I feel they don't know what they want. I'd just as soon have them learning things so they'll have some kind of experience.

The second theme had already been mentioned by Max: that is, that children get into trouble if their after-school time is not sufficiently structured.

The issue of supervision arose again when we discussed working mothers.

> **Susan:** That's just fine for them to work if they want. I have a lot of friends who are no good if they don't work. If they have someone

watching the kids, that's fine. Some people leave their kids running around, and that's no good.

Max said he approved of maternal employment, but with reservations similar to Susan's.

> **Max:** When they're really little, maybe it's better for someone to be home. Kids of grade school age shouldn't be left alone. It's okay if somebody's around. A fair number of the ones in this neighborhood get left after school till 5:00. Eight or ten year olds.

Susan agreed. She said these same unsupervised children are always trying to persuade her own boys to go with them to the local shopping center.

> **Susan:** They'll go and look at the *Playboys.* Just hanging around. You see a lot of kids doing that. They can get home before their mother gets home, and she'll never know.
>
> **Q:** So it's all right as long as they have supervision after school?

Susan hesitated, even though I was only paraphrasing what she had said.

> **Susan:** I used to do a lot of babysitting. I watched my girl friends' kids for several years. I treated them like my own. I told her if they were doing something I didn't like. If kids are going to have sitters, they really need someone who is willing to be responsible.

Susan continued talking and, rather to my surprise, echoed some of the frank comments of some of my earlier interviewees who had expressed doubts about a sitter being able to compensate for a mother's absence.

> **Susan:** When I was first married, I babysat a lot after our children were born. Sometimes I did it mainly for the money. I felt sorry for those parents. I had several babies [to take care of]. I didn't give them very much love or attention. Sometimes I'd let them cry. I didn't tell the parents stuff like that.

She continued to explain that, knowing all this—that is, how little love and attention the sitter's charges really get—had a strong bearing on her own reluctance to leave her own children with a sitter. Several times, she murmured to herself, remembering the past, comments like "It was terrible. I was only doing it for the money."

We went on to a long discussion of male and female roles. Susan had already said that she had no desire to go back to work. So her views came as no surprise when I asked how she would feel about exchanging roles with Max.

> **Susan:** I think he should work and I should stay home. I don't think I could handle a job every day. If someone else wants to reverse their roles, that's fine. If that's the way they like it. I don't think I could take the routine—having to get up a certain time. Maybe it's because I *had* a job and I didn't enjoy it.

But then she introduced a new concern.

> **Susan:** I have it set in my mind that beds are made and dishes done. If we both worked and shared it, he might not think it important, and it would bother me.

She talked some more about how she likes the flexible schedule that accompanies being a housewife. And concluded with, "Oh, maybe it's because I'm lazy."

Max was more open-minded in response to the question about reversing roles.

> **Max:** I think it's a personal choice. I don't have strong feelings one way or the other.

He denied, however, that his opinions had been affected by the women's movement.

> **Max:** I've always felt strongly about equal opportunities. I feel women can be in the home or have a job or anything. I may not have thought about it consciously. [That is, before the women's movement generated so much publicity about the issue.]

> **Susan:** It [i.e., the women's movement] probably has affected me. Especially with the kids. Before that, I probably never would have had them doing housework. It's made me feel I can voice my opinion more. I don't feel I have to carry the burden.

I asked who was responsible for the housework in their house. She gave a slight smile (as though the answer was obvious) and said "I am." We went through a list of items: cooking, dishes, cleaning, laundry, grocery shopping, clothes shopping. She said yes to each item, although she added that her husband usually buys his own clothes. As for bill paying, Susan said: "We both do it. I do the simple bills like the water bill. He does the insurance."

Max said he handles the "outside stuff." But Susan quickly interrupted:

Susan: I do all the yard work. Unless there's a project—like washing windows or cement work. The kids do the lawn. It's my responsibility to water, put the fertilizer on.

Max: When the appliances are down, or the car [i.e. he then fixes them]. I do the routine work on the cars. Mostly during the school year, my free time is pretty much tied up by the kids' activities. Sometimes I'm tied up all day Saturdays.

Susan: He does a lot of big jobs. He put in a big attic fan.

Unlike some women I spoke to, the amount of time Susan spends on housework in any week or on any day is quite variable, and her story changed several times in describing her weekly and daily activities. At first, she claimed to spend half a day each weekday on housework, with no housework at weekends. ("I don't consider beds and dishes housework.") She said, "Weekends we eat weird. Two meals or a snack." But then she decided she did maybe spend two or three hours a day on housework at the weekends also. She's pretty relaxed about how she approaches the whole business.

Susan: I don't do it all. I'll save it. One week, I'll spend that week cleaning, then let it go for a couple of weeks. I get in here [living room] once a month. The living room and dining room aren't used that much. The kitchen and family room have to be done every day.

Contradicting her earlier claim of half a day each weekday, she said:

I pick one day. Friday is housecleaning day. I don't do any volunteer work on Friday. The whole day is spent cleaning the house.

Susan stressed that she does not permit her housework schedule to tie her down (unlike another housewife who said she conformed to her schedule "with too great a passion"). She described an incident that occurred earlier that day. Susan had planned to clean the living room. Then, unexpectedly, she got a call from a woman friend who suggested they go out shopping together. Susan had decided that was the more appealing alternative and abandoned the living room cleaning until another day.

I asked a hypothetical question.

Q: If you *were* ever to return to work, would the two of you split the housework between you?

They both answered emphatically in the affirmative.

Susan: Even if I only made a dollar a week, if I was gone all day, we should share.

I commented on the fact that some working women I had talked to complained about their husbands' not helping out. She nodded knowingly and said, "I don't want to get into that bind." It seemed though that Max was not a likely candidate for getting her into "that bind." Susan admitted that in their early months of marriage when she had worked:

"He really did a lot. He got home before me. He got the dinner going. He handled all the bills. You'd [addressed to Max] run the vacuum. When I was pregnant, he washed the floors. I'll always remember that.

He was murmuring, half to himself, "My hours were more flexible." (At that time, he was a student.) Apparently he also helped out a lot after she left work and had young children.

Susan: I did all the bathing. He did a lot of the feeding. He was in school then. He would come home at 5:00 or 5:30 and go back to school at 8:30. So he fed them while he was home. Our second baby didn't sleep for five months. He used to stay up with me. He isn't the type that left me alone to take care of them.

Obviously, Susan was expressing approval of her husband, as she did overtly through other remarks. Her comments were stated matter-offactly, not with any emotion in the form of, for example, an affectionate smile in his direction. Max reacted to her last set of comments again by seemingly denigrating his helpfulness. He said, "I didn't have a set schedule then so I could help." However, this may have been by way of an explanation for his failure to do more in the house *now*— when he doesn't have much time and does have a set schedule.

Strangely, he almost immediately contradicted the suggestion that his school days gave him more time for the family. He estimates he now spends four to five hours every weekend on household chores. When I asked if this was very different from the time he spent as a student, he said quickly, "School was essentially a seven-day-a-week job." This seeming contradiction was resolved as we continued to talk.

Apparently there was less for him to do when they lived in married students' housing. The caretakers did most of the maintenance work. Also, although he did help out with the children when he was at home, they were too young then for all the extracurricular activities that so tie up his time now. Thus, in many ways, he feels he now spends more time with his family than he did in his student years. I commented that it was almost a shame that Susan, a nonworking woman, had a husband who was so willing to be helpful in the house while many working wives had such unhelpful husbands. Max and Susan laughed and exchanged smiles here and said they realized this and had discussed the fact.

Susan is the oldest in her family and the only girl. She has three brothers. Her mother was "the typical housewife—she didn't work"; her father never helped in the house—"he did the outside work." Max was also the oldest in his family; he had one brother and two sisters. His mother didn't work outside the home; she did most of the household chores. His father worked a ten-hour day; he took care of the car and did some yardwork. The kids did most of the yardwork starting at the age of ten or 11; they also took jobs around the neighborhood to earn money. Susan said, "You didn't have to fix your room." Max looked at her uncomprehendingly, and she prompted, "Like I have ours do," and he said, "Oh, no." When I asked if the boys and girls did different things around the house, or if they got paid for chores, he struggled for a while to try to remember but gave up. "It's been 15 years since I lived at home. I really can't remember."

Susan said she feels strongly that her sons should help out in the house. She added, rather interestingly, in view of her own nonemployed status:

> Susan: Their wives will probably work, and they'll have to do those things. I'm Italian. The boys [in her family] didn't have to do anything. The boys were gods. I'm doing the opposite. It helps me too.

The children mow the grass, cut the lawn edges, take out the garbage.

> Susan: I've started them recently cleaning their rooms. They've made their beds for a couple of years. They're more into the vacuuming and dusting now. I don't pay them an allowance yet [in response to my question]. I want them to feel they do the work because they want to.

She added that she had been thinking about starting an allowance some time soon. She stressed that she does not expect the kids to remember what chores they are to do.

> Susan: I tell them what to do when I want them to do it. Like I tell them "today you dust," so they have to do it. I make them.

There was some unintentional humor here in view of her expressed desire to have them feel "they do the work because they want to."

Max and Susan are clearly a family-oriented couple, given their willingness to spend so much time on the children's leisure activities and their reluctance to leave the boys with sitters. When I asked how they felt about the issue of family togetherness, however, Susan's reply was not what I had anticipated. She looked at me with raised eyebrows when I suggested that many families deliberately try to arrange activities with the immediate family, excluding outsiders in an attempt to foster some special family cohesiveness. Then she said crisply, "I bet that's in families where they both work." She and Max explained that most of their weekend activities—such as picnics and camping trips—are planned to include other families.

> Max: We do a fair amount of things as a family. We go for a drive, to the show. It's not forced [i.e., deliberately planned that way]. So much of our activity revolves around the kids anyway.

Susan picked up on his last comment. She says she is quite happy to go on an outing and spend all her time speaking with the adults, leaving the children to mingle with other children. She was sure that working parents were far more likely to be concerned about "togetherness" to assuage their feelings of guilt at leaving the children alone or with sitters so much.

> Susan: I spend enough time with the kids during the day anyway. There's no way I feel I neglect them.

Routinely, I asked every one of my interviewees to rank a list of factors that they considered to be most important in a marriage. One of these was "the chance to have children." Susan's reaction to this list uncovered a sentiment that I am convinced most parents would express from time to time. She said when she was first married, "the chance to have children" would have headed the list of important factors in marriage. Now, she says, "I'm kind of torn about it." I asked why.

> Susan: I'm having a bad time with the children. They're not doing anything right. I guess it's the age. Plus the fact that I have friends without children and they're doing perfectly fine. I envy them. But there are other times I'm glad I have them.

We talked about this a little more, with me expressing my sympathy, and she repeated the suggestion that it was possibly "just the age."

They talked about marriage and divorce and how things change between two people over time.

> Susan: You change so much. I think I'm a completely different person [now]. If you can keep getting along with the changes. We have some friends that are divorcing. People change. If I can't accept what he's doing now... you can't get along.

> Max: What seems to work well for us is we still seem to think alike about certain things. We buy a house. We like the same things and are looking for the same things. Planning a vacation. We enjoy the same things. We don't have any serious disagreements over those major things.

We discussed our interview a little and some of the ideas that had emerged. I commented that I was particularly interested in the way that people attempted to organize or structure their lives, and that it seemed that Susan clearly preferred a relatively unstructured situation, but that Max seemed fairly contented with a more structured schedule. The last statement was more in the form of a question to Max.

Max: Yes, that's right. I wouldn't call myself a workaholic. I don't necessarily prefer it [i.e., work to family life]. I guess it's maybe that I accept it. It isn't that my job is my whole life and my family life is subordinate. I feel the need to work on my career. It's a satisfying thing that I do.

Q: How do you find it satisfying, Max?

Max: I don't know. [spends some time thinking] Engineers seem to be a breed of people where they solve a problem or make a breakthrough. That's a reward aside from salary. It's an aspect of your life that is satisfied with that. There's a challenge there. To solve a problem.

Q: Do you think it would be ideal if you had the freedom to select your own hours—how often and when you worked?

Max: [after some hesitation] I don't know how long I'd be happy being able to do that.

He looked at Susan, and I looked questioningly from one to the other.

Max: Sometimes I'd love to take a day off. But I'm not sure what that would accomplish.

Susan could see I was still a little puzzled by his response.

Susan: He's better off when he has a schedule. I think his thesis would have gone on for 20 years if he didn't force himself.

Max picked up on this as if he were grateful to Susan for having suggested this as an example that he could describe to me. He explained how difficult that period of his life had been. In spite of the fact that he was holding a paying job for the first time, and the family had really needed the money, the fact that the thesis was hanging over him had taken a lot of pleasure out of life.

Susan: He used to work on the thesis after work. He had to do it nights and weekends. That takes discipline, which he didn't have.

Max: We'd go on a picnic on a Sunday, say. Come home, and there was the thesis reproaching us—as it were—because I hadn't worked on it that day.

I commented that it must have felt wonderful when finally the thesis was finished. Susan replied rather crisply:

> Well, it was the typical letdown. Not as wonderful as we'd thought. After he finished his Ph.D. we left [the Midwest] to come out here. He spent a lot more time than we expected.

That is, completing the thesis did not free up his time as much as they had hoped. This is because his first job in California had required a lot of overtime, even more than his present job.

It seemed that Max and Susan were suffering from the problem so many of the single-worker families I talked to reported. That is, the husband spends too much time on his job, and the wife feels "stuck" with the kids and house.

> Q: Max, what do you think an ideal work schedule would be for you?
>
> Max: A 40-hour week without having to concern myself with putting in the extra time [i.e., overtime]. I don't feel that way with my current job. If I had the money, I might consider—if there was a good neighborhood—moving closer to work with an easier commute.

He added later:

> If I don't have things specifically planned, like if I'm off for a day unexpectedly, I get kind of bored.
>
> Q: How about you, Susan? What would be a perfect schedule for Max from your point of view?
>
> Susan: I'd say from 8:00 to 5:00 sounds good. So he'd be at home at 5:30.
>
> Q: Five days a week?
>
> Susan: Yeah, the five-day week is all right with me because I've got enough things to do.

She is, in other words, quite content to have a daytime world that is quite separate from her husband's.

In looking back over this interview, I am struck by the fact of Max's anxiety over successfully combining career and parenthood. The pressures caused by the competing demands of work and family have been well publicized for today's career wives, who sometimes complain that only a "super mom" can possibly do everything well. Max's case reminds us that, even when their wives are full-time homemakers, some fathers today are caught up in a similar bind that only a "super pop" could resolve!

The issue of the place of children in today's families is one that deserves to have a whole book devoted to it. It is a relatively neglected topic. Although there are some interesting treatises on the child's place in the family (for example, the books by Shorter and Ariès), these are not empirical investigations of the actual roles played by children in today's families. In the present study, children's activities were incidental to my central interest and thus are not covered systematically. However, two child-related topics were discussed in almost every interview: children's organized extracurricular activities and the idea of "family togetherness."

CHILDREN'S ORGANIZED ACTIVITIES

Of the 22 families with at least one child of seven or older, children in 17 of them are regularly involved for several hours a week in some kind of organized activity outside school: sports, scouts, dance, music, or other classes. (See Table 3.2). In these 17 families, eight mothers are not employed, four are employed full-time, and four are students or are employed part-time.

It seems that the time involved is less when the mothers work full-time, although there are exceptions. (For example, see Interviews #9 and #20 in Table 3.2.) When both parents work, the children's participation is more contingent on such factors as the activity being close to home (within walking or biking distance), availability of neighbors or friends to drive them, or ability of the child to drive him or herself. Only one family mentioned the availability of public transportation as an important factor, which is, of course, to be expected in a car-oriented and car-dependent society.

It is not unusual for full-time housewives to spend very large amounts of time every week driving the children to and from after-school events and directly taking part by coaching, serving on committees, planning outings, and so on. Six women mentioned spending an average of three to five hours per week on such activities; one estimated that she spent nine hours a week and one as much as 20 hours a week. By contrast, the four employed mothers whose children engage in extracurricular activities say they personally spend no time at all on them. This, then, appears to be one kind of parental activity that is eliminated or reduced when a wife is employed.

The extent to which children engage in organized activities depends in large part on the extent to which they are available through such agencies as schools, churches, city park departments, and so on. Because most families in this sample live in contiguous suburban areas, they share a common institutional environment in this regard, and their similarities with respect to children's organizational involvement are not surprising. It is, however, interesting to note the sometimes vehement expressions of opinion by parents concerning the desirability of having their children's out-of-school time spent in this way and the extent to which they are willing to sacrifice their own time and energy to express their support.

Recall that Max, in spite of his demanding job, was heavily involved in his sons' after-school activities. Recall also that in spite of his complaining tone, both Max and his wife feel strongly that it is worth the time, effort, and money to have their sons involved—no matter how the sons feel about it!

Although Max and Susan's children appear to be somewhat reluctant participants in the recreational activities planned for them, the participation of older teenage children in the families I talked with is both voluntary and enthusiastic. While her parents beamed proudly, one 16-year old girl (Interview #20) described her after-school schedule to me. She is assistant editor of the yearbook and school newspaper. She is on the basketball and tennis teams and belongs to a young people's service organization. During the past school year, she got up every weekday morning at 6:00 a.m. for sports practice before school. Every other Monday, she stayed at school till 9:00 p.m. while she worked on the paper. She worked on the yearbook at lunchtime. During the sports season in the first half of the school year, she didn't get home till 6:30 or 7:00. Even during the rest of the year she's usually at school for at least an hour a day after classes working on various club activities. In addition, she has maintained close to a straight-A grade point average.

Two themes that emerged from the discussion with Max and Susan were echoed by other families also. One is that children need to be "exposed" to various kinds of activities—otherwise, they won't know what it is they are likely to enjoy. The other is that it is important for children to be kept occupied—otherwise they may turn to drugs, wander around the streets, and act in other undesirable ways. Of note is the fact that many parents report organized activities as being the most superior way of keeping children occupied. There was only one family (Interview #19) who showed their discomfort at living in an environment where even leisure time was structured. To quote the husband:

The kids are so strapped down. They have to go to organized activities in organized places. I'd like to move somewhere where they have stray dogs roaming around—you know what I mean. They'd have room to grow up loose, not so tied down.

When asked why they encouraged their children to participate in organized activities, this couple explained that they felt it unsafe in an urban area for the children to "wander around." In fact, the wife feels it necessary to accompany them to and from their after-school lessons and games because a child was molested in their neighborhood a while ago.

Although most families seem to feel strongly that it is desirable to have children help out with household chores (as discussed in Chapter 7), organized leisure activities appear to have prior claims on the child's time. For instance, one full-time housewife says she considers it highly desirable to have children share in the housework, but her own children do virtually nothing in the house. Even though they are in their mid to late teens, she makes their beds and cleans their rooms. I asked if she had ever requested their help.

Wife: I tried it for a while. Like we tried taking it in turn with the dishes at night. But it's hard when they're so busy. John would say, "But I've got a rally tonight," or someone would have a sport event to attend, so they couldn't be home for dinner, so how could you have them doing dishes? During school, it just isn't practical.

This same wife claims she would like to get a job but fears she could not handle both a job and the housework. I asked if the children could be asked to cut down on some of their extracurricular activities so as to help her more in the house. She was appalled at such an idea:

No, never. It's their lives. I would never tell them to cut down. I'd never tell them to give up an activity except possibly for the money. If something costs a lot, I might say, "Look, you'll have to find some way to pay for this."

Similarly, the busy 16-year old girl described above has far more after-school activities than her 13-year old brother. Both parents are employed and both children help a lot in the house. However, at those times when the daughter is extra busy after school, the son is expected to take over many of his sister's household chores. "It's only fair," the mother explains, "seeing Laura is so busy." The son apparently accepts this situation as a regrettable necessity.

Thus, in some of the families interviewed, affiliations with organized groups outside the family are fairly explicitly described as important and legitimate alternatives to an active housework role. For the children at least, the demands of the external activities often seem to receive higher priority than household duties.

Many housewives mentioned that one reason they would hesitate to take a full-time job is that this would necessitate limiting or eliminating their participation in their children's organized activities. It may be that the perceived importance of such parental participation really is an important factor that affects a woman's decision to work. It is also possible, of course, that the attitudes expressed by these women are simply reflections of an attempt to justify their present behavior.

Not one respondent explicitly said that they considered organizations outside the home—from schools to structured leisure groups—as prime avenues for their children's success or prestige. Yet I suspect that in many cases this is so. That is, most parents would feel more proud of a child's achievement in sports, for example, than of the child's ability to cook dinner or do the vacuuming. This is not surprising in view of the generally low status of housework in society. It is also not surprising in view of the fact that rational organizations establish clear-cut universalistic standards for achievement that are generally valued more than the particularistic criteria said to reign within the home. One wonders, however, how the emphasis on externally defined success affects ideas of family cohesiveness.

FAMILY TOGETHERNESS

Some years ago, a popular slogan proclaimed, "The family that prays together stays together." One quite closely held value of many families is that it is important for the family to do things together as a unit. In my interviews, all families were asked how they feel about "family togetherness" and the steps they take—if any—to insure "togetherness." Specifically, I asked, "Do you feel it's important for the family to be together and do things together without people outside the family being present?" The ensuing discussion generally uncovered many of the attitudes and emotions of respondents concerning the unique place of the family in their lives.

The majority of the couples interviewed (25 of the 30) expressed strong positive feelings about the value of "family togetherness." First, I shall discuss the comments of the minority who were sceptical about its value.

Antitogetherness Families

Three families said they feel that togetherness is somewhat overrated as a family aim and that it can stifle individual needs. One woman spoke with disfavor of families she knows who set aside a day or evening for family members only. She feels it is a bad mistake to insist on such an institution or ritual; it leads children to dislike their family life. It is far better, she feels, to let family members follow their own pursuits in whatever ways they choose. These negative comments were echoed in two other families. One couple, in fact, described family outings as occasions for constant bickering; they feel it is more desirable to "pair off" (husband with one child, wife with the other, and so on) than to strive for activities to include the whole group.

Another couple with two preschool children feels that children interfere somewhat with their solidarity as a couple. For this reason, their concern is to plan outings for the two of them, excluding the children. They also have the children eat separately from the parents, so dinnertime can be a time for husband and wife to communicate without interruption. When asked if they felt the children would benefit from a joint mealtime, the wife reminisced about her own childhood and the joint family meals:

> I never felt that dinnertime was too enjoyable. The clean-your-plate trip. Till we got to be teenagers—but *then* it was arguments all the time.

Recall that Susan (in the last case study) said rather scornfully that surely only working wives would be concerned with such an issue; her own children see so much of her every day that, if anything, *non*togetherness is what they might strive for at weekends. This underscores the point that in four of the five antitogetherness families the wives are not employed.

Protogetherness Families

Of the 25 families who expressed positive sentiments concerning family togetherness, most (19 of them) feel that there is something qualitatively different and important about the immediate family— parents and children only—spending time apart from friends and other relatives. The remaining few expressed the view that having friends along tends to enhance family feelings of cohesiveness. About half these families said they feel that togetherness becomes harder to attain as children grow older and come to prefer the company of friends to the company of family.

> When they're younger, it's no problem. Now it's more of a problem. It depends when we want to go and where. Just a drive isn't sufficiently exciting anymore (Interview #26).

Most seem to accept this as an inevitable part of the children's growth process. As one mother of three teenagers said:

> You know, they'd sooner be dead than be with their parents. We think it's great they have so many activities. They're doing a lot of interesting things (Interview #15).

Some parents, however, feel real sadness at this development. One couple (Interview #20) with two teenagers explained how they have always arranged days for family activities to which "outsiders" are specifically *not* invited. This family owns a cabin, a five-hour journey from home, and over the years they have spent many weekends there together. But such family weekends are not as frequent now as they used to be. Regretfully, as the husband said:

> They [children] have interests with their friends. And when parents compete with friends, that's tough. We're going to start allowing them to bring a friend along [i.e., to the cabin] because we don't want that to go sour.

His wife interrupted:

> It's just not the same thing when they have friends along. We enjoy their friends, but it's nice having just the four of us.

Her husband readily agreed with her but expressed the fear that if
the kids were forced to choose between going to the cabin without
a friend and staying home with the friend, they might choose the
latter course. As far as he is concerned, the compromise is better
than not having the children accompany them.

The most commonly mentioned "togetherness" activities were
weekend and vacation outings such as picnics and camping trips, eating dinner together every day, family shopping excursions, setting
aside a special "family day," which can be either reserved for activities planned by the parents or simply be a day that parents make
themselves available to do whatever the children request.

Most of these families make a special point of eating dinner together every night. Among the few exceptions are families where the
wife eats with the children on weekdays but the husband eats alone
because of his long working hours.

Although the majority of both dual-worker and single-worker
families expressed strong opinions about the desirability of family
togetherness, the latter were somewhat more likely to elaborate on
the subject than the former. This seems to support Susan's conten-
tion that only working wives are concerned about togetherness. She
thought that working mothers are likely to feel guilty about leaving
their children and to compensate by stressing the importance of joint
family activities during weekends and evenings. And, in fact, several
employed women and their husbands admitted that they had such
feelings of guilt.

As for why people consider "family togetherness" to be desirable:

We like us better than we like most people. We share things with each
other.

It cements the family relationship to have these times when you have
concentrated togetherness. We enjoy each other's company, and we
have fun as well as the opportunity to communicate.

We can keep the lines of communication open with the children, and
with teenagers that's really valuable.

I've seen a lot of people not have any impact on their children's achieve-
ments. If my kids go wrong, I want to be responsible, but if they go
right, I want to raise *my* hand too.

It's better when it's just us because [otherwise] we get to talking with
the grownups and not paying attention to the kids.

It does a lot to make a family feel like a family.

The last comment, "It helps us to feel like a family," was mentioned by several respondents. However, no matter how much I probed, I was unable to find anyone who could articulate this feeling more explicitly. This is reminiscent of Edward Shorter's (1975, chap. 6) claim that the nuclear family is really a state of mind, and undoubtedly the positive sentiment associated with "feeling like a family" is somewhat elusive and hard to express in words.

Togetherness as a Form of Control

It seems that not all the desire for togetherness is sentimental in nature. There are strong undercurrents of a desire for control in the parents' stress on joint family activities. For example, in many families, dinnertime serves a sort of roll-call function. When a common dinner hour is insisted on, the parents know where the children will be at that time each day and know that they can get their attention then. Several parents expressed concern that this kind of control is increasingly difficult to achieve as the children grow older. For example, one mother of a teenage daughter (Interview #26) noted that the daughter increasingly eats meals away from home with her friends. The mother tries to insist that the girl eat dinner at home regularly and spend some evenings at home every week.

> **Wife:** If she goes out a lot, I make an issue of it. We don't want to give her too much of a free rein.

I asked the mother if she feared that too many late nights would be bad for her daughter's health. She said:

> Not just her health. We don't want her to have that much freedom. We want to put limits on her.

SUMMARY

In order to socialize their children, to keep control over them and incalculate them with proper norms and values, parents must communicate with them. And setting aside time for family members exclusively to interact maximizes the opportunity for this communication.

But, as children grow older, they increasingly look outward, away from the family group. On the one hand, modern parents feel this is good—because children should become independent. But it is also bad —because children then move out of the reach of parental influence. One solution to this dilemma is for parents to encourage their children to take part in organized activities outside the home. No matter whether the activities relate to boy scouts, swimming team, or piano lessons in a teacher's private house, they have in common the fact that they ensure that for certain specified periods of time some adult or group will be responsible for those children. The more of these activities the child has, the less time he or she will have to wander out of reach and out of control of parents.

The importance parents place on organized activities is probably more than simply a desire for control, however. For as with all rational organizations, these leisure groups also use universalistic criteria to measure achievement. Probably it is this feature of such activities that leads so many families to assign them a priority second only to schoolwork, and certainly higher than helping with the housework. Perhaps, like schools, these structured leisure activities are another way of preparing youngsters for the adult world of work organizations—with its hierarchies of authority, status based on achievement, rules, and timetables.

PART THREE: CONCLUSIONS

CHAPTER **X**

Conclusions

In the first part of this book, I reviewed some theoretical perspectives that I feel tend to perpetuate the myth of the separate worlds of work and family. For most people in modern societies, work— that is, paid employment—normally occurs in an organizational setting. Because organizations are treated as rational social structures and families as emotionally-oriented expressive groups, the tendency is for families and organizations to fall into separate fields of study. My argument is that the norms of rationality that guide organizations guide certain family activities also and that the degree of a family's rationality is at least partly a function of the number and strength of its links to organizations.

This earlier discussion will now be assessed in terms of the interview findings. First, there is the issue of family functions. Is family work inherently different from work performed in organizations? Second, is there such a thing as family rationality analogous to organizational rationality? And do families become more rational as their links with organizations increase? Third, is today's family inward-turning, as some would claim, in an attempt to preserve an emotional haven free from the influence of its organizational environment? Or is it becoming ever more outward-turning as its links to organizations increase?

FAMILY FUNCTIONS

Undoubtedly, there is widespread consensus that a most important, if not *the* most important, function of the family unit is to nourish affective, holistic concern for its members. This is in contrast to the prototypical bureaucracy where such personal concern, where it exists, tends to have a strong instrumental underpinning—that is, the organization is kind to its employees so that they will work harder or be more loyal. However, families have instrumental functions too. And, in fact, these are the ones around which the "battle of the sexes" in the home generally revolves, especially when the wife is employed.

These interviews have not uncovered any evidence that family *work* (instrumental activity) is qualitatively different from work performed in organizations. There is, thus, no reason to believe that organizational solutions are not appropriate for family work problems. Quite the contrary, in fact, as our interviews have demonstrated. One interview after another illustrates the fact that the simple and repetitious nature of much family work is, like similar work in organizations, highly amenable to such rational devices as preplanning and scheduling.

Recall one suggestion that only organizations are likely to rely on professional expertise (cf. Litwak, 1968). However, this is really not true. Families, like organizations, often seek professional advice— whether from reference to "how-to-do-it" manuals (cooking, gardening, money management) or through consultation with experts outside the family (for example, marriage and family counselors). Moreover, as these interviews demonstrate, expertise permeates family life in another important way. This is that family members with particular skills or training tend to utilize these in the family setting. Because of variations in the expertise of individual members, different families tend to perform different functions at very different levels of effectiveness.

This brings us to a common but misleading assumption, which is that families are relatively homogeneous in the kinds of functions they perform. In fact, families vary a great deal in the extent to which, for instance, they engage in carpentry, home decorating, or landscaping; cook from scratch rather than use ready-mix products; eat in restaurants; grow and can their own foods; mend broken television sets or rewire the house; develop an investment portfolio; and so on. It is true that family income or wealth determines how much a family can afford to pay outsiders for any of these services. It is also true that many people take pride and pleasure in being a "do-it-yourselfer," even though they can afford to hire others. Moreover, the nature of a worker's occupation will often determine the extent to which he or she perceives a particular function to be valuable. (So, for example, a division controller spends many hours a week on his family's financial investments and instructs his young children to keep "books" and balance them regularly.)

The special skills of individuals also have some impact on the division of labor. For example, a husband's skill at carpentry appears to let him "off the hook" as far as the housework is concerned. This is the case even though his wife works full-time and spends far more time on the housework than he does on the carpentry.

In short, families can benefit as well as organizations from the expertise of members. An obvious difference between the family and the organization is that certain kinds of expertise are often required for membership in the latter, and this is not usually the case with the former. Of course, it was once said that a woman's good cooking was a factor in attracting a husband, and a man's career prospects a factor in attracting a wife, but I suspect that the overarching emphasis on "love" in modern times has tended to blur such practical concerns.[1]

This is not to claim that there are no problems that a family unit is better equipped to handle than an impersonal organization. A family setting is undoubtedly the most appropriate for handling situations that call for emotional or affective responses—such as verbal and physical expressions of sympathy to an unhappy individual. Although such situations arise within the context of organizational life also, the appropriate responses must be limited so as to not to interfere with the work of the organization. Families, on the other hand, are *supposed* to place highest priority on attending to such matters.

FAMILY RATIONALITY

If the families interviewed here are typical, we might conclude that there are many instances of "organizational rationality" in family life. Under certain conditions, families organize, schedule, and coordinate their activities in ways similar to those of more formal bureaucratic structures. Such organizing tendencies seem to grow

---

[1] Such factors may, nevertheless, affect the success of a marriage. I have no evidence on this, but it might be an interesting issue to explore.

in response to time pressures and, in fact, were explicitly described by many respondents as essential to dealing with time constraints. Employed wives, of course, are pressured by the dual requirements of a job and homemaking. The organized full-time housewives interviewed here apparently felt pressured also, but for a different reason. They had exceptionally high standards of household cleanliness that created the time pressures that led to the "need" to be organized.

It also seems clear, however, that the ability to organize successfully is not possessed by everyone. The most successful organizers in the home seem to be those whose jobs require organizing skills also. Thus, we find that an assembly line worker is less likely to report successful home organization than a company executive. This isomorphism of home and job activities is, of course, another instance of the way that an individual's skills on the job are likely to appear in the home. The relationship between time pressures and a tendency to rationalize housework still holds, however. Women who report being completely relaxed about housework when they are not employed say they switch to a "super organized" mode when they become employed, and vice versa.

A further strain toward rationality in the interviewed families is evidenced by the attempts by many to make their lives as predictable as possible. The discussion on flexible scheduling is a case in point. Life is simpler for all concerned if schedules are predictable, and, thus, our respondents do not utilize this flexibility to the fullest —by frequently varying their work hours, taking time off in the middle of the day, and so on. They tend, rather, to establish a suitable schedule and stick to it. The problems that may arise in terms of coordinating children's, spouse's, and sometimes sitter's schedules, when work hours are changed frequently far outweigh any possible advantages of a varied schedule.

More evidence of a desire for predictability is the emphasis so many families place on having their children engage in structured activities outside school. These activities are scheduled at set times, which, on the one hand, makes household timetables predictable, but, on the other hand, constrains the individuals concerned—and indeed the whole family—by the time demands they impose.

In these homes, there seems to be a certain amount of discomfort at the thought of the children having large blocks of totally unscheduled time. Fears were expressed that such latitude is likely to lead, at worst, to delinquency or drug addiction, and, at best, to laziness and boredom and the failure to experience fully all the possibilities available for self-improvement. Ironically, the nonemployed mothers were the most vociferous in expressing such concerns; yet, these same women often cited the relative freedom and lack of constraint in their own timetable as one of the prime advantages of being a full-time housewife rather than a working wife. A further anomaly here is that the employed women have more opportunity to supervise their children—and keep them away from crime and drugs—than do the employed wives who appear to be less emphatic, on the whole, about the need to organize their children's free time.

One is tempted to speculate that some housewives may structure their children's time as one way to introduce "organization" into their own activities, keeping in mind the association between being organized and doing "real work" that some people feel exists. The situation is not clear cut, however, for sometimes husbands with very demanding job schedules—and thus surely no need to seek further sources of organization in their lives—place the same emphasis as their wives do on the desirability of structured activity for children.

Finally, if we assume that a rational response to the wife's employment is a shift away from the traditional toward a more equal allocation of housework among family members, then we have some further evidence of rationality. In the families interviewed, the wife's employment most assuredly does increase the time spent by husbands on domestic chores, although mostly the men's contributions can more accurately be described as "helpfulness" rather than "role sharing." This is one issue on which there is a fair amount of evidence from other studies (as summarized in Chapter 2). Most of it points to a similar pattern of findings as we have here. In fact, in studies using large samples, the differences found between husbands in dual-worker and single-worker families on time spent in housework are extremely small. Note that the families interviewed here are most likely to explain a husband's increased helpfulness in terms of time constraints on the wife. That is, they use a *rational* explanation rather than invoking normative beliefs about family roles.

INWARD- OR OUTWARD-TURNING?

Today's families look *outward* to the organizational environment for income, for the performance of many essential functions, for nonmonetary rewards like recognition, prestige, and challenge, and for all manner of activities that make life interesting and fun. Most of the 30 families in this study seem to thrive in their organizational environment.

How, then, about the image of the modern family as inward-turning—a refuge from the world outside? There do seem to be attempts to keep the outside world at bay. Our interviews suggest that people resent a work organization's intrusion into family time. Employer-generated pressure to do overtime or even to attend a company picnic is often perceived as such intrusion. Also, there is the emphasis placed by so many people on the importance of "family togetherness," with time set aside for family members to interact among themselves without distraction from outsiders.

All this is not necessarily evidence of a desire to "turn inward," however. For example, many people who resent company demands for overtime do so because it interferes with their ability to engage in some other kind of *external* activity—like coaching the children's soccer team or signing up for night classes. The resentment, in other words, may arise from the family's desire for *control* over its organizational affiliations. Unfortunately, control over a work organization is particularly likely to be elusive because generally membership is so critical to the individual and the family. Similarly, much family togetherness sentiment may be more indicative of a desire for control than a desire to "turn inward." Organized after-school activities may be viewed as a proxy for parental control, being relatively predictable and visible and appealing to older children who seek the company of their peers.

We, thus, see a picture emerging from these interviews of family life in which the organizational lives of members inevitably affect domestic activities—the functions performed in the home, the timing of activities, the tendency to organize or rationalize domestic tasks, and to some extent the way that work is allocated among family members. Not only do organizations—in particular, work organizations—affect family life, but sometimes they seem to dominate it. At the same time, most families are not unaware of organizational influence on their lives and do make attempts to reserve certain activities or segments of time over which the family has control.

A TENTATIVE MODEL OF FAMILY PROCESSES

Figure 10.1 is an attempt to summarize some of the processes that appear to result in family rationality. Both organizational affilia-

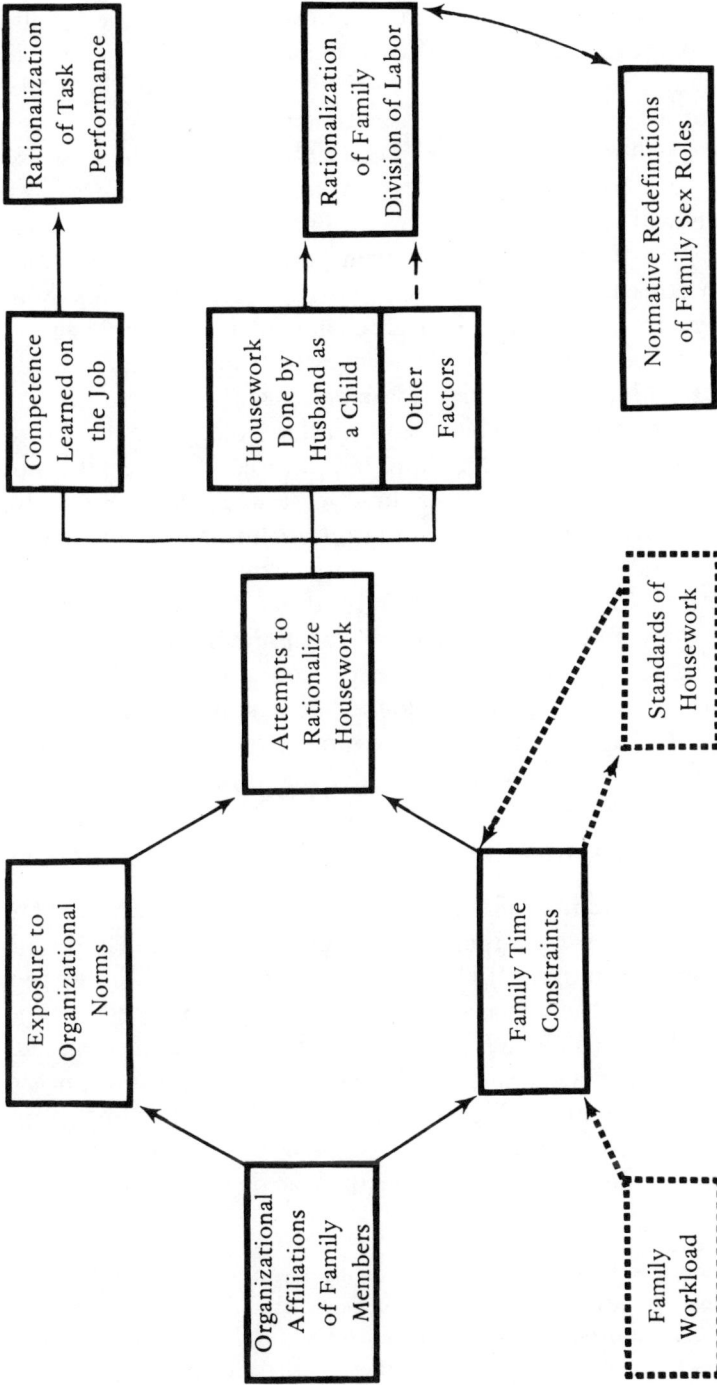

Figure 10.1 Processes by which organizational affiliations lead to rationalization of family activities.

tions and workload factors affect time pressures within the family. Standards for housework both affect, and are affected by, overall time constraints. For example, a factor that increases workload, like the arrival of a new baby, or increases time pressures, like the wife's employment, will most likely result in lower standards for housework.

Both time constraints on the family and exposure to organizational norms will lead to *attempts* to rationalize housework. Success at doing so will be mediated at least in part by competency: thus, people who effectively organize their activities at work are likely to do so at home too; husbands who learned how to do household chores as children can be recruited by their wives to help out more readily than can husbands without such prior experience.

There is some association between sex-role ideology and sex-linked behavior. As my discussion in Chapter 8 indicated, however, it is not clear that there is any simple causal linkage between them. Probably, changes in the marketplace are responsible for most of the variation in the rates of labor force participation of married women. Differing rates of participation, in turn, probably affect normative attitudes toward sex roles. But changed normative attitudes do not necessarily lead to changes in domestic roles. People can quite happily resolve inconsistencies between their ideological beliefs and their behavior in the home. Changes in the latter are more likely to occur through the processes outlined above than through ideological shifts.

SUGGESTIONS FOR FUTURE RESEARCH

One topic that warrants investigation is the extent to which there is a trade-off between time spent on instrumental activities and time spent on expressive activities. This study has concentrated on the former, but obviously the latter are time-consuming too. It takes time and effort to listen to and advise others: to be sympathetic, congratulatory, or otherwise meet emotional needs. Does too great a concern with running a household efficiently lead to the neglect of important affective interaction among family members? Or does being organized save them precious time that can then be devoted to expressive activities?[2]

---

[2] To complicate the issue further, in a family setting it may not always be easy to distinguish instrumental from expressive activity. In some cases, for example, preparing a meal or changing a diaper may be an expression of loving concern. But we cannot assume this. In other cases, these may simply be perceived as menial chores that evoke resentment rather than love.

A second issue that needs to be investigated more fully is the possible isomorphism between an individual's activities in a work setting and his or her activities in the home. Many skills can be learned at work—such as the ability to process complex information to arrive at a decision—that can then usefully be applied in domestic situations. Of course, the reverse is also true.

Third, there is the issue of a husband's willingness to do housework. One factor that affects this appears to be the husband's having had to do such work as a child. This is seemingly more important than, for example, the division of labor between his parents. This childhood experience does not, in itself, inevitably result in a helpful husband but does seem to be a predisposing factor that makes some husbands more likely to share the wife's household burden when time pressures arise. If this finding is confirmed in a larger study, it will usefully guide the parents of today who are desirous of producing helpful husbands of the future.

The issue of children's extracurricular activities is another that deserves further investigation. Most of the families interviewed here are middle class, and all live in fairly dense suburban areas. No doubt, a fairly large population is needed to support activities like this on a large scale. Also, possibly, this is largely a middle-class phenomenon. There may be a certain amount of "keeping up with the Joneses" involved, in that no one likes to feel their own children are being deprived of some special skill that most of the neighborhood children are acquiring.

Even if this phenomenon is confined to certain socioeconomic groups, it would still be of interest to determine the factors that lead families to place greater or lesser emphasis on having their children involved in organized activities and the long-range effects on children of having greater or lesser proportions of their time structured. For example, do such children adapt more readily and successfully to the world of work than children who were allowed to amuse themselves?

Finally, much more investigation is needed on the potential of work organizations to affect the quality of family life and the reciprocal effects on the employee's relationship with his or her employer. One writer suggests that the only solutions available to the time-pressured dual-worker families of today are: (1) they must turn increasingly to the market to find substitutions for goods and services that formerly were the responsibility of the mother, or (2) the workplace must be reorganized to "place the needs of people first and the goals of corporate America and the state second" (Glazer, 1980,

p. 268). Realistically, it is difficult to believe that a profit-minded employer would be willing to accept this last alternative for purely altruistic motives. It would be valuable to determine in what ways and under what circumstances employers are willing to accommodate the family needs of their employees.

IN CLOSING

Linkages with organizations form an integral part of modern family life. The world "outside" and the world "inside" are closely intertwined. Admittedly, the family is an expressive group, united by bonds of affection and mutual concern. But it also has the responsibility for carrying out quite instrumental tasks and duties. Most of us recognize the fact that individuals can be irrational or emotional on the job as well as in the home. In like vein, there is no justification for assuming that family "work"—that is, instrumental activity—is exempt from the kinds of rational principles that are said to govern work in organizations.

The popular conceptual boundary between the "affective family" and the "rational organization" has been too rigidly established. It is dysfunctional because it tends to blur the important fact that family life itself is structured by the organizational ties of members. If we remove this artificial boundary and recognize that both family and organization are legitimate arenas, perhaps to varying degrees, of both affective and rational behavior, we can greatly increase the value of future explorations of family life.

Appendix:

Panel Study of Effects of Employment on Housework Time of Family Members

This study was a secondary analysis of survey data gathered for the University of Michigan's Panel Study of Income Dynamics (PSID). The purpose of the analysis was to test the hypothesis that changes in the wife's employment hours would lead to changes in housework hours of family members. The PSID data set contains interview responses from a cross-national sample of approximately 5,000 U.S. families who were interviewed every year from 1968 to 1976.[1] For my study, I selected 863 families from the larger sample and examined their responses for three years: 1972, 1974, and 1976.[2]

My criteria for selecting families were: (1) families had to be husband-wife intact, (2) there had to be at least one child under the age of 18 living at home, and (3) the marriage had to have been stable

---

[1] For full information concerning this data set, refer to *A Panel Study of Income Dynamics*, Survey Research Center, University of Michigan, Ann Arbor, Michigan, Vols. I through VI, 1968 through 1976. Additional waves of data have been collected since 1976.

[2] The reasons for selecting the three years of 1972, 1974, and 1976 were as follows. The 1976 wave was the only time that wives were interviewed. In previous years, husbands had been asked to report on their wives' activities. The

over the four-year period involved. The reasons for the first two requirements are fairly obvious, given that the aim here is to examine
changes in housework patterns of husband, wife, and children. The
third requirement was made because it is possible that different
housework patterns may arise when an individual divorces and re-
marries. By choosing a relatively stable sample of families, we are
putting our change hypothesis to the most stringent test possible.

Respondents were asked, "Which people in the family do any
housework?", and, for every person named, "About how much time
does he/she/you spend on this housework in an average week—such
as, time spent cooking, cleaning and other work around the house?"
This method of measuring time spent on housework is undoubtedly
not as precise as that used in time budget studies, but it does avoid
one criticism of the latter, which is that the day sampled may not
have been typical for that family (Pleck, 1977).

First, I examined the mean hours of housework reported for husbands, wives, and others in the family—broken down by employment
status of the wife. These figures are reported in Table A.1. The means
indicate that, for this sample, wives are primarily responsible for
housework regardless of their employment status. In 1976, for instance, the mean for the whole sample of husbands was 4.98 hours
per week, as compared to the mean for all wives of 32.55 hours per
week. There was, however, a tendency over time for husbands to
increase their average housework hours and wives to decrease theirs,
again regardless of the wife's employment status. For example, for
nonemployed wives, the husband's average weekly housework increased from 1.68 hours in 1972 to 3.66 hours in 1976, while the
nonemployed women decreased theirs from 43.73 in 1972 to 36.81
in 1976. Possibly, these trends reflect an increased emphasis over
these years on the desirability of viewing housework as a shared,
rather than a segregated, role activity.

1976 wave also contained information on the wife's background not obtainable
in earlier waves.

Because the 1975 data wave contained no information on housework, it was
not suitable for inclusion. Thus 1974 variables were needed to predict 1976 dependent variables. Because it is possible that the two measures of the wife's housework are not comparable, one being based on the wife's report and the other on
the husband's, the 1972 data were included also so that a panel analysis using
1972 variables to predict 1974 dependent variables could be performed as a
check against 1974–76 results.

These means also reflect differences by wife's employment status. In 1976, nonemployed wives reported an average of 36.81 hours per week of housework, as compared to an average of 29.32 hours per week for employed wives. Husbands of nonemployed wives in 1976 reported an average of 3.66 hours per week, as compared to an average of 5.99 hours per week for husbands of employed wives. These differences are intensified when we compare means for those families where the wife was employed at all three time periods with families where the wife was nonemployed at all three times. For husbands, the respective means are 6.04 hours per week as compared with 3.09; for wives, 27.37 as compard with 37.59.

Finally, the means suggest that it is those women who tend to do less housework when they are not employed who are most likely to take jobs at a later time; these women also appear to have husbands who do somewhat more than the husbands of women who remain housewives. (Refer to figures reported under "Changes in Wife's Employment" in Table A.1.) This implies that the husband's somewhat greater willingness to help in the home might encourage a woman to go out to work; or perhaps the women who do relatively little housework when they are not employed are those who find it particularly unrewarding—motivating them to seek employment at a future time.

There are, of course, many factors that might independently affect the amount of time spent on housework, apart from the employment hours of husbands and wives. Among these are family size and the presence of young children. The latter tend to cause much work for others, while being unable to help much themselves. In addition, socioeconomic factors, such as the education and occupation of respondents, may have an effect on the willingness of husbands to help with the housework.[3]

In order to obtain more precise estimates of the effects of a wife's employment on housework patterns, while simultaneously controlling for workload and socioeconomic variables, the statistical technique of multiple regression was used. Both cross-sectional and longitudinal analyses were performed. The former utilizes variables measured at the same time point; there are, thus, three such analyses, for 1972, 1974, and 1976. The longitudinal analyses determined the effects of

---

[3] Although many studies suggest that men with higher education and social status do more housework than lower status men, the evidence is not entirely consistent. See the summary of this literature in Pleck, 1976, pp. 14–16.

Table A.1.
Mean Weekly Hours of Housework of Husbands, Wives, and Others in the Family by Working Status of Wife, Over Time

Working Status of Wife	(N)	1972	1974	1976
Husband's Housework				
Whole sample	(863)	2.42	2.80	4.98
Wife currently working	(——)[a]	3.09	3.72	5.99
Wife currently nonworking	(——)[b]	1.68	1.86	3.66
Wife working all times	(295)	3.72	4.22	6.04
Wife nonworking all times	(233)	1.38	1.16	3.09
Changes in Wife's Employment				
Nonworking 1972, working 1974	(86)	2.61	3.18	
Nonworking 1972 and 1974	(321)	1.43	1.46	
Nonworking 1974, working 1976	(131)		2.60	5.97
Nonworking 1974 and 1976	(295)		1.52	3.48
Nonworking 1972, working 1976	(153)	2.24		5.62
Nonworking 1972 and 1976	(254)	1.34		3.35
Wife's Housework				
Whole sample	(863)	36.83	34.83	32.55
Wife currently working	(——)[a]	30.68	28.83	29.32
Wife currently nonworking	(——)[b]	43.73	40.91	36.81
Wife working all times	(295)	26.78	27.50	27.37
Wife nonworking all times	(233)	44.36	41.28	37.59

	N			
Changes in Wife's Employment				
Nonworking 1972, working 1974	(86)	39.92	31.11	
Nonworking 1972 and 1974	(321)	44.75	41.53	
Nonworking 1974, working 1976	(131)		39.52	34.03
Nonworking 1974 and 1976	(295)		41.53	37.06
Nonworking 1972, working 1976	(153)	43.21		31.91
Nonworking 1972 and 1976	(254)	44.03		37.68
Housework of Others in the Family				
Whole sample	(863)	5.49	5.63	7.32
Wife currently working	(——)[a]	5.51	6.09	7.81
Wife currently nonworking	(——)[b]	5.47	5.15	6.66
Wife working all times	(295)	6.20	6.26	7.75
Wife nonworking all times	(233)	6.04	6.16	7.36
Changes in Wife's Employment				
Nonworking 1972, working 1974	(86)	5.97	6.67	
Nonworking 1972 and 1974	(321)	5.33	5.80	
Nonworking 1974, working 1976	(131)		4.46	7.39
Nonworking 1974 and 1976	(295)		5.45	6.63
Nonworking 1972, working 1976	(153)	4.87		8.49
Nonworking 1972 and 1976	(254)	5.83		7.36

[a]N for each year is as follows: 1972 = 456, 1974 = 436, 1976 = 491.
[b]N for each year is as follows: 1972 = 407, 1974 = 426, 1976 = 372.

Table A.2.
Cross-Sectional Regression Analyses of the Effects of Selected Variables on the Husband's Annual Hours of Housework for 1972, 1974, and 1976

Independent Variables	b	beta	S.E. b	F
1972 (N = 804)				
Wife annual working hrs.	.08	.19	.01	29.84[a]
Husband annual working hrs.	- .07	-.16	.01	21.42[a]
Children annual hrs. housework	- .03	-.06	.02	1.74
Wife education	13.81	.07	7.04	3.84[b]
Family size	2.24	.01	8.80	.07
Constant	182.16			
R^2	.08			
1974 (N = 812)				
Wife annual working hrs.	.06	.16	.01	21.90[a]
Family size	- 31.34	-.15	8.65	13.13[a]
Children annual hrs. housework	.05	.09	.02	5.23[b]
Husband annual working hrs.	- .02	-.04	.01	1.31
Wife education	17.93	.09	8.07	4.93[b]
Husband education	7.64	.05	6.56	1.36
Constant	164.81			
R^2	.07			

1976 (N = 805)[c]

Wife annual working hrs.	.08	.18	.02	24.83[a]
Husband annual working hrs.	– .06	-.13	.02	13.81[a]
Children annual hrs. housework	.05	.08	.03	3.66[b]
Family size	12.57	.04	11.56	1.18
Wife education	7.18	.03	10.62	.46
Husband education	1.87	.01	8.72	.05
Constant	237.13			
R^2	.06			

[a] $p < .01$.
[b] $p < .05$.
[c] Uses the wife's report of her housework hours, but the husband's report of other variables. Results are almost identical when the wife's report of her employment hours are substituted in equation for the husband's report of the wife's employment hours.

Table A.3.
Longitudinal Regression Analyses of the Effects of Selected Variables on the Husband's Annual Hours of Housework

Variables	b	beta	S.E. b	F
Regression of 1974 Husband Annual Hrs. Housework on 1972 Independent Variables				
Autoregression (1972 husband annual hrs. housework)	.35	.37	.03	122.96[a]
Family size	− 25.30	−.13	7.76	10.63[a]
Wife annual working hrs.	.04	.10	.01	9.02[a]
Children annual hrs. housework	.03	.06	.02	2.07
Husband annual working hrs.	− .01	−.03	.01	.99
Wife education	15.26	.08	7.51	4.12[b]
Husband education	6.21	.04	6.08	1.04
Constant	121.46			
R^2	.21			
R^2 autoregression only	.16			

Regression of 1976 Husband Annual Hrs. Housework on 1972 Independent Variables

Autoregression (1974 husband annual hrs. housework)	.37	.28	.05	61.00^a
Husband annual working hrs.	− .05	−.10	.02	7.82^a
Family size	13.60	.05	11.30	1.45
Wife annual working hrs.	.03	.05	.02	2.34
Children annual hrs. housework	.02	.02	.03	.23
Husband education	− 4.69	−.02	8.52	.30
Wife education	− 1.99	−.01	10.43	.04
Constant	281.96			
R^2	.10			
R^2 autoregression only	.08			

$^a p < .01.$
$^b p < .05.$

Table A.4.
Cross-Sectional Regression Analyses of the Effects of Selected Variables on the Wife's Annual Hours of Housework for 1972, 1974, and 1976

Independent Variables	b	beta	S.E. b	F
1972 (N = 804)				
Wife annual working hrs.	-.46	-.35	.04	115.40[a]
Family size	143.45	.21	27.29	27.63[a]
Husband annual working hrs.	.13	.09	.05	8.12[a]
Children annual hrs. housework	-.20	-.10	.08	6.70[b]
Wife education	-56.21	-.08	26.38	4.54[b]
Husband education	45.25	.08	21.28	4.52[b]
Constant	1327.93			
R^2	.21			
1974 (N = 812)				
Wife annual working hrs.	-.44	-.38	.04	131.94[a]
Family size	124.71	.18	26.33	22.44[a]
Husband annual working hrs.	.06	.05	.04	2.12
Children annual hrs. housework	-.10	-.05	.07	1.80
Wife education	-37.68	-.06	24.56	2.35
Husband education	19.94	.04	20.00	1.00
Constant	1472.82			
R^2	.20			

1976 (N = 805)[c]

Wife annual working hrs.	-.38	-.37	.03	121.78[a]
Family size	86.34	.13	25.06	11.87[a]
Husband annual working hrs.	.10	.09	.04	7.24[a]
Children annual hrs. housework	-.06	-.04	.06	1.01
Husband education	-38.61	-.08	18.89	4.18[b]
Wife education	-21.15	-.04	23.02	.84
Constant	1647.21			
R^2	.17			

[a] $p < .01$.
[b] $p < .05$.
[c] Uses the wife's report of her housework hours, but the husband's report of other variables.

Table A.5.
Longitudinal Regression Analyses of the Effects of Selected Variables on the Wife's Annual Hours of Housework

Variables	b	beta	S.E. b	F
Regression of 1974 Wife Annual Hrs. Housework on 1972 Independent Variables				
Autoregression (1972 wife annual hrs. housework)	.34	.37	.03	105.39[a]
Wife annual working hrs.	-.10	-.08	.04	5.18[b]
Family size	63.06	.10	26.07	5.85[b]
Children annual hrs. housework	-.18	-.10	.07	6.02[b]
Husband annual working hrs.	.04	.03	.04	.73
Wife education	-33.49	-.05	24.88	1.81
Husband education	20.98	.04	20.13	1.09
Constant	946.62			
R^2	.21			
R^2 autoregression only	.19			

Regression of 1976 Wife
Annual Hrs. Housework on
1974 Independent Variables

Autoregression (1974 wife annual hrs. housework)	.28	.31	.03	71.49[a]
Husband annual working hrs.	.17	.14	.04	17.28[a]
Wife annual working hrs.	– .14	-.13	.04	12.66[a]
Children annual hrs. housework	– .10	-.06	.07	2.06
Family size	– 28.35	.04	25.25	1.26
Husband education	– 32.01	-.07	18.92	2.86
Wife education	– 10.35	-.02	23.17	.20
Constant	959.52			
R^2	.19			
R^2 autoregression only	.14			

[a] $p < .01$.
[b] $p < .05$.

Table A.6.
Cross-Sectional Regression Analyses of the Effects of Selected Variables
on the Children's Annual Hours of Housework for 1972, 1974, and 1976

Independent Variables	b	beta	S.E. b	F
1972 (N = 804)				
Family size	197.51	.57	10.27	370.12[a]
Age youngest child	27.43	.21	3.70	54.85[a]
Wife annual working hrs.	.05	.08	.02	6.03[b]
Husband annual working hrs.	.03	.04	.02	2.39
Wife annual hrs. housework	−.03	−.05	.02	2.47
Husband annual hrs. housework	−.03	−.02	.05	.30
Wife education	16.85	.05	11.90	2.01
Husband education	−9.90	−.04	9.57	1.07
Constant	−845.99			
R^2	.40			
1974 (N = 812)				
Family size	197.69	.55	10.53	352.78[a]
Age youngest child	31.26	.29	3.17	97.13[a]
Wife annual working hrs.	.03	.05	.02	2.56
Husband annual working hrs.	.01	.01	.02	.14
Husband annual hrs. housework	.17	.10	.05	11.35[a]

	b	β	SE	F
Wife annual hrs. housework	- .01	-.02	.02	.31
Wife education	8.99	.03	11.45	.62
Husband education	- 5.72	-.02	9.25	.38
Constant	-879.27			
R^2	.37			
1976 (N = 805)[c]				
Family size	216.31	.53	11.95	327.78[a]
Age youngest child	37.89	.36	3.12	147.13[a]
Wife annual working hrs.	.03	.05	.02	2.80
Husband annual working hrs.	.00	.00	.02	.00
Husband annual hrs. housework	.11	.07	.04	6.59[b]
Wife annual hrs. housework	.01	.02	.02	.41
Husband education	- 22.77	-.08	10.08	5.11[b]
Wife education	3.47	.01	12.33	.08
Constant	-897.38			
R^2	.37			

[a] $p < .01$.
[b] $p < .05$.
[c] Uses the wife's report of her housework hours, but the husband's report of other variables.

Table A.7.
Longitudinal Regression Analyses of the Effects of Selected Variables on the Children's Annual Hours of Housework

Variables	b	beta	S.E. b	F
Regression of 1974 Children Annual Hrs. Housework on 1972 Independent Variables				
Autoregression (1972 children annual hrs. housework)	.38	.39	.03	130.76[a]
Family size	101.80	.31	11.51	78.16[a]
Age youngest child	12.90	.11	3.55	13.21[a]
Husband annual working hrs.	− .02	−.02	.02	.64
Wife annual working hrs.	− .03	−.04	.02	1.86
Husband annual hrs. housework	.16	.10	.05	11.72[a]
Wife annual hrs. housework	.00	.01	.01	.11
Husband education	7.92	.02	11.05	.51
Wife education	− 1.81	−.01	8.90	.04
Constant	−357.49			
R^2	.43			
R^2 autoregression only	.35			

Regression of 1976 Children
Annual Hrs. Housework on
1974 Independent Variables

Autoregression (1974 children annual hrs. housework)	.35	.32	.04	84.99[a]
Family size	135.59	.35	13.26	104.49[a]
Age youngest child	18.51	.16	3.51	27.65[a]
Wife annual working hrs.	.05	.07	.02	5.14[b]
Husband annual working hrs.	.03	.04	.02	1.60
Wife annual hrs. housework	.02	.04	.02	2.01
Husband annual hrs. housework	.04	.02	.05	.46
Husband education	−18.00	−.02	8.06	4.99[b]
Wife education	.00	.00	.00	.00
Constant	−554.23			
R^2	.41			
R^2 autoregression only	.31			

[a] $p < .01.$
[b] $p < .05.$

employment and control variables measured at one time point on housework variables measured at a later time.

The measurement of change is a far from straightforward matter. A panel design approximates a matched longitudinal design in that by using the same group of subjects one is matching, or holding constant, variables related to characteristics of the subjects—such as, ethnicity, parental background, and so on.

One way of estimating change in the dependent variable is to use multiple regression techniques, regressing the dependent variable at time t on predictor variables at time t – 1, while holding constant the value of the dependent variable at t – 1 (by including it in the regression equation on the right-hand side). This is the method used here. By measuring the dependent variables at a later time point than the predictor variables, one is assuming that change in the former follows the latter. By including the value of the dependent variable from the earlier time in the equation, one can ascertain the stability of the dependent variable over time and thus estimate the amount of change likely to have been induced by the predictor variables.

This method does have drawbacks, notably the fact that there is likely to be autocorrelation of error terms when different measures of the same variable are included on both sides of the equation. This violates one of the assumptions of regression analysis. Typically, however, it is the coefficient for the lagged dependent variable that is biased upward, with coefficients for the predictor variables being biased downward. Thus, the researcher is not likely to falsely overestimate the effects of the predictor variables.[4]

Two longitudinal analyses were performed for each housework variable: one in which 1972 measures of employment, housework, and control variables are used to predict housework in 1974, and one in which 1974 measures of the independent variables are used to predict housework in 1976. Results can be summarized as follows.

HUSBAND'S HOUSEWORK (TABLES A.2 AND A.3)

The wife's employment hours are strongly and consistently related to the amount of housework done by the husband. In terms of

---

[4] For some comprehensive discussions of the issues involved in attempts to measure change, see Coleman, 1968; Hibbs, 1974; Linn and Slinde, 1977.

actual differences in time spent, the results appear somewhat less impressive than the statistically significant coefficients imply. In the 1976 cross-sectional analysis (Table A.2), for instance, the husband's housework time increased by nearly five minutes for every hour the wife worked outside the home. (As would be expected, the husband's own working hours are negatively related to his housework time—for every hour of the former, the latter is reduced by about five and one-half minutes.) Looking at the longitudinal data (Table A.3), we find that for every hour the wife was employed in 1972, the husband did two and one-half minutes more of housework in 1974; the results were similar for the 1974–76 longitudinal analysis.

WIFE'S HOUSEWORK (TABLES A.4 AND A.5)

A wife's employment appears dramatically to decrease her housework time. In 1976, for instance, the cross-sectional analysis (Table A.4) indicates that every hour of the wife's employment reduced her housework time by almost 23 minutes. Family size was strongly related to her housework time: in 1976, every additional family member reported raised the wife's housework time by about one and one-third hours per week. This relationship held in the longitudinal analyses (Table A.5). A one-hour increase in the wife's 1972 employment resulted in a six-minute reduction in her 1974 housework hours; each hour of her employment in 1974 was associated with an eight and one-half minute reduction in 1976 housework.

CHILDREN'S HOUSEWORK (TABLES A.6 AND A.7)

Unfortunately, it was not possible to obtain separate estimates for different children in the household, so the measure of the children's housework reflects an average reported for all children in the family. Disaggregation by age of children would have been particularly useful because it is likely that only older children contribute much to housework. The wife's working hours were positively related to the amount of housework reported for children (Table A.6), although this was not as influential a factor as family size and the age of the youngest child. There were no longitudinal effects of the wife's employment on the children's housework. This is a somewhat unexpected finding, because it would seem that working mothers would be especially likely to encourage their children to help in the house and that the help provided would increase as the children grew older.

To summarize then, these panel study findings confirm other findings insofar as the working wives reported far less time spent on housework than the nonworking wives. As far as the husband's housework is concerned, although the changes associated with the wife's employment are small, they are quite consistently positive.

Bibliography

Adams, B.N. *The American Family.* Chicago: Markham, 1971.

Aldous, J. "Wives' Employment Status and Lower-Class Men as Husband-Fathers." *Journal of Marriage and the Family* 31(1969):469.

Anshen, R.N. *The Family: Its Functions and Destiny.* New York: Harper, 1949.

Ariès, P. *Centuries of Childhood.* New York: Vintage, 1962.

Bahr, S.J. "Effects on Power and Division of Labor in the Family." In *Working Mothers,* edited by L.W. Hoffman and F.I. Nye, pp. 167–85. San Francisco: Jossey-Bass, 1974.

Berk, S.F. and A. Shih. "Contributions of Household Labor: Comparing Husbands' and Wives' Reports." In *Women and Household Labor,* edited by S.F. Berk, pp. 191–227. Beverly Hills, Calif.: Sage, 1980.

Bernard, J. *The Future of Marriage.* New York: Bantam Books, 1972.

Blood, R.O., Jr. and D.M. Wolfe. *Husbands and Wives.* New York: The Free Press, 1960.

Bose, C. "Social Status of the Homemaker." In *Women and Household Labor,* edited by S.F. Berk, pp. 69–87. Beverly Hills, Calif.: Sage, 1980.

Bureau of Labor Statistics, U.S. Department of Labor. *Employment and Earnings,* vol. 25, no. 9, September 1978.

Burns, J. and G.M. Stalker. *The Management of Innovation.* London: Tavistock, 1961.

Chafe, W.H. *The American Woman.* New York: Oxford, 1972.

Clark, R.A., F.I. Nye, and V. Gecas. "Husband's Work Involvement and Marital Role Performance." *Journal of Marriage and the Family* 40(1978):9–21.

Coleman, J.S. "The Mathematical Study of Change." In *1968 Methodology in Social Research.* Edited by H.M. Blalock, Jr. and A.B. Blalock. New York: McGraw-Hill, 1968.

Collins, R. "A Conflict Theory of Sexual Stratification." *Social Problems* 19 (1971):3–12.

229

Cooley, C.H. *Social Organization*. New York: Scribner's, 1923.

Durkheim, E. *The Division of Labor in Society*. New York: The Free Press, 1933.

Friedan, B. *The Feminine Mystique*. New York: Dell, 1963.

Galbraith, J. *Designing Complex Organizations*. Reading, Mass.: Addison-Wesley, 1973.

Glazer, N. "Everyone Needs Three Hands: Doing Unpaid and Paid Work." In *Women and Household Labor*, edited by S.F. Berk, pp. 249–73. Beverly Hills, Calif.: Sage, 1980.

Goldberg, M.P. "Housework as a Production Activity." Ph.D. dissertation, University of California at Berkeley, 1977.

Gronau, R. "Leisure, Home Production and Work—The Theory of the Allocation of Time Revisited." *Journal of Political Economy* 85(1977):1099–124.

Hall, F.T. and M.P. Schroeder. "Effects of Family and Housing Characteristics on Time Spent on Household Tasks." *Journal of Home Economics* 62 (1970).

Henderson, A.M. and T. Parsons. *Max Weber. The Theory of Social and Economic Organization*. Glencoe, Ill.: Free Press, 1947.

Hibbs, D.A., Jr. "Problems of Statistical Estimation and Causal Inference in Time-Series Regression Models." In *Sociological Methodology*. Edited by H.L. Costner, chapter 10. San Francisco: Jossey-Bass, 1974.

Hoffman, L.W. and F.I. Nye, eds., *Working Mothers*. San Francisco: Jossey-Bass, 1974.

Holter, H. "Sex Roles and Social Change." In *Toward a Sociology of Women*. Edited by C. Safilios-Rothschild. Lexington, Mass.: Xerox, 1972.

Kanter, R.M. *Work and Family in the United States: A Critical Review and Agenda for Research and Policy*. New York: Russell-Sage Foundation, 1977.

Katz, E. and P.F. Lazarsfeld. *Personal Influence*. Glencoe, Ill.: Free Press, 1955.

Kohn, M.L. *Class and Conformity*. Homewood, Ill.: Dorsey Press, 1969.

Kohn, M.L. and C. Schooler. "Occupational Experience and Psychological Functioning: An Assessment of Reciprocal Effects." *American Sociological Review* 38(1973):97–118.

Lawrence, P.R. and J.W. Lorsch. *Organization and Environment*. Boston: Harvard Business School, 1967.

Linn, R.L. and J.A. Slinde. "The Determination of the Significance of Change between Pre- and Posttesting Periods." *Review of Educational Research* 47(1977):121–50.

Litwak, E. "Technological Innovation and Theoretical Functions of Primary Groups and Bureaucratic Structures." *American Journal of Sociology* 73(1968):468–81.

Lynch, M. "Sex-Role Stereotypes: Household Work of Children." *Human Ecology Forum* 5(Winter 1975):22–26.

Meissner, M., E.W. Humphreys, S.M. Meis, and W.J. Scheu. "No Exit for Wives:

Sexual Division of Labor and the Cumulation of Household Demands."
Canadian Review of Sociology and Anthropology 12(1975):424–39.

Mortimer, J.T. and R.G. Simmons. "Adult Socialization." *Annual Review of Sociology* 4(1978).

Nye, F.I. and L.W. Hoffman. *The Employed Mother in America.* Chicago: Rand McNally, 1963.

Oakley, A. *The Sociology of Housework.* New York: Pantheon Books, 1974.

———. "Prologue: Reflections on the Study of Household Labor." In *Women and Household Labor,* edited by S.F. Berk, pp. 7–14. Beverly Hills, Calif.: Sage, 1980.

Ogburn, W.F. and M.F. Nimkoff. *Technology and the Changing Family.* New York: Houghton Mifflin, 1955.

Ogburn, W.F. and C. Tibbitts. "The Family and Its Functions." In *Recent Social Trends in the U.S.* New York: McGraw-Hill, 1933.

Olsen, M.E. "Distribution of Family Responsibilities and Social Stratification." *Marriage and Family Living* 22(1960):60–65.

A Panel Study of Income Dynamics. Vol. I: *Study Design, Procedures and Available Data.* Vol. II: *Tape Code and Indexes.* Survey Research Center, Institute for Social Research, University of Michigan, Ann Arbor, Michigan, 1972.

———. Vol. IV: *Procedures and Tape Codes, 1974 Interviewing Year.* Survey Research Center, Institute for Social Research, University of Michigan, Ann Arbor, Michigan, 1974.

———. Vol. VI: *Procedures and Tape Codes, 1976 Interviewing Year.* Survey Research Center, Institute for Social Research, University of Michigan, Ann Arbor, Michigan, 1976.

Parsons, T. *The Social System.* New York: The Free Press, 1951.

Perrow, C. *Organizational Analysis: A Sociological View.* Belmont, Calif.: Wadsworth, 1970.

Pleck, J.H. "Men's New Roles in the Family: Housework and Child Care." Revised version of a paper prepared for the Ford Foundation/Merrill-Palmer Institute Conference on the Family and Sex Roles, Detroit, November 10–12, 1975. Revised 1976.

———. "The Work-Family Role System." *Social Problems* 24(1977):417–27.

Powell, K.S. "Family Variables." In *The Employed Mother in America,* edited by F.I. Nye and L.W. Hoffman, pp. 231–40. Chicago: Rand McNally, 1963.

Rapoport, R. and R.N. Rapoport. *Dual Career Families Reexamined.* New York: Harper & Row, 1976.

Robinson, J.P. "Housework Technology and Household Work." In *Women and Household Labor,* edited by S.F. Berk, pp. 53–67. Beverly Hills, Calif.: Sage, 1980.

Safilios-Rothschild, C. "Dual Linkages between the Occupational and Family Systems." *Signs* 1(1976):51–60.

Scanzoni, J. and G.L. Fox. "Sex Roles, Family and Society: The Seventies and Beyond." *Journal of Marriage and the Family* 42(1980):743–56.

Schooler, C. "Social Antecedents of Adult Psychological Functioning." *American Journal of Sociology* 78(1972):299–322.

Shorter, E. *The Making of the Modern Family.* New York: Basic Books, 1975.

Sokoloff, N.J. *Between Money and Love.* New York: Praeger, 1980.

Sorokin, P.A. *Social and Cultural Dynamics* 5(1937).

———. *The Crisis of our Age.* New York: E.P. Dutton, 1941.

Strasser, S.M. "An Enlarged Human Existence? Technology and Household Work in Nineteenth-Century America." In *Women and Household Labor,* edited by S.F. Berk, pp. 29–51. Beverly Hills, Calif.: Sage, 1980.

Szalai, A., ed. *The Use of Time.* The Hague, Netherlands: Mouton, 1972.

Thompson, J.D. *Organizations in Action.* New York: McGraw-Hill, 1967.

Tiger, L. and J. Shepher. *Women in the Kibbutz.* London: Harcourt Brace Jovanovich, 1975.

Tönnies, F. *Gemeinschaft und Gesellschaft,* 1887. Translated and edited by C.P. Loomis as *Community and Society.* New York: Harper & Row, 1963.

Vincent, C.E. "Familia Spongia: The Adaptive Function." *Journal of Marriage and the Family* 28(1966):29–36.

Wade, M. *Flexible Working Hours in Practice.* New York: Halsted Press, 1974.

Walker, K.E. "Time Used by Husbands for Household Work." *Family Economics Review* (June 1970).

Walker, K.E. and W.H. Gauger. *The Dollar Value of Household Work.* Information Bulletin 60. New York State College of Human Ecology. Ithaca: Cornell University, 1972.

———. "Time and Its Dollar Value in Household Work." *Family Economics Review* (Fall 1973).

Young, M. and P. Willmott. *The Symmetrical Family.* New York: Pantheon Books, 1973.

Zelditch, M., Jr. "Role Differentiation in the Nuclear Family." In *Family, Socialization and Interaction Process,* edited by T. Parsons and R.F. Bales. Glencoe, Ill.: Free Press, 1955.

Zimmerman, C.C. *Family and Civilization.* New York: Harper, 1947.

Index

Adams, Bert N., 4, 6
Aldous, Joan, 18

Berk, S.F., 128
Biological theories of sex-typing, 8–9
Bose, C., 14
Boundaries, family, 58–60

Case studies, 34
Chafe, W.H., 157–58
Child care (*see also* Sitters), 44, 114–15
Children: effects of mother's employment
   on, 17–19; housework done by, 44–45,
   98–99, 116–20, 134–36, 144–45, 183–
   84; organized activities, 54, 92, 95–96,
   169, 175–78, 188–91, 195–96, 202–3;
   roles of, 10
Clark, R.A., 106
Cohesion, social, 3–4
Collins, R., 9
Cooley, C.H., 3
Conflict theories of sex-typing, 9–10

Decentralization of family work, 17, 84–86
Dinnertime, 53–54, 192, 194–95, 109–40
Division of labor, 8–10, 41–43, 69, 93–94,
   96, 143–45, 181–84; effects of wife's
   employment on, 17–19
Durkheim, E., 4

Egalitarian ideology, 158–59; couples with,
   162–65
Employer: attitude toward, 38–39, 171;
   interference in family life, 38–39
Employment: effects on family, 35–60,
   170–74; intentions of wife, 67–69 (*see*

also Wife's employment); effects on
   housework, 17–19, 109, 128–32; of
   married women, 15; of mother and
   effects on children, 50–51 (*see also*
   Mother's employment); of wife and
   ideology, 159–60
Expressive: activities (definition), 5; leader
   in family, 5; roles, 5
External commitments: constraints imposed
   by, 13–14; effects on family, 15; of wife,
   14

Familial employer, 38
Family boundaries, 58–60
Family division of labor and wife's employ-
   ment, 17–19 (*see also* Division of labor)
Family functions, 4–5, 89–107, 199–201;
   effects of employment on, 105–6;
   societal norms regarding, 8
Family life, impact of organizations on,
   13–19 (*see also* Organizations)
Family processes, model of, 204–6
Family rationality, implications of, 16–17,
   46–47
Family togetherness, 50–51, 71, 184–85,
   191–95
Families interviewed, characteristics of,
   25–34
Finances, 43, 94
Flexible scheduling, 39–40, 56–58

Gauger, W.H., 106
Gecas, V., 106
Gemeinschaft, 4
Generalization theory, 16, 86–87
Gesellschaft, 4

233

About the Author

MARGARET R. DAVIS is a Sociologist in the Socioeconomic Research Center at SRI International (formerly Stanford Research Institute).

Dr. Davis has written numerous technical reports on the structure and technology of organizations and on the effects of institutional factors on family life, and has published in professional sociological journals.

Dr. Davis received her bachelor's degree, master's degree, and doctorate in sociology from Stanford University.